T0207437

Lecture Notes in Computer Science 14482

Founding Editors

Gerhard Goos
Juris Hartmanis

Editorial Board Members

The series Lecture Notes in Computer Science (LNCS), including its subseries Lecture Notes in Artificial Intelligence (LNAI) and Lecture Notes in Bioinformatics (LNBI), has established itself as a medium for the publication of new developments in computer science and information technology research, teaching, and education.

LNCS enjoys close cooperation with the computer science R & D community, the series counts many renowned academics among its volume editors and paper authors, and collaborates with prestigious societies. Its mission is to serve this international community by providing an invaluable service, mainly focused on the publication of conference and workshop proceedings and postproceedings. LNCS commenced publication in 1973.

Samia Bouzefrane · Soumya Banerjee ·
Fabrice Mourlin · Selma Boumerdassi ·
Éric Renault
Editors

Mobile, Secure, and Programmable Networking

9th International Conference, MSPN 2023
Paris, France, October 26–27, 2023
Revised Selected Papers

Springer

Editors
Samia Bouzefrane ⓘ
Cedric Lab, Cnam
Paris, France

Soumya Banerjee ⓘ
Trasna Solutions
Rousset, France

Fabrice Mourlin ⓘ
University Paris-Est Créteil
Créteil, France

Selma Boumerdassi ⓘ
Cedric Lab, Cnam
Paris, France

Éric Renault ⓘ
LIGM, ESIEE
Noisy-le-Grand, France

ISSN 0302-9743   ISSN 1611-3349 (electronic)
Lecture Notes in Computer Science
ISBN 978-3-031-52425-7   ISBN 978-3-031-52426-4 (eBook)
https://doi.org/10.1007/978-3-031-52426-4

This Springer imprint is published by the registered company Springer Nature Switzerland AG
The registered company address is: Gewerbestrasse 11, 6330 Cham, Switzerland

Paper in this product is recyclable.

Preface

The rapid deployment of new generations of networks and the exponential increase of connected objects trigger new applications and services that in turn generate new constraints such as security and/or mobility. The International Conference on Mobile, Secure and Programmable Networking aimed at providing a forum for researchers and industrial practitioners to present and discuss emerging trends in networking infrastructures, distributed yet intelligent protocols, security, services and applications while focusing manifold vertical tools on machine leaning and artificial intelligence, network programming and cloud computing, industrial Internet of Things, digital twins, etc.

MSPN 2023 was hosted by Cnam (Conservatoire National des Arts et Métiers), a French public institute created in 1794 and dedicated to long-life education. Cnam is based in the heart of Paris and is associated with the Arts et Métiers Museum. It was organized by the CEDRIC Lab of Cnam, the University of Limoges, and the association ASELKIM with the cooperation of IFIP WG 11.2 Pervasive Systems Security.

We had 31 submissions and the program committee accepted 15 papers. Every submission was assigned to three members of the program committee for single blind review process. The accepted papers originated from: Algeria, Czech Republic, France, Germany, Japan, Luxembourg, Senegal, USA, and Vietnam. Four brilliant invited speakers completed the technical program. The first speaker was Hiroaki Kikuchi, Associate Dean of the School of Interdisciplinary Mathematical Sciences, Meiji University of Japan. His talk dealt with the improvement of secure and private Key-Value data sharing. The second speaker was Philipp Brune, who is research professor for Artificial Intelligence and Natural Language Processing at Neu-Ulm University of Applied Sciences (HNU) in Germany. His talk was entitled "Towards an Enterprise-Ready Implementation of Artificial Intelligence-Enabled, Blockchain-Based Smart Contracts". The third speaker was Marc-Oliver Pahl, an expert in cybersecurity at IMT Atlantique, France. There he holds the industrial chair in Cybersecurity for Critical Networked Infrastructures. His talk was about a Holistic Approach to Cybersecurity from the sound of Robot Arms over collaborating competitors to Human Retinas. The fourth invited speaker was Haifa Touati of the University of Gabès (Tunisia). She gave a good overview of the security in named data networking.

We would like to thank the authors for their high-quality paper contributions, the chairs and the members of the Technical Program Committee for reviewing the submitted papers and selecting a high-quality program, and the general chairs for their support. Our special thanks go also to the Organizing Committee members for their great help and to the sponsor institutions.

We hope that all the participants enjoyed this hybrid conference, especially those who came to visit Cnam and Paris.

October 2023

Samia Bouzefrane
Soumya Banerjee
Fabrice Mourlin
Selma Boumerdassi
Eric Renault

Organization

General Chairs

Samia Bouzefrane   Cnam, France
Soumya Banerjee   Transa Solutions, Ireland
Fabrice Mourlin   UPEC, France

Steering Committee

Samia Bouzefrane   Cnam, France
Eric Renault   ESIEE Paris, France
Selma Boumerdassi   Cnam, France

Program Chair

Damien Sauveron   University of Limoges, France

Technical Program Committee

Emad Abd-Elrahman	National Telecommunication Institute, Egypt
Amar Abane	NIST, USA
Iness Ahriz	Cnam, France
Keyvan Ansari	University of the Sunshine Coast, Australia
Lynda Boukela	Nanjing University of Science and Technology, China
Mohand-Cherif Boukala	USTHB, Algeria
Julien Cordry	Teesside University, UK
Claude Duvallet	University of Le Havre, France
Nour El Medhoun	ISEP, France
Mohammed Erritali	Sultan Moulay Slimane University, Morocco
Hend Fourati	University of Manouba, Tunisia
Chrystel Gaber	Orange Labs, France
Bamba Gueye	Cheikh Anta Diop de Dakar (UCAD) University, Senegal
Nasreddine Hajlaoui	Qassim University, Saudi Arabia

Ghazaleh Khodabandeh	UPEC, France
Thinh Le Vinh	HCMC University of Technology and Education, Vietnam
Mohammed Nafi	University of Béjaia, Algeria
Karima Oukfif	University Mouloud Mammeri of Tizi-Ouzou, Algeria
Nouredine Tamani	ISEP, France
Haifa Touati	Gabès University, Tunisia

Organizing Committee

Rezak Aziz	Cnam, France
Lydia Ouaili	Cnam, France
Mustapha Kamal Benramdane	Cnam, France
Yulliwas Ameur	Cnam, France
Taysir Ismail	Cnam, France

Sponsoring Institutions

Conservatoire National des Arts et Métiers, France
University of Limoges, France

Contents

IoTDisco: Strong yet Lightweight End-to-End Security for the Internet of Constrained Things

Hao Cheng$^{(\boxtimes)}$, Georgios Fotiadis, Johann Großschädl, and Peter Y. A. Ryan

DCS and SnT, University of Luxembourg,
6, Avenue de la Fonte, 4364 Esch-sur-Alzette, Luxembourg
{hao.cheng,georgios.fotiadis,johann.groszschaedl,peter.ryan}@uni.lu

Abstract. Most widely-used protocols for end-to-end security, such as TLS and its datagram variant DTLS, are highly computation-intensive and introduce significant communication overheads, which makes them impractical for resource-restricted IoT devices. The recently-introduced Disco protocol framework provides a clean and well-documented basis for the design of strong end-to-end security with lower complexity than the (D)TLS protocol and no legacy baggage. Disco consists of two sub-protocols, namely Noise (known from e.g., WhatsApp) and Strobe, and is rather minimalist in terms of cryptography since it requires only an elliptic curve in Montgomery form and a cryptographic permutation as basic building blocks. In this paper, we present IoTDisco, an optimized implementation of the Disco protocol for 16-bit TI MSP430 microcontrollers. IoTDisco is based on David Wong's EmbeddedDisco software and contains hand-written Assembly code for the prime-field arithmetic of Curve25519. However, we decided to replace the Keccak permutation of EmbeddedDisco by Xoodoo to reduce both the binary code size and RAM footprint. The experiments we conducted on a Zolertia Z1 device (equipped with a MSP430F2617 microcontroller) show that IoTDisco is able to perform the computational part of a full Noise NK handshake in 26.2 million clock cycles, i.e., 1.64 s when the MSP430 is clocked at 16 MHz. IoTDisco's RAM footprint amounts to 1.4 kB, which is less than 17% of the overall RAM capacity (8 kB) of the Zolertia Z1.

Keywords: Internet of Things (IoT) · Security protocol · Elliptic curve cryptography · Cryptographic permutation · Efficient implementation

1 Introduction

The concept of *End-to-End (E2E) security* refers to the protection of data in transit, i.e., while being transmitted from a source to the intended destination (usually over an insecure network like the Internet) [29]. Strong E2E security is crucial for a wide spectrum of Internet applications and services, ranging from various kinds of e-commerce over personal communication to Web-based leisure and entertainment, e.g., social networks. In general, E2E security involves E2E

© The Author(s), under exclusive license to Springer Nature Switzerland AG 2024
S. Bouzefrane et al. (Eds.): MSPN 2023, LNCS 14482, pp. 1–16, 2024.
https://doi.org/10.1007/978-3-031-52426-4_1

authentication, E2E key agreement, and E2E encryption and integrity protection, all of which has to be implemented in a way that no third party, not even the Internet Service Provider (ISP), can learn anything about the transmitted data (except of communication meta-data), which is far from trivial to achieve in practice [22]. The de-facto standard for E2E-secure communication over the Internet is the *Transport Layer Security (TLS)* protocol [26], previously known as *Secure Sockets Layer (SSL)* protocol. Originally developed in the 1990s, the TLS/SSL protocol has undergone various revisions since then to strengthen its security, e.g., by adding new ciphers to replace broken ones like RC4 [1]. TLS is a modular protocol comprising a few sub-protocols, of which the handshake protocol and the record protocol are particularly important [26]. The former is responsible for authentication and key establishment and uses classical public-key cryptosystems (e.g., RSA and Diffie-Hellman) or more recent elliptic-curve schemes (ECDSA, ECDH [15]). On the other hand, the record protocol ensures data encryption and integrity through symmetric algorithms, e.g., AES.

TLS is a highly complex protocol and challenging to implement for a couple of reasons. First, as stated above, achieving E2E security in general, and E2E authentication in particular, is a difficult problem for which no easy or simple solution exists (and likely never will exist [22]). In addition, also certain design decisions like *algorithm agility* have added to the complexity of TLS. Algorithm agility means that the TLS protocol supports various combinations of cryptographic algorithms, called *cipher suites*, and the client and server agree on one of them dynamically during the handshake phase. For example, in version 1.3 of the TLS protocol, a server can authenticate itself to a client via certificates based on three different signature algorithms (RSA, ECDSA, EdDSA [4]), and each of them comes with at least two levels of security. Another reason for the complexity of TLS implementations is that old(er) versions of the protocol, in particular TLS v1.2, are still widely used and have to be supported to ensure backwards compatibility. Furthermore, in the course of approximately 30 years of development (i.e., bug fixing) and evolution, the protocol became overloaded with niche features and extensions for very specific purposes with questionable relevance in real-world settings. The enormous complexity of TLS has been the root cause for a multitude of problems. First, it has been key enabler of various security flaws and vulnerabilities in the protocol itself (e.g., the re-negotiation attack analyzed in [12]), the underlying cryptography (e.g., the attacks known as BEAST and Lucky13 [13]), and different implementations of TLS (e.g., the "Heartbleed" bug found in OpenSSL [11]). Second, the high complexity of the protocol translates directly to high resource consumption, i.e., large code size and memory (RAM) footprint, which makes TLS relatively unattractive for the *Internet of Things (IoT)* and its billions of constrained devices.

The Internet Engineering Task Force (IETF) describes in RFC 7228 [7] three classes of constrained devices, depending on the code complexity (i.e., the size of ROM or flash) and the size of state/buffers (i.e., RAM) they can handle, see Table 1. Class 0 devices (C0 for short) are so limited in terms of memory and processing capabilities that they will "not have the resources required to

Table 1. Classes of constrained devices according to RFC 7228 [7].

Name	Data size (e.g., RAM)	Code size (e.g., flash)
Class 0, C0	$\ll 10\,\text{kB}$	$\ll 100\,\text{kB}$
Class 1, C1	$\sim 10\,\text{kB}$	$\sim 100\,\text{kB}$
Class 2, C2	$50\,\text{kB}$	$250\,\text{kB}$

communicate directly with the Internet in a secure manner". Class-1 (C1) devices are also constrained and can not easily communicate with other Internet nodes through a complex protocol like TLS. However, they are capable enough to use protocols specifically designed for such devices and participate in conversations without the help of a gateway node. Indeed, a full-fledged TLS implementation like OpenSSL [31] contains over 500,000 lines of code and has a (binary) code size of several 100 kB, which is even beyond the resources of C2 devices. There exist a few optimized (D)TLS libraries for embedded systems, such as ARM's mbedTLS, but they nonetheless need a code space of around 50 kB as reported in [27]. Such code size is theoretically feasible for C1 devices, but not practical since it leaves only about half of the total ROM (resp., flash) capacity for the operating system and application(s). Two examples of E2E security protocols that have been specifically developed to be suitable for limited devices are the so-called Diet EXchange (DEX) variant [23] of IETF's Host Identity Protocol (HIP) and the Ephemeral Diffie-Hellman Over COSE (EDHOC) [28] protocol (which is still in development). While both protocols can be optimized to have a binary code size of less than 20 kB, they are still (unnecessarily) complex due to algorithm agility. Some EDHOC cipher suites are (unnecessarily) slow since they use cryptosystems that are nowadays considered dated and efficiency-wise not state-of-the-art anymore (e.g., ECDH with NIST curves or AES-GCM).

Disco is a protocol framework developed by David Wong [34] with the goal of simplifying the design and implementation of lightweight security protocols with high efficiency, but without making compromises regarding security. The Disco framework is specified as an extension of the well-known *Noise* protocol framework of Trevor Perrin [25]. Disco can be seen as a clean-slate approach to achieve end-to-end secure communication with much lower complexity and less legacy overheads than TLS. It has the potential to become a viable alternative to (D)TLS in the IoT, especially in settings where all communication endpoints are managed or controlled by one single entity. Disco supports a subset of the Noise handshakes for key exchange and (optionally) authentication. Noise has been widely adopted in the past couple of years; for example, it is used by the instant messenger WhatsApp [32] and the WireGuard VPN tunnel (part of the Linux kernel since version 5.6). WhatsApp is estimated to have more than two billion users worldwide, who send each other tens of billions of text messages per day [22]. Every Noise protocol starts with a handshake phase in which two parties exchange their Diffie-Hellman (DH) public keys and perform a sequence of DH operations, hashing the DH results into a shared secret key. The Noise framework comes with a collection of common "handshake patterns" with well-defined security properties (i.e., various kinds of confidentiality, integrity, and authenticity guarantees). Besides Noise, Disco also uses *Strobe*, a framework to build symmetric cryptosystems and protocols [14]. Strobe goes beyond modes of operation (or modes of use) and supports the design of secure bi-directional communication channels. Disco is rather minimalist in terms of cryptosystems since the full protocol, including both Noise and Strobe, requires just two basic low-level components: Curve25519 [2] and the Keccak permutation [6].

EmbeddedDisco is a prototype implementation of Disco developed by David Wong that targets embedded environments [35]. The protocol itself (i.e., Noise and Strobe) consists of just about 1000 lines of C code, excluding the low-level cryptographic functions. EmbeddedDisco uses the Curve25519 implementation of TweetNaCl [5], a compact cryptographic library that supports variable-base scalar multiplication and fits into just 100 tweets. The Keccak implementation of EmbeddedDisco is also very compact (i.e., "tweetable") and fits in only nine tweets. Unfortunately, these tweetable implementations are extremely slow on microcontrollers, which makes EmbeddedDisco rather inefficient. We present in this paper *IoTDisco*, the first optimized implementation of the Disco protocol for C1 devices equipped with an ultra-low-power 16-bit MSP430(X) microcontroller [30]. IoTDisco replaces the Keccak permutation by *Xoodoo* [9], a modern permutation (designed by largely the same team as Keccak) with a state of 48 bytes instead of 200 bytes, thereby reducing the RAM consumption. Both the prime-field arithmetic for Curve25519 and the Xoodoo permutation are written in MSP430 Assembly to achieve high speed and small code size. The IoTDisco prototype we benchmarked performs a Noise NK handshake, which means the server gets authenticated to the client via a static public key that is known in advance (e.g., pre-deployed on the device), but the client is not authenticated to the server. Our experimental results show that Disco-based E2E security is not only feasible for C1-class IoT devices, but actually practical for real-world applications since the computational part of the handshake can be executed in just 1.64 s when our target device (an MSP430F2617 microcontroller) is clocked at 16 MHz. IoTDisco consumes 1.4 kB RAM and has a binary code size of 11.6 kB, which is less than 15% of the RAM/flash capacity of a C1 device.

2　Preliminaries

Wong's Disco specification [33] is written as an extension of Noise (and not as a self-contained protocol specification), which makes sense since the handshake phase of Disco is largely based on the Noise protocol framework. However, the subsequent transport phase, in which symmetric cryptosystems are utilized, is based on Hamburg's Strobe protocol framework. In this section, we first give an overview of both Noise and Strobe, and thereafter explain how Disco combines them into a single protocol framework.

2.1　Noise Protocol Framework

Noise, as specified in [25], is not a protocol but rather a framework to facilitate the creation of custom E2E security protocols that are tailored for certain use cases. This protocol framework has shown to be especially beneficial in settings where a single entity controls/manages all communication endpoints, as is the case for a range of Internet applications, e.g., WhatsApp (the first widespread adoption of a Noise-based protocol) and also for many IoT applications. There are different reasons why designing a custom E2E security protocol can make sense; for example, the target application may need a special feature that none of the existing protocols (e.g., TLS, SSH, IKE/IPSec) offers and extending one of them turns out to be a non-trivial task. Likely more common is the situation where an application only needs a subset of the features of, e.g., TLS and the application developers would prefer a simpler and "lighter" solution. The Noise framework facilitates the design and security analysis of custom E2E protocols through the definition of a small set of basic elements called *tokens* (in essence DH keys or DH operations) along with well-documented rules for combing and processing them. A Noise-based protocol is composed of three layers: (i) a thin negotiation layer, (ii) a DH-based handshake layer (which, in fact, uses ECDH as underlying primitive), and (iii) a transport layer for the secure transmission of application data. Apart from ECDH, Noise-based protocols also employ two symmetric cryptosystems, namely an algorithm for Authenticated Encryption with Associated Data (AEAD) and a hash function, the latter of which serves to compute protocol transcripts and to derive AEAD keys.

One of the distinguishing features of Noise is a clear separation between the negotiation phase, in which initiator and responder agree on a common handshake pattern (including whether/how the parties are authenticated), and the actual execution of the handshake. This contrasts with TLS, where negotiation and handshake are "intertwined" and, therefore, the sequence of cryptographic operations performed by the client and server depends on negotiation decisions (e.g., protocol version, cipher suite, client authentication, etc.) made *during* the handshake [26]. When using Noise, many of such run-time decisions become, in fact, design-time decisions within a framework, i.e., the protocol designer has to decide which handshake structure fits best for the target application; this includes decisions like who is authenticated to whom and which cryptosystems are employed. Remaining run-time decisions, if any, are separated out from the rest of the protocol and combined together, thereby enabling the handshake to become a straight (linear) sequence of messages and cryptographic operations without any branches apart from error handling. Such a linear execution profile reduces the run-time complexity of the handshake (compared to TLS) and also simplifies the implementation and testing of Noise-based protocols.

The core component of every Noise handshake is an *Authenticated Key Exchange (AKE)* protocol based on DH (in fact ECDH) that can be instantiated with two different elliptic curves: Curve25519 and Curve448. Depending on the concrete handshake pattern, either none, one, or both involved parties become authenticated. Each party has an ephemeral key pair, which is used to generate a fresh shared secret, and, optionally, a long-term (i.e., static) key pair for the purpose of authentication. Many classical AKE protocols in the literature have in common that the static keys are signature keys, i.e., authentication is done through the generation and verification of digital signatures. Examples for this kind of AKE range from basic "Signed DH," where each party simply signs its own ephemeral DH key using the static private key, to advanced protocols like SIGMA [18], which requires each side to generate a signature over both public DH keys and compute a Message Authentication Code (MAC) of the signer's identity with a secret key derived from the shared DH secret. Alternatively, an AKE protocol can use DH for both key exchange and authentication (i.e., the static key-pairs are DH key-pairs); well-known examples are NAXOS [19] and MQV [20]. Also Noise follows this approach, which has two advantages: (i) an implementation only needs DH but no signature scheme[1] and (ii) the messages can be significantly shorter (see, e.g., Fig. 1 in [28]). The basic idea is to derive the shared secret not solely from the result of ephemeral-ephemeral DH, but to also include DH values combining ephemeral with static keys. For example, in order to authenticate the responder to the initiator, the latter has to perform a DH operation using its own ephemeral private key and the responder's static public key, whereas the responder uses its static private key and the initiator's ephemeral public key. The only responding party that is able to compute the correct shared secret is the party in possession of the static private key.

Another common feature of Noise-based handshakes is that the handshake messages are not limited to (public) DH keys but may also contain application data as "handshake payloads." These early payloads can be AEAD-encrypted as soon as at least one DH operation has been carried out; in certain cases it is even possible to encrypt the payload of the very first message of the handshake (e.g., if the responder's static public key was pre-distributed). The AEAD keys and nonces are derived from a so-called *chaining key*, which gets updated (and gradually evolves) with the output of each DH operation. Thus, the handshake payloads have normally weaker security guarantees than the transport payloads that follow after the handshake. Besides the chaining key, the two parties also maintain a *handshake hash* (essentially a transcript of handshake messages) to ensure they have a consistent view of the handshake.

2.2 Strobe Protocol Framework

The transport layer of Noise corresponds to the record layer of TLS; both protect the exchange of application data with the help of symmetric cryptographic

---

[1] Depending on the application, signatures (e.g., in the form of certificates) may still be necessary to confirm a cryptographically-secure binding between a static public key and the identity of an entity. However, in such case, a Noise-based protocol has to support only signature verification, but not the signing operation. Note that the provision of evidence for the binding of an identity to a static public key is outside the scope of the Noise specification. More concretely, [25, Sect. 14] states that "it is up to the application to determine whether the remote party's static public key is acceptable." Sect. 14 of [25] also outlines some methods to ensure a static public key is genuine and trustworthy: certificates (which may be passed in a handshake payload), pre-configured lists of public keys, or pinning/key-continuity approaches where parties remember the public keys they encounter.

algorithms. Transport payloads in Noise are secured through an AEAD scheme and a hash function; the latter is also the main component of a Key-Derivation Function (KDF). Strobe is based on the idea that all symmetric cryptographic operations needed for a secure transport protocol can be efficiently designed on top of a single low-level primitive, namely an un-keyed permutation. Similar to Noise, Strobe is not a protocol but a protocol framework; more concretely, it is framework for building secure transport protocols [14]. Strobe-based protocols operate on a "wrapper" around the *duplex construction* [9], which elevates the duplex into a stateful object, i.e., an object that maintains its state across an arbitrary sequence of absorb and squeeze phases. The specification [14] defines a simple API for a Strobe object to perform authenticated encryption, pseudo-random number generation, hashing, and key derivation. Strobe's main design principle is that the cryptographic output from any step shall not only depend on the directly-provided input (e.g., plaintext, nonce, and key if the operation is encryption), but also all preceding inputs processed in the session. The state of the permutation holds a "running hash" of the protocol transcript, which is the sequence of all operations and data as seen by the application layer. Strobe maintains such a running hash on both sides, making it easy to find out when one side diverged from the protocol, e.g., due to a corrupted or lost message.

Besides the messages that are sent back and forth, the running hash of the protocol transcript also includes metadata to ensure the semantic integrity of the cryptographic operations. The behavior of any operation is determined by five flags (one indicating metadata operations) for which Strobe reserves a byte in the rate-part of the permutation. A further rate-byte is used for tracking the start-position of an operation within the rate-part, i.e., the number of bytes in a Strobe block is always two bytes less than the rate of the permutation.

2.3   Disco Protocol Framework

Disco merges Noise and Strobe into one single protocol framework that aims to facilitate the design (and implementation) of custom security protocols. Disco improves Noise in two main aspects: it simplifies the symmetric cryptographic operations performed in the handshake phase and reduces the number of low-level primitives. A Noise handshake as described in [25] requires each party to maintain three objects, two of which contain hashes, keys, and nonces that are inputs or outputs of symmetric cryptographic operations. Disco replaces these two objects by a single *StrobeState* object, acting as an opaque cryptographic scheme based on the Keccak-f[1600] permutation. Using a permutation allows for simpler transcript hashing (because all the data from previous operations is naturally absorbed) and simpler encryption/decryption of handshake payloads (since no dedicated key derivation has to be carried out).

Disco also replaces the original transport layer of Noise by a Strobe-based transport mechanism. After completion of the handshake, the final StrobeState object is split up into two objects if full-duplex communication is desired, one for each direction. Each channel operates individually in half-duplex mode.

3   Implementation Details

Our target platform to assess the computational cost of IoTDisco is a Zolertia
Z1 IoT device housing a low-power 16-bit MSP430F2617 microcontroller from
Texas Instruments. The MSP430(X) architecture is based on the von-Neuman
memory model, which means code and data share a unified address space, and
there is a single address bus and a single data bus that connects the CPU core
with RAM, ROM/flash memory, and peripheral modules. Its instruction set is
rather minimalist, consisting of merely 27 core instructions, and supports seven
addressing modes, including modes for direct memory-to-memory operations
without an intermediate register holding (similar to CISC architectures). Some
MSP430 models, such as the MSP430F2617, have a memory-mapped hardware
multiplier capable to carry out (16×16)-bit multiply and multiply-accumulate
operations [30]. The MSP430F2617 is equipped with 8 kB SRAM and features
92 kB flash memory, i.e., it can be seen as a typical C1 device.

Our IoTDisco prototype is largely based on David Wong's EmbeddedDisco
software, but we modified its Noise and Strobe component in order to improve
efficiency on 16-bit MSP430(X) microcontrollers. First, we replaced the plain C
implementation of Curve25519, which is based on TweetNaCl, by an optimized
C implementation with hand-written Assembly code for the underlying prime-
field arithmetic. Furthermore, we replaced the Keccak permutation by Xoodoo
and also modified Strobe to become *Strobe Lite* as described in Appendix B.2
of [14]. In this section, we first describe our optimized Curve25519 and Xoodoo
implementations, and then explain how a Noise-NK handshake is executed.

3.1   Curve25519

Our implementation of Curve25519 is a modified and improved version of the
ECC software for MSP430(X) microcontrollers presented in [21]. This library is
not purely optimized for speed but aims for a trade-off between execution time
and binary code size. The elements of the underlying 255-bit prime field $\mathbb{F}_p$ are
stored in arrays of unsigned 16-bit integers, i.e., arrays of type uint16_t. All
low-level field-arithmetic functions are written in MSP430 Assembly language
to reduce the execution time. Apart from inversion, the arithmetic functions do
not execute operand-dependent conditional statements like jumps or branches
(i.e., their execution time is constant), which contributes to achieve resistance
against timing attacks. The $\mathbb{F}_p$-inversion is based on the Extended Euclidean
Algorithm (EEA), but uses a "multiplicative masking" technique to randomize
its execution time and thwart timing attacks (see [21] for details).

A scalar multiplication on Curve25519 can be implemented using either the
Montgomery form or the birationally-equivalent *Twisted Edwards (TE)* model
of the curve [3]. The former is beneficial for variable-base scalar multiplication
(e.g., to derive a shared secret in ECDH key exchange) thanks to the so-called
Montgomery ladder [8], which is not only fast but also provides some intrinsic
resistance against timing attacks due to its highly regular execution profile. On
the other hand, when a fixed-base scalar multiplication needs to be performed

(e.g., to generate an ephemeral key pair), our ECC software uses the TE form and takes advantage of Hişil et al's fast and complete addition formulae based on extended coordinates [16]. To be more concrete, the scalar multiplication is carried out via a so-called *fixed-base comb method* [15] with a radix-2^4 signed-digit representation of the scalar and uses a lookup table of eight pre-computed points. Similar to the Montgomery ladder, our fixed-base comb method is able to resist timing attacks. The pre-computed points are given in extended affine coordinates and occupy 768 bytes altogether in flash memory.

3.2 Xoodoo

Xoodyak [9] is a versatile cryptographic scheme that was developed by a team of cryptographers led by Joan Daemen, who is also one of the designers of the two NIST standards AES and SHA-3. At the heart of Xoodyak is Xoodoo, an extremely lightweight permutation that shares some similarities with Keccak's permutation and can potentially serve as "drop-in replacement". However, the state of Xoodoo is much smaller (384 versus 1600 bits), making it more IoT-friendly since it can be optimized to occupy less space in RAM and flash than Keccak. IoTDisco instantiates Xoodoo with a capacity of 256 bits (to achieve 128-bit security), which means the rate is 128 bits (16 bytes). As mentioned in Subsect. 2.2, Strobe dedicates two bytes in the rate-portion of the permutation to special purposes; one byte holds five flags and the other is used to track the beginning of a Strobe operation, see [14, Sect. 4.1] for further details. Since the operations for metadata are small in Strobe, it is normally not very efficient to execute the permutation for each operation, especially when the rate is large as in Keccak-f[1600]. To reduce overheads, Strobe packs multiple operations into one block when possible, which explains why keeping track of the start-position of an operation is necessary. However, when using a small permutation, such as Xoodoo, it makes sense to always begin a new block for every new operation (the resulting Strobe variant is called *Strobe Lite* in [14, Sect. B.2]). IoTDisco follows this approach and, therefore, a Strobe block is 15 bytes long (i.e., one byte less than the nominal rate of Xoodoo with a capacity of 256 bits).

We implemented Xoodoo from scratch in MSP430 Assembly language. One of the main challenges was to find a good register allocation strategy so as to reduce the number of load/store operations. Another challenge was to perform multi-bit shift and rotations of 32-bit words efficiently, which is important since MSP430 microcontrollers can only shift or rotate a register one bit at a time.

3.3 Noise NK Handshake

Noise-NK is one of 12 so-called *fundamental handshake patterns* for interactive protocols that are described in the Noise specification [25] and implemented in EmbeddedDisco and also IoTDisco. This handshake pattern authenticates the responder through a long-term, i.e., static, public DH key, which is known (and trusted) by the initiator. On the other hand, the initiator is not authenticated and does, therefore, not have a static public key. A real-world example for this

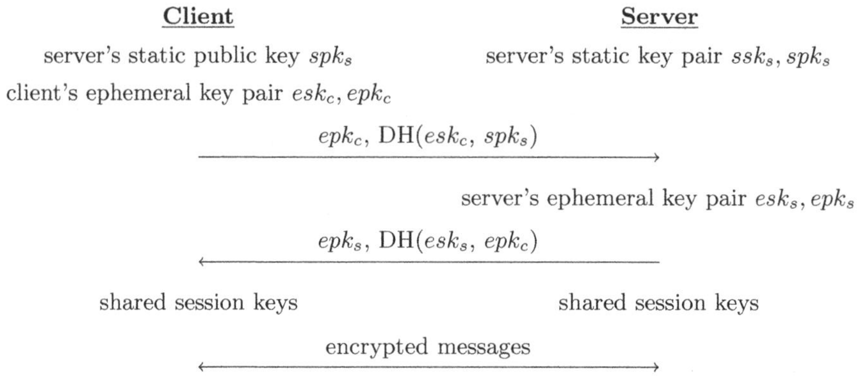

Client   **Server**

server's static public key spk_s server's static key pair ssk_s, spk_s

client's ephemeral key pair esk_c, epk_c

epk_c, DH(esk_c, spk_s)

$\longrightarrow$

server's ephemeral key pair esk_s, epk_s

epk_s, DH(esk_s, epk_c)

$\longleftarrow$

shared session keys   shared session keys

encrypted messages

$\longleftrightarrow$

Fig. 1. Simplified Noise-NK handshake pattern.

kind of authentication scenario is a mobile-device application that connects to a webserver using certificate (i.e., public-key) pinning. An example with more relevance for the IoT is secure software update, i.e., a device regularly connects to a server to check whether software updates are available and, if this is the case, downloads and installs them. While it is obvious that authenticating the server to the client is an important security requirement, there is normally no need to authenticate the client because most software vendors provide patches for free. A minimalist implementation of such a secure software update service could pre-distribute the server's static public key, e.g., by "hard-coding" it in the IoTDisco software before the device gets deployed.

Figure 1 illustrates the main operations and messages when performing an NK handshake with IoTDisco/EmbeddedDisco. The handshake layer operates on a *HandshakeState* object that contains, among some other things, the local ephemeral and static key pair (if such keys exists) as well as the other party's ephemeral and static public key. At first, the client and the server initialize the HandshakeState by calling the function `Disco_Initialize()` with the server's static key and a token representing the NK pattern. Then, the client assembles its handshake message through the function `Disco_WriteMessage()`, using the HandshakeState object as input. This function generates the client's ephemeral key pair esk_c, epk_c, performs a DH computation on esk_c and spk_s, and absorbs the results of all these operations into the client's StrobeState object, which is contained in the HandshakeState object. The client sends this first handshake message, consisting of the key epk_c and the DH result of esk_c and spk_s, to the server. Having received the message, the server uses `Disco_ReadMessage()` to (i) extract epk_c, (ii) compute the DH result of ssk_s and epk_c, and (iii) update the StrobeState object in the server's HandshakeState. The server produces its handshake message by invoking `Disco_WriteMessage()` as well. In addition to generating the server's ephemeral key pair and computing the DH of esk_s and epk_c, the `Disco_WriteMessage()` function also outputs shared session keys in two new StrobeState objects. The first object is named *s_write* and can be used to encrypt all messages that the server sends to the client, whereas the second object, *s_read*, enables the server to decrypt messages of the client. Finally, the server sends the generated (second) handshake message to the client, who upon reception invokes `Disco_ReadMessage()` to retrieve the shared session keys in two new StrobeState objects, called *c_read* and *c_write*, which can be used in the same way as on the server side.

4   Experimental Results

We compiled the source code and evaluated the performance of both IoTDisco and EmbeddedDisco using version 7.21.1 of IAR Embedded Workbench for the MSP430 architecture. This development environment includes a cycle-accurate Instruction Set Simulator (ISS) and also provides some utilities for tracking the stack usage during debugging, enabling developers to easily measure execution time and RAM footprint. The binary code size of all modules of an application is reported in a map file after compilation of the source code. In this section, we present, analyze, and compare implementation results of different components of IoTDisco and EmbeddedDisco, which we determined with IAR Embedded Workbench using the TI MSP430F2617 [30] as target device. From a software-architectural point of view, the Disco framework can be (roughly) divided into three layers; the bottom layer includes the main functions of the cryptographic primitives, i.e., fixed/variable-base scalar multiplication on Curve25519 and the function to permute the state of Keccak or Xoodoo. The medium layer covers all Disco functions for the different handshakes (i.e., Noise) and for the secure transport of application data (i.e., Strobe). Finally, the top layer consists of the full handshakes supported by Disco, but we limit our attention to Noise-NK in this paper. We compare IoTDisco and EmbeddedDisco layer-wise from bottom to top and, thereafter, we also compare IoTDisco with implementations of two other E2E security protocols for the IoT.

Table 2. Execution time (in clock cycles on a MSP430F2617), throughput (in cycles per rate-byte), RAM usage, and code size of Keccak-f[1600] and Xoodoo.

Permutation	Lang.	Exec. time (cycles)	Throughput (c/rb)	RAM (bytes)	Size (bytes)
Keccak (24 rounds)	C	577,808	3481	536	2174
Xoodoo (12 rounds)	Asm	10,378	692	262	1312

Table 2 shows the results of the Keccak permutation used in the Embedded-Disco software (written in C) and our Assembly implementation of the Xoodoo permutation. Since the permutations use different rates, it makes more sense to compare the throughputs (e.g., in cycles per rate-byte) than the raw execution times. As already mentioned in previous sections, the original Strobe protocol

Table 3. Execution time (in clock cycles on a MSP430F2617), RAM usage, and code size of some implementations of scalar multiplication on Curve25519.

Implementation	Lang.	Exec. time (cycles)	RAM (bytes)	Size (bytes)
TweetNaCl [5]	C	221,219,800	2014	2510
Düll et al. [10]	Asm	7,933,296	384	13,112
This work (fixed-base)	Asm	4,428,920	588	5260
This work (variable-base)	Asm	10,843,907	562	4717

of EmbeddedDisco dedicates two rate-bytes for a special purpose, which means the actual rate (i.e., the length of a Strobe block) is $(1600 - 256)/8 - 2 = 166$ bytes. On the other hand, IoTDisco uses *Strobe Lite* and, hence, only one byte in the rate-part is reserved, i.e., the rate is $(384 - 256)/8 - 1 = 15$ bytes. The throughput figures obtained on basis of these rate values indicate that Xoodoo outperforms Keccak by a factor of five. In addition, the RAM usage and code size of Xoodoo is much smaller.

Table 3 shows the results of some implementations of scalar multiplication on Curve25519 executed on a MSP430(X) microcontroller. Besides TweetNaCl (used by EmbeddedDisco) and our implementation, we also list the currently-fastest software of Curve25519 for MSP430(X), which was introduced by Düll et al. [10]. However, their field-arithmetic operations are aggressively optimized for speed (e.g., by fully unrolling inner loops), thereby inflating the binary code size. For example, the field-arithmetic library alone occupies some 10 kB of the flash memory, which is quite a lot for typical C1 devices. Our ECC software is optimized to achieve a trade-off between speed and code size instead of speed alone; therefore, we did not unroll the inner loop(s) of performance-critical operations. This makes our implementation slower, but also much smaller than that of Düll et al. More concretely, when compared to Düll et al., our variable-base scalar multiplication is requires 2.9 million cycles more, but the fixed-base scalar multiplication 3.6 million cycles less than their software, which supports only variable-base scalar multiplication. However, when comparing binary code size, our implementation is around 2.6 times smaller. Note that our fixed-base and variable-base scalar multiplication share a lot of the low-level components (e.g., the field arithmetic); thus, the overall size of both is only 6650 bytes.

We summarize in Table 4 the execution time of some of the Disco functions needed for a Noise-NK handshake and for the secure transport of application data. The `disco_WriteMessage()` function performs a fixed-base scalar multiplication (to generate an ephemeral key-pair) and, thereafter, a variable-base scalar multiplication. On the other hand, the `disco_WriteMessage()` function includes just the latter. IotDisco outperforms EmbeddedDisco by more than an order of magnitude (up to a factor of almost 30), which is not surprising since TweetNaCl is not optimized at all for MSP430 and, therefore, quite slow. The `disco_EncryptInPlace()` function executes an authenticated encryption of 65 bytes of application data. Its execution time can be seen as benchmark for the efficiency of the Strobe implementation and its permutation.

Table 4. Execution time (in clock cycles on a MSP430F2617) of EmbeddedDisco and IoTDisco when executing the Disco functions for a Noise-NK handshake and for the secure transport of 65 bytes of application data using Strobe (resp., Strobe Lite).

Disco function	EmbeddedDisco (C impl.)	IoTDisco (Asm impl.)
Initialization		
disco_Initialize()	583,052	55,699
client → server handshake (Noise)		
disco_WriteMessage()	443,604,514	15,218,721
disco_ReadMessage()	222,379,982	10,825,192
server → client handshake (Noise)		
disco_WriteMessage()	444,768,307	15,299,704
disco_ReadMessage()	223,543,472	10,903,793
client ↔ server secure transport (Strobe)		
disco_EncryptInPlace()	1,158,706	75,774
disco_DecryptInPlace()	1,158,677	75,745

Table 5. Execution time (in clock cycles on a MSP430F2617) of EmbeddedDisco and IoTDisco when executing the a full Noise-NK handshake.

Implementation	Lang.	Side	Exec. time (cycles)	RAM (bytes)	Size (bytes)
EmbeddedDisco	C	client	667,731,038	3366	8911
		server	667,731,341	3366	8911
IoTDisco	Asm	client	26,178,213	1382	11,602
		server	26,180,595	1382	11,602

The running time, RAM consumption, and binary code size of a full Noise-NK handshake computation performed by EmbeddedDisco and IoTDisco are shown in Table 5. On each side (i.e., client and server), a Noise-NK handshake invokes the three functions disco_Initialize(), disco_WriteMessage(), and disco_ReadMessage() to obtain a shared secret. IoTDisco requires 26.2 million cycles for a full NK handshake on each the client and the server side, which is more than 25 times faster than EmbeddedDisco. Furthermore, IoTDisco is also much more efficient than EmbeddedDisco in terms of RAM footprint (1383 vs 3366 bytes). A part of this saving comes from the smaller state of the Xoodoo permutation. The RAM footprint given in Table 5 also includes two 128-byte buffers (for sending and receiving messages) on each side. Note that the 1.4 kB of RAM consumed by IoTDisco represents only about 14% of the overall RAM available on a typical C1 device, which leaves about 86% of the RAM for the operating system and the actual target application. The code size of IoTDisco amounts to 11.6 kB, which is 2.7 kB higher than that of EmbeddedDisco. This means IoTDisco occupies less than 12% of the total flash memory available on a typical C1 device.

Table 6. Handshake computation time (in clock cycles) of implementations of E2E security protocols for the IoT.

Protocol	Sec. (bits)	Device	Side	Exec. time (cycles)	RAM (bytes)	Size (bytes)
HIP DEX [24]	112	32-bit ARM9 @180 MHz	client	192,960,000	n/a	n/a
			server	192,960,000	n/a	n/a
μEDHOC [17]	128	32-bit Cortex-M0 @16 MHz	client	274,816,000	2381	18,950
			server	274,832,000	2624	18,950
IoTDisco (This work)	128	16-bit MSP430X @8 MHz	client	26,178,213	1382	11,602
			server	26,180,595	1382	11,602

Finally, in Table 6 we compare IoTDisco with implementations of the two other E2E protocols mentioned in Sect. 1, i.e., the HIP DEX protocol by Nie et al. [24] and μEDHOC by Hristozov et al. [17]. Even though a 32-bit ARM9 microcontroller has more computing power than a 16-bit MSP430, IoTDisco is about 7.4 times faster than HIP DEX. It should also be noted that DEX was designed to offer only up to 112-bit security. When compared to μEDHOC on an ARM Cortex-M0, IoTDisco is more than an order of magnitude faster and also consumes 1.0 kB less RAM and 7.3 kB less flash memory.

5   Summary and Conclusion

Although E2E-secure communication is nowadays omnipresent in the classical Internet, it still represents a massive challenge for the IoT due to the resource constraints of the connected devices. We presented in this paper an optimized implementation and practical evaluation of Disco, a modern E2E security protocol combining Noise (a DH-based two-party handshake protocol) and Strobe (a permutation-based secure transport protocol). Disco is a "clean-slate" design and, therefore, unencumbered by most of the problems and issues that plague legacy protocols such as TLS, in particular backwards compatibility, algorithm agility, and/or inefficient cryptographic primitives. The IoTDisco prototype we introduced is optimized for MSP430-based C1 devices and contains carefully-tuned Assembly functions for the prime-field arithmetic of Curve25519 and the Xoodoo permutation, which serves as lightweight replacement for Keccak. Due to these optimizations, IoTDisco is capable to complete the full computational part of a Noise NK handshake in only 26.2 million cycles on our target device (a TI MSP430F2617 microcontroller), which compares very favorably with the implementations of other E2E protocols described in the literature. IoTDisco occupies only about 11.6 kB flash memory and roughly 1.4 kB RAM, which is less than 14% of the total flash capacity and less than 17% of the RAM of the MSP430F2617. All these results make IoTDisco an important milestone on the road towards strong E2E security in the Internet of constrained things, i.e., the Internet of C1 devices.

References

1. AlFardan, N.J., Bernstein, D.J., Paterson, K.G., Poettering, B., Schuldt, J.C.: On the security of RC4 in TLS. In: King, S.T. (ed.) Proceedings of the 22th USENIX Security Symposium (USS 2013), pp. 305–320. USENIX Association (2013)
2. Bernstein, D.J.: Curve25519: new Diffie-Hellman speed records. In: Yung, M., Dodis, Y., Kiayias, A., Malkin, T. (eds.) PKC 2006. LNCS, vol. 3958, pp. 207–228. Springer, Heidelberg (2006). https://doi.org/10.1007/11745853_14
3. Bernstein, D.J., Birkner, P., Joye, M., Lange, T., Peters, C.: Twisted Edwards curves. In: Vaudenay, S. (ed.) AFRICACRYPT 2008. LNCS, vol. 5023, pp. 389–405. Springer, Heidelberg (2008). https://doi.org/10.1007/978-3-540-68164-9_26
4. Bernstein, D.J., Duif, N., Lange, T., Schwabe, P., Yang, B.Y.: High-speed high-security signatures. J. Cryptogr. Eng. $2(2)$, 77–89 (2012)
5. Bernstein, D.J., van Gastel, B., Janssen, W., Lange, T., Schwabe, P., Smetsers, S.: TweetNaCl: a crypto library in 100 tweets. In: Aranha, D.F., Menezes, A. (eds.) LATINCRYPT 2014. LNCS, vol. 8895, pp. 64–83. Springer, Cham (2015). https://doi.org/10.1007/978-3-319-16295-9_4
6. Bertoni, G., Daemen, J., Peeters, M., Van Assche, G.: The Keccak reference, version 3.0 (2011). http://keccak.team/files/Keccak-reference-3.0.pdf
7. Bormann, C., Ersue, M., Keranen, A.: Terminology for constrained-node networks. IETF, Light-Weight Implementation Guidance Working Group, RFC 7228 (2014)
8. Costello, C., Smith, B.: Montgomery curves and their arithmetic. J. Cryptogr. Eng. $8(3)$, 227–240 (2018)
9. Daemen, J., Hoffert, S., Peeters, M., Van Assche, G., Van Keer, R.: Xoodyak, a lightweight cryptographic scheme. IACR Trans. Symmetric Cryptol. 2020(S1), 60–87 (2020)
10. Düll, M., et al.: High-speed Curve25519 on 8-bit, 16-bit and 32-bit microcontrollers. Des. Codes Crypt. $77(2–3)$, 493–514 (2015)
11. Durumeric, Z., et al.: The matter of Heartbleed. In: Williamson, C., Akella, A., Taft, N. (eds.) Proceedings of the 14th Internet Measurement Conference (IMC 2014), pp. 475–488. ACM (2014)
12. Giesen, F., Kohlar, F., Stebila, D.: On the security of TLS renegotiation. In: Sadeghi, A., Gligor, V.D., Yung, M. (eds.) Proceedings of the 20th ACM Conference on Computer and Communications Security (CCS 2013), pp. 387–398. ACM (2013)
13. Guha Sarkar, P., Fitzgerald, S.: Attacks on SSL: a comprehensive study of BEAST, CRIME, TIME, BREACH, Lucky 13 & RC4 biases. Technical report, iSEC Partners Inc. (Part of NCC Group) (2013). http://www.nccgroup.com/globalassets/our-research/us/whitepapers/ssl_attacks_survey.pdf
14. Hamburg, M.: The STROBE protocol framework. Cryptology ePrint Archive, Report 2017/003 (2017). http://eprint.iacr.org
15. Hankerson, D.R., Menezes, A.J., Vanstone, S.A.: Guide to Elliptic Curve Cryptography. Springer, Heidelberg (2004). https://doi.org/10.1007/b97644
16. Hisil, H., Wong, K.K.-H., Carter, G., Dawson, E.: Twisted Edwards curves revisited. In: Pieprzyk, J. (ed.) ASIACRYPT 2008. LNCS, vol. 5350, pp. 326–343. Springer, Heidelberg (2008). https://doi.org/10.1007/978-3-540-89255-7_20

17. Hristozov, S., Huber, M., Xu, L., Fietz, J., Liess, M., Sigl, G.: The cost of OSCORE and EDHOC for constrained devices. In: Joshi, A., Carminati, B., Verma, R.M. (eds.) Proceedings of the 11th ACM Conference on Data and Application Security and Privacy (CODASPY 2021), pp. 245–250. ACM (2021)
18. Krawczyk, H.: SIGMA: the 'SIGn-and-MAc' approach to authenticated Diffie-Hellman and its use in the IKE protocols. In: Boneh, D. (ed.) CRYPTO 2003. LNCS, vol. 2729, pp. 400–425. Springer, Heidelberg (2003). https://doi.org/10.1007/978-3-540-45146-4_24
19. LaMacchia, B., Lauter, K., Mityagin, A.: Stronger security of authenticated key exchange. In: Susilo, W., Liu, J.K., Mu, Y. (eds.) ProvSec 2007. LNCS, vol. 4784, pp. 1–16. Springer, Heidelberg (2007). https://doi.org/10.1007/978-3-540-75670-5_1
20. Law, L., Menezes, A., Qu, M., Solinas, J.A., Vanstone, S.A.: An efficient protocol for authenticated key agreement. Des. Codes Crypt. 28(2), 119–134 (2003)
21. Liu, Z., Großschädl, J., Li, L., Xu, Q.: Energy-efficient elliptic curve cryptography for MSP430-based wireless sensor nodes. In: Liu, J.K., Steinfeld, R. (eds.) ACISP 2016. LNCS, vol. 9722, pp. 94–112. Springer, Cham (2016). https://doi.org/10.1007/978-3-319-40253-6_6
22. Menezes, A.J., Stebila, D.: End-to-end security: when do we have it? IEEE Secur. Priv. 19(4), 60–64 (2021)
23. Moskowitz, R., Hummen, R., Komu, M.: HIP Diet EXchange (DEX). IETF, Internet draft draft-ietf-hip-dex-24 (2021)
24. Nie, P., Vähä-Herttua, J., Aura, T., Gurtov, A.V.: Performance analysis of HIP diet exchange for WSN security establishment. In: Chen, H., Ben-Othman, J., Cesana, M. (eds.) Proceedings of the 7th ACM Symposium on QoS and Security for Wireless and Mobile Networks (Q2SWinet 2011), pp. 51–56. ACM (2011)
25. Perrin, T.: The Noise protocol framework (revision 34). Specification (2018). http://noiseprotocol.org/noise.pdf
26. Rescorla, E.K.: The transport layer security (TLS) protocol version 1.3. IETF, Network Working Group, RFC 8446 (2018)
27. Restuccia, G., Tschofenig, H., Baccelli, E.: Low-power IoT communication security: on the performance of DTLS and TLS 1.3. In: Proceedings of the 9th IFIP International Conference on Performance Evaluation and Modeling in Wireless Networks (PEMWN 2020), pp. 1–6. IEEE (2020)
28. Selander, G., Preuß Mattsson, J., Palombini, F.: Ephemeral Diffie-Hellman over COSE (EDHOC). IETF, Internet draft draft-ietf-lake-edhoc-22 (2023)
29. Stallings, W.: Cryptography and Network Security: Principles and Practice, 7th edn. Pearson (2016)
30. Texas Instruments Inc: MSP430x2xx Family User's Guide (Rev. J). Manual (2013). http://www.ti.com/lit/ug/slau144j/slau144j.pdf
31. The OpenSSL Project: OpenSSL: Cryptography and SSL/TLS Toolkit (2021). http://www.openssl.org
32. WhatsApp LLC: WhatsApp encryption overview. Technical white paper (2020). http://www.whatsapp.com/security/WhatsApp-Security-Whitepaper.pdf
33. Wong, D.: Noise extension: disco (revision 6). Specification (2018). http://www.discocrypto.com/disco.pdf
34. Wong, D.: Disco: modern session encryption. Cryptology ePrint Archive, Report 2019/180 (2019). http://eprint.iacr.org
35. Wong, D.: EmbeddedDisco (2020). http://embeddeddisco.com

StrucTemp-GNN: An Intrusion Detection Framework in IoT Networks Using Dynamic Heterogeneous Graph Neural Networks

Imed Eddine Boukari[1,2](✉)[iD], Ihab Abderrahmane Derdouha[1,2][iD],
Samia Bouzefrane[1,2][iD], Leila Hamdad[1,2], Safia Nait-Bahloul[1,2][iD],
and Thomas Huraux[1,2]

[1] Higher National School of Computer Science (ESI), Algiers, Algeria
`ii_boukari@esi.dz`
[2] CEDRIC Lab, Conservatoire National des Arts et Metiers, Paris, France

Abstract. Deep Learning (DL) techniques are effective for designing network intrusion detection systems (NIDS) but they lack leveraging IoT network topology. In the meanwhile, Graph Neural Networks (GNNs) consider both statistical properties and topological dependencies outperforming DL in complex IoT systems. However, three improvements are required: 1) Scalability as GNNs are more suitable for offline analysis with a static dependency graph. 2) Current GNNs focus on homogeneous graphs with topological dependencies; thus, including temporal aspects in heterogeneous graphs would improve the overall performance. 3) IoT time and resource constraints require optimized resource usage for efficient intrusion detection. To address these challenges, we propose **StrucTemp-GNN** a dynamic heterogeneous GNN-based NIDS for IoT networks. The method leverages both structural and temporal dependencies, giving rise to its name, **Structural-Temp**oral GNN. Real-time intrusion detection is enabled by constructing a dynamic graph from incoming IoT data flows, incorporating structural and temporal information. The lightweight GNN model achieves fast and accurate intrusion detection. It has been evaluated on four new IoT datasets and has proven efficient in both binary and multiclass classification.

Keywords: Deep Learning · Graph Neural Network · Intrusion Detection System · Heterogenous Graph · Line Graph

1 Introduction

The Internet of Things (IoT) is rapidly disrupting our daily lives and professional environments. With the exponential growth of internet-connected devices, IoT has expanded into a wide range of application domains, from Industrial IoT to the Internet of Vehicles, not to mention smart homes. All these application domains have the potential to significantly improve our productivity, well-being, and quality of life. Furthermore, the COVID-19 pandemic has accelerated the growth of IoT by pushing a significant number of people to adopt a more digitized lifestyle and work environment. This has increased the demand for smart devices and caused a rapid expansion of the IoT industry. The proliferation of IoT devices has raised serious cybersecurity concerns as the risk of cyberattacks and data breaches has increased [1]. Effective and advanced Network Intrusion Detection Systems (NIDS) are therefore necessary to ensure the security of the IoT network. Intrusion Detection Systems (IDS) can be defined as platforms (software or hardware) that recognize, detect, and respond to attacks that may impact a given system [13]. Machine learning has shown particularly promising results in the field of anomaly detection and intrusion detection, indeed learning-trained models can learn from complex behaviors [7]. It has become a viable solution for identifying malicious packets, and many works in the same domain have emerged. Regarding supervised methods, authors in [12] used classification methods such as Logistic Regression (LR), Decision Trees (DT), and Support Vector Machines (SVM) for detection, and the results showed the performance of DT. Authors of [4] also used LR, SVM, and RF, and their tests revealed the effectiveness of RF followed by LR and SVM. As for unsupervised learning methods, they are less explored with some contributions using the K-means algorithm [10]. Reinforcement learning is generally combined with deep learning for subsequent use in intrusion detection.

However, the volume of data generated by IoT devices surpasses the scope of traditional NIDS, necessitating the exploration of more innovative options to address these challenges such as deep learning approaches [6]. There are several deep learning techniques applied to the intrusion detection problem, as mentioned in [2], where the authors classified the techniques based on the type of learning:

- For supervised learning, Long Short-Term Memory Networks (LSTM), LSTM + Recurrent Neural Network (RNN), LSTM + Convolutional neural network (CNN), CNN alone, CNN + Auto-encoders (AE), Deep Feedforward Neural Networks (DFFNN), and GNN have been used.
- For unsupervised learning, Deep Belief Network (DBN), AE, CNN + AE, CNN + AE + LSTM, and Decentralized Machine Learning (DML) have been employed.
- AE, Variational AE, and CNN have been used for semi-supervised learning.

It's worth noting that Accuracy, Precision, Recall, False Positive Rate (FPR), False Negative Rate (FNR), and F-measure are the most commonly used model evaluation techniques in the context of deep learning [18,20].

Nevertheless, despite the promising performance of deep learning, it still fails to capture the topological dependencies between IoT devices. Graph-based deep learning approaches, on the other hand, can leverage the interactions between different entities in the network to detect any abnormal activity. Graph Neural Networks (GNNs) are a variant of deep neural networks that can be used for training on graphs [15] and enable the discovery of attack patterns that standard deep learning would have little chance of detecting, making it a promising research topic. Several NIDS architectures using GNNs have been designed (see

Sect. 2) and have demonstrated the effectiveness of GNNs in intrusion detection. However, although these models have made significant progress, they still have limitations. These limitations include scalability issues during deployment, managing heterogeneity of dependencies within the GNN model itself, and optimizing time and resources to meet the constraints of the IoT environment. Therefore, it is necessary to develop a new GNN-based NIDS architecture that aims to overcome the aforementioned limitations.

- **Improving scalability:** Despite the dynamic nature of recent models and the fact that they take into account the temporal aspect between data, some of them are not scalable and cannot be improved to integrate new flows. Indeed, adding new flows often requires a complete rebuild of the graph, making these models unscalable. As a result, it is essential to develop scalable models capable of adapting to and efficiently handling new data flows that may emerge in the network.
- **Exploring new dependencies:** Current GNNs build a homogeneous graph with only one type of dependency, structural dependencies. It is interesting to explore the possibility of building heterogeneous graphs with different types of dependencies, which could enable more accurate and complete modelling of the relationships between the nodes in the network.
- **Managing time and resources:** Given that IoT devices, including Edge nodes, have resource constraints, it is essential to develop methods that optimize the use of available resources. This will reduce the load on devices and improve the overall efficiency of the intrusion detection system.

To address these issues, we propose a new architecture for Network Intrusion Detection Systems (NIDS) in IoT networks, based on a dynamic heterogenous GNN model. This architecture allows capturing the specific characteristics of IoT data flows by leveraging different types of dependencies between nodes. It is designed to be scalable, capable of integrating new data flows, and optimizes resource management to reduce the burden on IoT devices. This advanced approach overcomes the limitations of current GNN models, opening up new perspectives for protecting IoT networks against cyber-attacks.

2   Related Works

Unlike traditional DL methods, GNNs can handle complex network topologies and dynamic interactions, which has led to GNN-based NIDSs. On the other hand, GNN is a relatively new deep learning approach, so its application to NIDS has been little researched. The chronological axis in Fig. 1 below differentiates current work according to two key criteria: node/edge classification and static/dynamic approach. On the one hand, the first classification criterion is linked to graph modelling, where flows are represented as nodes (node classification) or edges (edge classification). On the other hand, the second criterion concerns the type of graph, static or dynamic, and therefore the model's ability to exploit the structural and/or temporal dependencies hidden in the network flows.

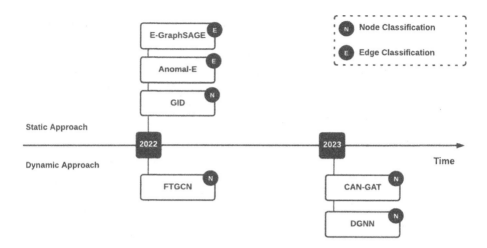

Fig. 1. Timeline of recent GNN-based NIDS

E-GraphSAGE [14] is the first model to implement a GNN-based NIDS in an IoT network. This model relies on the GraphSAGE filter to categorise network flows represented by edges in a static graph. In addition, authors in [5] take this approach a step further by integrating semi-supervised learning via auto-encoders. The solution proposed in [24] provides a global scheme for intrusion detection based on GNNs, and differs from the previous approaches by adapting the static graph during learning for better flow classification. However, despite their effectiveness, these models cannot take into account the temporal and dynamic characteristics of the network due to their static representation, hence the birth of dynamic approaches.

In [8], the FT-GCN model exploits both the topological and temporal aspects of the network by representing flows in the form of a graph with a temporal constraint. This model uses the GCN (Graph Convolutional Network) filter and an attention mechanism to prioritise key information, and is adapted to poorly labelled data thanks to semi-supervised learning. On the other hand, CAN-GAT [22] is a model used for intrusion detection in a vehicle network. This model represents flows as a DTDG graph (see Sect. 3.2.4) composed of snapshots of fixed size and uses a GAT to identify temporal dependencies between flows. Similarly, the semi-supervised DGNN model [9] represents flows as a DTDG with a sliding window and combines the GCN and Gated Recurrent Unit (GRU) models to exploit structural and temporal dependencies.

To summarize, the common approach to flow modelling is to treat flows as nodes, which leads to node classification. In terms of graph type, the dynamic graph is a better representation of network flows because it incorporates topological and temporal information. Structural dependencies of flows are usually captured using a GCN model, while temporal dependencies can be treated using a GAT filter or a recurrent model such as GRU.

3 Dynamic Heterogenous GNN-Based NIDS

3.1 Overall Architecture of the Model

The proposed solution aims to strengthen the security of IoT networks by integrating an intrusion detection system at gateways and/or Edge nodes inspired by the novel approach shown in [3]. The architecture is based on two distinct modes: training and evaluation.

Training Mode: The system is configured to learn from a database of labelled data streams. This enables the system to recognise patterns and characteristics associated with known intrusions, gradually improving its ability to identify malicious behaviour in IoT data streams.

Evaluation Mode: The system performs real-time analysis of IoT data streams. New data streams are assessed and analysed instantly to detect any suspicious activity. The aim is therefore to quickly identify data flows likely to contain intrusions, triggering an alarm if necessary. So, by combining these two modes, the intrusion detection system offers dual functionality: learning from tagged data to improve detection accuracy, and monitoring and analysing IoT data streams in real time to identify potential intrusions. As a result, this detection system provides a proactive defence against threats, helping to prevent security incidents in IoT networks.

As shown in Fig. 2, the proposed GNN-based NIDS architecture relies on two main data sources: a labelled flow database and a real-time flow generator. The database contains records of previously collected IoT data streams, labelled to enable the model to be trained. The stream generator transforms real-time network traffic into an IoT data stream that can be exploited and evaluated by the model to detect intrusions.

Given the use of a GNN model, the architecture incorporates a graph modeller to build a dependency graph from the flow metadata. This graph modeller acts on batches of flows generated by the sliding window mechanism, producing a dynamic graph as input to the GNN model. The GNN model, which forms the core of the architecture, distinguishes between normal and malicious flows by analysing the dynamic graph in real time. Initially trained using the base of labelled flows, the GNN model is then deployed to evaluate new flows from the IoT network, enabling effective intrusion detection.

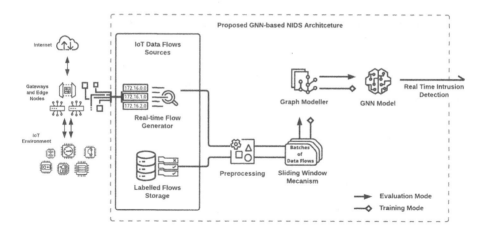

Fig. 2. Global architecture of the proposed GNN-based NIDS

3.2 Architecture Components

Having described the overall architecture, we will now delve into the details of each component. We will justify the choices made to ensure the relevance of the decisions taken. The five components at our disposal are as follows: Sources of IoT Data Streams, Preprocessing, Sliding Window Mechanism, Graph Embedder, and GNN Model. Throughout the following subsections, we will explain the rationale behind our choices, thus justifying the decisions made.

3.2.1 Sources of IoT Data Streams

The proposed NIDS system has two main sources of data streams: a labeled data stream repository and a real-time data stream generator.

- **Labeled Data Stream Base:** An essential resource for our model. It contains previously collected IoT data streams, each labeled to indicate whether it represents an intrusion or not. These labeled data streams form the basis for effective training of our model. By leveraging this repository, we can expose the model to a wide range of data instances, enabling it to learn and generalize patterns associated with intrusions and non-intrusions.
- **Real-Time Data Stream Generator:** In addition to the labeled data stream repository, we have a real-time data stream generator. This component plays a crucial role in capturing and processing real-time network traffic, converting it into readily usable IoT data streams for the learning models. The generator is responsible for continuously collecting and storing network packets, aggregating them into coherent IoT data streams, and applying necessary transformations (see Sect. 3.2.2). By simulating real-time conditions, this generator allows us to assess and evaluate the performance of our model in dynamic and evolving environments. The generator's ability to capture and process data in real-time enhances the responsiveness and adaptability of the system, enabling it to take necessary actions against new malicious streams.

3.2.2 Preprocessing

Data preprocessing is a crucial step in any machine learning project as it prepares raw data in a way that can be effectively utilized by models. This phase typically consists of two main steps: data cleaning and data transformation.

- **Data Cleaning:** It is an integral part of data preprocessing with the primary goal of ensuring data integrity and reliability. This step involves:
  - ensuring data consistency, addressing inconsistencies, and examining duplicates.
  - Handling missing values includes strategies like deletion of rows or columns, mean/median imputation, or advanced machine learning methods.
  - Removing irrelevant attributes is used to enhances data quality, boosting confidence and validity in learning processes.
- **Data Transformation:** Once cleaned, data undergo transformations to suit the model. Among the well-known transformations are:
  - Categorical feature encoding: involves converting categorical data (often strings) into numerical values, such as ordinal encoding where categories are assigned integers from 0 to $(N - 1)$, with N being the number of categories.
  - Normalization (standardization): is a critical transformation, especially for algorithms assuming normally distributed data. For a given features X it is performed as follows: $\tilde{X} = \frac{X - \bar{X}}{\sigma}$ where σ is the standard deviation, $\tilde{X}$ is the normalized feature and $\bar{X}$ is the mean.
  - Scaling confines numerical values between 0 and 1. This is particularly useful in neural network training, especially in backpropagation, which is sensitive to large values. Scaling is done as follows: $\tilde{X} = \frac{X - min}{max - min}$ where: $\tilde{X}$ is the scaled feature, min is the minimum value, and max is the maximum value of X.

3.2.3 Sliding Window Mechanism

Preprocessed IoT data streams undergo a sliding window mechanism [25] to organize them into batches. Sliding windows are employed to analyze and monitor short-term trends in real-time IoT data [17], making them commonly used for intrusion detection. A sliding window possesses two key characteristics: window size and overlap rate.

- **Window Size:** Corresponds to the batch size, indicating the number of IoT data streams in each batch (It is generally defined as a power of two for computational efficiency 512 in our case).
- **Overlap Rate:** Used to more effectively capture transitions and variations, facilitating the analysis of temporal trends (It is generally defined as 50% of the batch size 256 in our case) (Fig. 3).

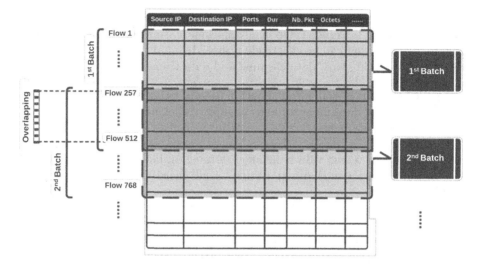

Fig. 3. Batch Generation of IoT Streams through the Sliding Window Mechanism.

3.2.4   Graph Modeler

A fundamental step in building a GNN model is creating a dependency graph that leverages the relationships between IoT data streams. Existing approaches have demonstrated the utility of modeling streams with a Line Graph (see Sect. 2). Additionally, to account for the dynamic aspect, they use discrete-time dynamic graphs (see Sect. 2). However, most of these methods present two types of constraints:

- They are not scalable because they simulate the model's operation on a limited number of data streams and do not consider the arrival of new streams when constructing the graph. The arrival of new streams often requires a complete graph reconstruction.
- The snapshots of the dynamic graph support only one type of dependency between streams. Exploring other types of dependencies is an area for improvement.

The graph modeler we propose is based on a construction strategy that addresses scalability and heterogeneity issues. In the following sections, we will explain how the graph is constructed from the streams, indicating how this resolves the aforementioned problems.

1. **Scalability: Construction of Discrete-Time Dynamic Graphs.** To ensure system scalability and efficiency, we employ an innovative approach that involves building a discrete-time dynamic graph [16] from batches of IoT data streams. Unlike conventional methods that handle only a limited number of streams, our technique ensures that even when new batches of streams arrive, they can be evaluated efficiently. For each batch produced

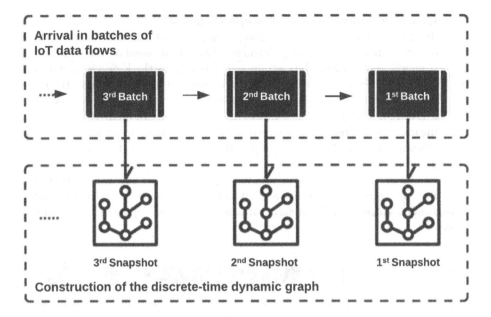

Fig. 4. Construction of Discrete-Time Dynamic Graph

by the sliding window, we generate its snapshot accordingly, as illustrated in Fig. 4. Moreover, the size of each batch, and thus the snapshot, is carefully controlled by the sliding window's size. This dynamic window adapts to available resources, allowing for seamless and efficient management. It expands when additional resources are available and contracts when resources become limited.

2. **Heterogeneity: Building Dependencies within a Snapshot**
   Existing work typically focuses on a single type of dependency within a snapshot. In contrast, our approach considers each snapshot as a heterogeneous graph with two types of dependencies: structural and temporal. These temporal dependencies, along with structural dependencies, are leveraged by appropriate GNN filters. Node representation in the graph follows the Line Graph-based modeling approach. In other words, each data stream is represented by a node identified by source and destination (IP address, port) pairs. Dependencies are constructed as follows:

   • **Construction of Structural Dependencies:**
     This type of dependency incorporates topological information from the IoT network. A structural dependency between two data streams, i.e., an edge connecting two nodes, exists if they share a common identifier. In other words, if at least one of the two (IP address, port) pairs is present in both nodes. As illustrated in Fig. 5, a structural dependency is established between data streams 1 and 3 because they share the pair (45.3.12.6,7), unlike data streams 3 and 4, which do not have a common pair.

- **Construction of Temporal Dependencies:**
  Temporal dependencies encompass temporal information between IoT data streams. Temporal dependencies are created based on the contextual principle. For a given data stream, it depends on the k previous streams and the k subsequent streams. The hyperparameter k determines the context size and, consequently, the number of streams temporally linked to a given stream. In Fig. 5, temporal dependencies are created with k = 1, meaning each stream is connected to two others: the previous and the next stream. This clarifies, for example, the edge established between stream 2 and streams 1 and 3.

In summary, the modeler constructs a discrete-time dynamic graph by transforming each stream batch into a snapshot. Each snapshot constitutes a heterogeneous graph with both structural and temporal dependencies simultaneously.

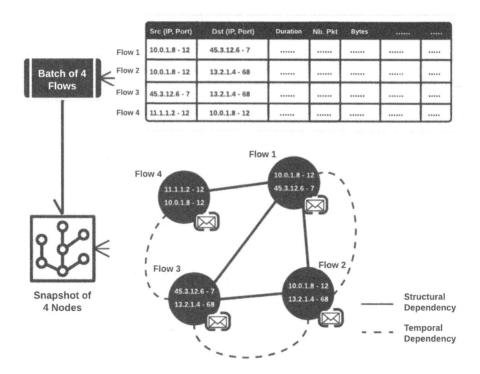

Fig. 5. Construction of Structural and Temporal Dependencies within a Snapshot

3.2.5   GNN Model

The GNN model constitutes the core of the architecture as it is the intelligent system responsible for distinguishing between normal and malicious data streams. This model takes the dynamic graph generated by the modeler as input and detects intrusions in real-time. Initially, the model is trained using the labeled data stream database. Once trained and deployed, it is responsible for evaluating new streams coming from the IoT network.

The proposed architecture of the GNN model processes snapshots of the dynamic graph, one snapshot at a time. The architecture allows for the simultaneous use of structural and temporal information present in the structural and temporal dependencies of the snapshot, respectively. The Fig. 6 illustrates the detailed architecture of the proposed GNN model:

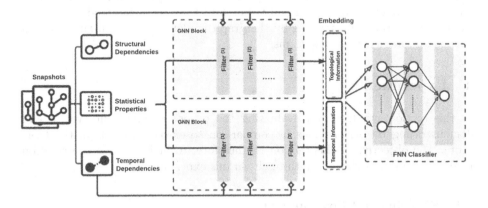

Fig. 6. Detailed Architecture of the Proposed GNN Model

- **Model Description**
  The model consists of two main parts: embedding and classification. On one hand, the embedding phase aims to encode dependencies and efficiently capture the underlying structural and temporal relationships between IoT data streams while projecting them into a low-dimensional vector space. This phase comprises two distinct GNN blocks. The first block captures the topological information of structural dependencies, while the second block captures temporal information between successive data streams. Structural and temporal information is then concatenated to produce a single embedding for the entire snapshot. This embedding is subsequently introduced into a Feedforward Neural Network (FNN) for binary classification of streams, determining whether they represent intrusions or not.

  The embedding step allows for a compact representation of complex relationships within each snapshot, facilitating the subsequent classification task. Moreover, the GNN blocks used for this purpose can employ various GNN filters, including the GCN filter [23], GraphSAGE filter [11], GAT filter [21], or any combination of these filters.

- **Training and Model Evaluation**
  Snapshots from the labeled data stream database are used to train the model, while new snapshots produced by the real-time stream generator are used for evaluation. Snapshots are introduced into the model one by one, allowing for mini-batch learning. This approach speeds up learning while gradually improving the model's performance.

3.2.6   Summary

Throughout this section, we have provided a comprehensive explanation of the key components of the architecture. The architecture integrates various data sources, including a labeled data stream database for model training and a real-time data stream generator for evaluating new streams. Data preprocessing plays an essential role in ensuring the integrity and reliability of IoT data streams by performing cleaning and transformation operations. To facilitate short-term trend analysis, the sliding window mechanism is used to efficiently organize data streams into batches. At the core of the architecture, the GNN model examines the dynamic graph constructed by the graph modeler to differentiate between normal and malicious data streams.

4   Experiments

In this section, we focus on evaluating the proposed intelligent system and demonstrating its performance in comparison to existing models in the literature. The objective of this section is, therefore, to highlight the contribution made by the new architecture through various experiments.

4.1   Experimental Environment

The tests were conducted on a virtual machine using the Linux Ubuntu operating system, version 22.04.2 LTS (Jammy Jellyfish). The specifications of the machine are detailed in Table 1.

Table 1. Specifications of the Test Environment

Memory (RAM)	32 Go
Processor (CPU)	Intel(R) Core(TM) i7-8700 CPU @ 3.20 GHz
Storage (Disk)	1 To
graphics card (GPU)	NVIDIA GeForce RTX 2080 Ti - CUDA 12.1

4.2   Datasets

In previous studies, datasets have often been modified to remove sensitive features such as IP addresses and ports to ensure privacy and prevent overfitting [9]. However, in the present work, we have selected four recently published datasets that include topological information to evaluate our GNN-based intrusion detection system. These datasets, namely NF-BoT-IoT, NF-ToN-IoT, NF-BoT-IoT-V2, and NF-ToN-IoT-V2 [19], offer different distributions, with some closely resembling realistic scenarios. This allows us to effectively assess the performance of our model.

The first two datasets, denoted as V1 versions, share the same limited set of 8 NetFlow-based features. In contrast, the NF-BoT-IoT-V2 and NF-ToN-IoT-V2 datasets, designated as V2 versions, are extensions of the original datasets and include 43 NetFlow features. Specifically, the NF-BoT-IoT and NF-ToN-IoT datasets are based on NetFlow and generated from PCAP files. The NF-BoT-IoT dataset was created by constructing a realistic network environment within the UNSW Canberra Cyber Range Laboratory. As for NF-ToN-IoT, it encompasses heterogeneous data from IoT and IIoT sensor telemetry, Windows 7 and 10 operating system data, Ubuntu 14 and 18 TLS data, and network traffic data. Some details of the two datasets are presented in Table 2. The number of data flows indicates the size of each dataset, while the percentage of normal flows provides an indication of the proportion of normal flows and intrusions. These properties are crucial for evaluating the complexity and diversity of scenarios present in each dataset.

Table 2. Specifications of the Datasets used

Dataset	Number of data flows	Percentage of normal flows
NF-BoT-IoT-V1	600,100	2.31%
NF-BoT-IoT-V2	37,763,497	0.36%
NF-ToN-IoT-V1	1,379,274	19.6%
NF-ToN-IoT-V2	16,940,49	36.01%

4.3   Evaluation Metrics

Performance or evaluation metrics are indicators used to evaluate the model at various stages, such as training, validation, and testing. When it comes to classification problems, particular attention is given to the confusion matrix. Indeed, a confusion matrix, also known as an error matrix, represents, in tabular form, the predicted and actual classes of a dataset and summarizes the effectiveness of the classification model. In the context of binary classification, a confusion matrix typically comprises four cells:

- **True Positive (TP):** The number of samples correctly identified by the model as positives.
- **False Positive (FP):** The samples incorrectly identified by the model as positives when they are actually negatives.
- **True Negative (TN):** The number of samples correctly identified by the model as negatives.
- **False Negative (FN):** The samples incorrectly predicted by the model as negatives when they are actually positives.

Furthermore, the confusion matrix allows for the calculation of various metrics, such as the accuracy rate, precision, recall, F1 score, and F-beta score as follow:

$$Accuracy = \frac{TP + TN}{TP + TN + FP + FN} \tag{1}$$

$$Precision = \frac{TP}{TP + FP} \tag{2}$$

$$Recall = \frac{TP}{TP + FN} \tag{3}$$

$$F1\text{-}Score = \frac{2 * Precision * Recall}{Precision + Recall} \tag{4}$$

F-beta Score: The F-beta Score is a generalization of the F1-Score, allowing for the adjustment of the importance given to precision and recall by introducing a beta parameter (Baeza-Yates Ribeiro-Neto, 2011). A beta value greater than 1 gives more weight to recall, while a beta value less than 1 emphasizes precision. It is measured by the following formula:

$$F\text{-}Beta\ Score = \frac{Beta * Precision * Recall}{Precision + Recall} \tag{5}$$

Precision Recall and F1 score have been widely used, e.g., in [9,14], These metrics provide an overall assessment of the performance of a classification model, taking into account various aspects. It is crucial to choose the appropriate evaluation metric to measure the specific performance of the problem under study. The evaluation metric is considered the primary performance measure, while other metrics act as supplementary indicators, also known as satisfaction metrics. However, it should be noted that the evaluation metric typically receives greater importance and confidence compared to other metrics when assessing the model's effectiveness. In the context of intrusion detection, an NIDS is considered effective if it maximizes the detection rate, i.e., recall, while maintaining a good balance with precision. Therefore, we have chosen the F-beta score as the **evaluation metric**. This metric is primarily used for model validation during training. Other measures, such as accuracy, recall, precision, and F1 score, are considered **satisfaction metrics**. We have set thresholds for these satisfaction metrics to evaluate the model's performance during testing. The threshold values for the satisfaction metrics are determined through empirical study, and their values are summarized in Table 3.

Table 3. Threshold of satisfaction metrics used

	F1-score	Recall	Precision	Accuracy
Threshold	>0.95	>0.99	>0.95	>0.95

4.4   Exprimental Setup (Hyperparameters)

To maximize the performance of our model, we carefully selected and applied the hyperparameters listed in Table 4 during our testing phase.

Table 4. Selected hyperparameters

Hyperparameter	Value
Data Split	60/20/20
Number of Neurons per Layer	64
Embedding Size	32
Number of GNN Filters per Block	3
Classifier FNN Depth	1
GNN filter combination	SAGEConv/SAGEConv
Number of epochs	15
Optimization algorithm	Adam
Learning rate	Variable learning rate with initial value 0.001, following exponential decay
Régularization	None

These hyperparameters were carefully chosen after an extensive empirical study. We adopted a "baby-sitting" approach to configure the selected models and choose their hyperparameters. This approach involves testing various parameter combinations and gradually improving the model's performance. To determine the optimal model hyperparameters, we used the F-beta score as an **evaluation metric**. Additionally, we have defined satisfaction thresholds for metrics such as the F1 score, recall, precision, and accuracy. The model must meet these thresholds for each **satisfaction metric**. Results of the tests of each of hyperparameters are shown in Fig. 7, let's consider the example of the choice of the ratio of training, validation and test hyperparameter. We explored different data split ratios and recorded the results. The results of this exploration demonstrate that the optimal ratio for achieving good performance is 60% for training, 20% for validation, and 20% for testing the model, as it achieves the best F-beta score and meets other metric criteria. We proceeded in a similar manner to fine-tune and select other parameters.

4.5 Experimental Results

In the context of our study, we evaluated our model by applying it to the previously defined four datasets: NF-BoT-IoT, NF-ToN-IoT, NF-BoT-IoT-V2, and NF-ToN-IoT-V2. For the V1 version datasets, we utilized all available data flows. However, due to the substantial size of the V2 version datasets, we followed an approach supported by existing literature [9] by selecting 800,000 flows from each dataset. In the following sections, we address two significant contributions of our work. Firstly, we present the results of tests conducted on these datasets to demonstrate our model's performance. Secondly, we highlight the efficiency of our model in terms of time and resource management. Finally, we conduct a comparison between our model's performance and state-of-the-art approaches, showcasing its competitiveness.

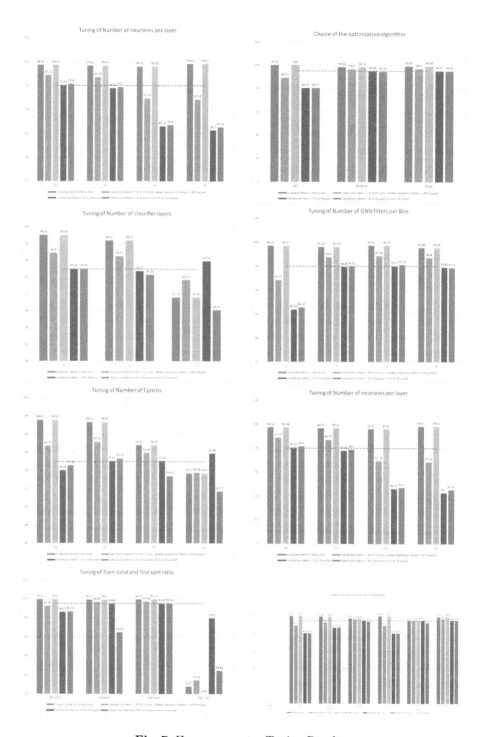

Fig. 7. Hyperparameter Tuning Results

4.5.1   Contribution 1: Evaluation Results

The model is trained and evaluated using the hyperparameters mentioned in Table 4. Throughout the training and validation epochs, we record the evolution of the loss function and the evaluation metric, which is the F-beta score. We focus particularly on the NF-ToN-IoT-V2 dataset as it represents the most recent dataset for intrusion detection in IoT networks.

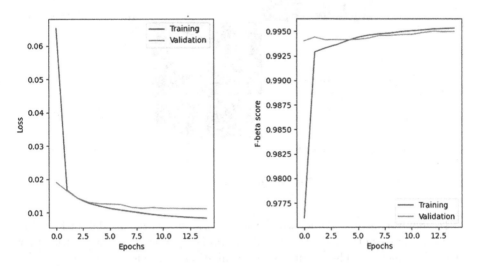

Fig. 8. Curves Illustrating Training and Validation Loss evolution, Alongside F-beta Score

Figure 8 illustrates the evolution of the loss function, we observe a gradual decrease in the training loss, approaching zero, which demonstrates the effectiveness of training, notably due to the well-chosen Adam optimizer and the use of an exponentially decaying learning rate. Similarly, the validation loss closely aligns with the training loss, indicating the absence of overfitting. As for the evolution of the F-beta score, we observe a progressive increase with each epoch until it reaches a stable and high value, thus demonstrating the successful training process.

The confusion matrix obtained during the model's testing on the NF-ToN-IoT-V2 dataset is displayed in Fig. 9. At first glance, the model's performance can be considered high, given the low classification error rates for normal flows (0.61%) and intrusions (0.42%).

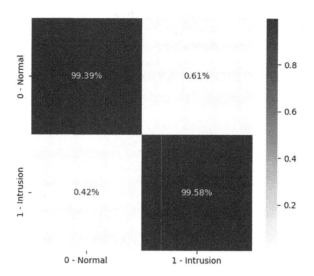

Fig. 9. Confusion Matrix

To comprehensively demonstrate the performance of our model during testing, we also utilize the F-beta score as an evaluation metric as long as the other satisfaction metrics. The results of this evaluation on the four datasets are presented in Table 5.

Table 5. Model Evaluation Results on Four Datasets

Dataset	Evaluation Metric	Satisfaction metrics			
		>95%	>99%	>95%	>95%
	F-beta score	F1 score	Recall	Precision	Accuracy
NF-Bot-IoT	99.92	99.32	99.92	98.74	98.67
NF-ToN-IoT	99.36	97.21	99.36	95.14	95.40
NF-Bot-IoT-V2	99.98	99.89	99.98	99.79	99.96
NF-ToN-IoT-V2	99.58	99.47	99.58	99.37	99.48

The results demonstrate very high intrusion detection performance, with F-beta score and recall values ranging from 99.36% to 99.98%. The model successfully captures almost all intrusions, with F1 score values ranging from 97.21% to 99.98%, accuracy varying from 95.40% to 99.96%, and precision exceeding the 95% satisfaction threshold. Thus, the model proves to be a promising contribution to intrusion detection in IoT networks.

4.5.2   Contribution 2: Time and Resource Optimization

Another significant contribution relates to the efficient management of time and resources. Given that the NIDS is deployed in an IoT environment with constraints on time and resources, it is essential for the system to consider these constraints, particularly regarding storage and network latency. In this regard, we measured the average time required to predict a data flow on both CPU and GPU. Additionally, we assessed the storage space needed to save the model in PyTorch's .pt format. The measurements obtained are summarized in Table 6.

Table 6. Prediction Times on GPU and CPU and Model Size for Different Datasets

Dataset	Prediction Time GPU (μs/flow)	Prediction Time CPU (μs/flow)	Model Size (.pt) (Ko)
NF-Bot-IoT	6.07	27.2	167
NF-ToN-IoT	5.3	21.99	167
NF-Bot-IoT-V2	5.03	21.43	167
NF-ToN-IoT-V2	5.37	21.96	167

Analyzing the results, it is clear that prediction times are generally faster on the GPU than on the CPU for all datasets. This demonstrates the advantage of using the GPU to accelerate prediction operations. However, it is important to note that even on the CPU, prediction times remain relatively short. Furthermore, the model size is negligible, which can be attributed to the fact that the proposed GNN model is lightweight and has a reduced number of parameters while maintaining excellent performance. Due to IoT network resource constraints, a heavy model can impact latency, highlighting the necessity of lightweight models in terms of both time and memory.

4.5.3   Comparison with Similar Works

We have evaluated the performance of the proposed intelligent system for real-time intrusion detection while optimizing prediction time and resources. We now proceed to compare our results with some currently available state-of-the-art approaches. The goal of this comparison is to highlight our contributions. We conducted comparisons with the DLGNN model [9], E-GraphSAGE [14], and a deep neural network (DNN) [9].

The results of this comparison are summarized in Table 7. Comparison criteria include performance measures such as F1 score, recall, precision, and accuracy, as well as prediction time per flow on the GPU. It is important to note that time measurements were taken on the same type of GPU. These results demonstrate that our model achieves high performance in terms of F1 score, recall, precision, and accuracy while maintaining fast prediction times for each dataset. Our model stands out particularly in the NF-Bot-IoT-V2 and NF-ToN-IoT-V2 datasets, where it outperforms other compared methods, including DLGNN and DNN. This can be explained by the fact that these datasets more realistically simulate data flows generated in a real IoT environment.

Table 7. Model Comparison with State-of-the-Art Methods

Method	Dataset	Performance Metrics				Prediction Time (μs/flow)
		F1 score	Recall	Precision	Accuracy	
Our Model	NF-Bot-IoT	99.32	99.92	98.74	98.67	6.07
DLGNN		99.87	99.89	99.84	99.85	640
E-GraphSAGE		97	93.43	100	93.57	1300
Our Model	NF-ToN-IoT	97.21	99.36	95.14	95.40	5.3
DLGNN		98.55	97.46	99.68	99.15	820
E-GraphSAGE		100	99.85	100	99.69	1600
Our Model	NF-Bot-IoT-V2	99.89	99.98	99.79	99.96	5.03
DLGNN		99.89	99.98	99.79	99.78	–
DNN		100	99.54	100	99.54	–
Our Model	NF-ToN-IoT-V2	99.47	99.58	99.37	99.48	5.37
DLGNN		98.87	97.94	99.82	98.69	–
DNN		96	95.27	96.74	94.74	–

The results obtained highlight the excellent performance of our model in terms of both quality and execution time. Its ability to process data quickly and accurately opens up promising new prospects in the field of intrusion detection. Therefore, our model positions itself as a preferred solution for applications that require an optimal combination of quality, speed, and resource optimization.

5   Conclusion and Future Works

This research has introduced a novel architecture for addressing the challenges associated with intrusion detection in IoT networks. By leveraging the unique characteristics of IoT data streams and harnessing the capabilities of GNNs to process them, the architecture lays the foundation for an intelligent intrusion detection system specifically designed for IoT networks. The developed intelligent system overcomes three main limitations:

1. Scalability: The model is designed to be scalable, allowing it to adapt to environmental changes during deployment by efficiently managing the reception of new IoT data streams.
2. Dependency Management: The model addresses the challenge of managing dependencies within data by using heterogeneous snapshots that capture both structural and temporal dependencies within the data streams.
3. Resource Optimization: The system effectively manages prediction time while minimizing resource consumption. This makes it suitable for IoT environments where resources may be limited. The architecture's effectiveness has been demonstrated through superior performance in terms of model quality, reduced detection time, and resource optimization, making it well-suited for deployment in IoT environments. This architecture introduces an advanced approach to intrusion detection in IoT networks, providing new avenues to enhance the security of these networks against cyberattacks.

The proposed architecture underwent rigorous evaluation, comparison with existing models, and empirical studies. The identification of optimal hyperparameters enhances the reliability and stability of the proposed architecture. Furthermore, potential improvements have been considered, including the integration of semi-supervised learning using GNN-based autoencoders, which can address the challenge of sparsely labeled data. Labeling each IoT data stream as intrusion or non-intrusion often requires expert intervention and can be cumbersome. Therefore, it would be advantageous to label a small portion of data streams and employ semi-supervised learning techniques on these labeled data. Future progress and enhancements to this architecture will contribute to the development of more effective and reliable NIDS solutions for IoT networks, protecting them against intrusion attempts and improving overall IoT network security.

References

1. Abid, M.: IoT Security Challenges and Mitigations: An Introduction, October 2022
2. Alsoufi, M.A., et al.: Anomaly-based intrusion detection systems in IoT using deep learning: a systematic literature review. Appl. Sci. **11**(18), 8383 (2021). ISSN 2076-3417. https://doi.org/10.3390/app11188383. https://www.mdpi.com/2076-3417/11/18/8383. Accessed 12 Apr 2022
3. Altaf, T., et al.: A new concatenated Multigraph Neural Network for IoT intrusion detection. Internet Things **22**, 100818 (2023). ISSN 2542-6605. https://doi.org/10.1016/j.iot.2023.100818. https://linkinghub.elsevier.com/retrieve/pii/S2542660523001415. Accessed 20 Oct 2023
4. Bagui, S., Wang, X., Bagui, S.: Machine learning based intrusion detection for IoT Botnet. IJMLC **11**(6), 399–406 (2021). ISSN 2010-3700. https://doi.org/10.18178/ijmlc.2021.11.6.1068. https://www.ijmlc.org/index.php?m=content&c=index&a=show&catid=117&id=1256. Accessed 30 Dec 2022
5. Caville, E., et al.: Anomal-E: a self-supervised network intrusion detection system based on graph neural networks. Knowl.-Based Syst. **258**, 110030 (2022). ISSN 0950-7051. https://doi.org/10.1016/j.knosys.2022.110030. https://linkinghub.elsevier.com/retrieve/pii/S0950705122011236. Accessed 24 Jan 2023
6. Chalapathy, R., Chawla, S.: Deep learning for anomaly detection: a survey (2019). arXiv Version Number: 2. https://doi.org/10.48550/ARXIV.1901.03407. https://arxiv.org/abs/1901.03407. Accessed 04 Jan 2023
7. da Costa, K.A.P., et al.: Internet of Things: a survey on machine learning based intrusion detection approaches. Comput. Netw. **151**, 147–157 (2019). ISSN 1389-1286. https://doi.org/10.1016/j.comnet.2019.01.023. https://linkinghub.elsevier.com/retrieve/pii/S1389128618308739. Accessed 04 Jan 2023
8. Deng, X., et al.: Flow topology-based graph convolutional network for intrusion detection in label-limited IoT networks. IEEE Trans. Netw. Serv. Manage. 1 (2022). ISSN 1932-4537, 2373-7379. https://doi.org/10.1109/TNSM.2022.3213807. https://ieeexplore.ieee.org/document/9919790/. Accessed 24 Jan 2023
9. Duan, G., et al.: Application of a dynamic line graph neural network for intrusion detection with semisupervised learning. IEEE Trans. Inform. Forensic Secur. **18**, 699–714 (2023). ISSN 1556-6013, 1556-6021. https://doi.org/10.1109/TIFS.2022.3228493. https://ieeexplore.ieee.org/document/9980414/. Accessed 24 Jan 2023

10. Gadal, S., et al.: Machine learning-based anomaly detection using K-mean array and sequential minimal optimization. Electronics **11**(14), 2158 (2022). ISSN 2079-9292. https://doi.org/10.3390/electronics11142158. https://www.mdpi.com/2079-9292/11/14/2158. Accessed 30 Dec 2022

11. Hamilton, W.L., Ying, R., Leskovec, J.: Inductive representation learning on large graphs (2017). arXiv Version Number: 4. https://doi.org/10.48550/ARXIV.1706.02216. https://arxiv.org/abs/1706.02216. Accessed 24 Jan 2023

12. Hasan, M., et al.: Attack and anomaly detection in IoT sensors in IoT sites using machine learning approaches. Internet Things **7**, 100059 (2019). ISSN 2542-6605. https://doi.org/10.1016/j.iot.2019.100059. https://linkinghub.elsevier.com/retrieve/pii/S2542660519300241. Accessed 30 Dec 2022

13. Heidari, A., Jamali, M.A.J.: Internet of Things intrusion detection systems: a comprehensive review and future directions. Cluster Comput., October 2022. ISSN 1386-7857, 1573-7543. https://doi.org/10.1007/s10586-022-03776-z. Accessed 04 Dec 2022

14. Lo, W.W., et al.: E-GraphSAGE: a graph neural network based intrusion detection system for IoT. In: 2022 IEEE/IFIP Network Operations and Management Symposium, NOMS 2022, Budapest, Hungary, pp. 1–9. IEEE, April 2022. ISBN 978-1-66540-601-7. https://doi.org/10.1109/NOMS54207.2022.9789878. https://ieeexplore.ieee.org/document/9789878/. Accessed 12 Jan 2023

15. Ma, Y., Tang, J.: Deep Learning on Graphs, 1st edn. Cambridge University Press, September 2021. ISBN 978-1-108-92418-4 978-1-108-83174-1. https://doi.org/10.1017/9781108924184. https://www.cambridge.org/core/product/identifier/9781108924184/type/book. Accessed 08 Jan 2023

16. Ma, Y., Tang, J.: Deep Learning on Graphs. Cambridge University Press, Cambridge (2021)

17. Mahalingam, A., et al.: ROAST-IoT: a novel range-optimized attention convolutional scattered technique for intrusion detection in IoT networks. Sensors **23**(19), (2023). ISSN 1424-8220. https://doi.org/10.3390/s23198044. https://www.mdpi.com/1424-8220/23/19/8044

18. Powers, D.M.W.: Evaluation: from precision, recall and F-measure to ROC, informedness, markedness and correlation. arXiv:2010.16061 [cs, stat], October 2020. https://arxiv.org/abs/2010.16061. Accessed 11 Sept 2023

19. Sarhan, M., Layeghy, S., Moustafa, N., Portmann, M.: NetFlow datasets for machine learning-based network intrusion detection systems. In: Deze, Z., Huang, H., Hou, R., Rho, S., Chilamkurti, N. (eds.) BDTA/WiCON -2020. LNICST, vol. 371, pp. 117–135. Springer, Cham (2021). https://doi.org/10.1007/978-3-030-72802-1_9

20. Sokolova, M., Lapalme, G.: A systematic analysis of performance measures for classification tasks. Inf. Process. Manage. **45**(4), 427–437 (2009). ISSN 0306-4573. https://doi.org/10.1016/j.ipm.2009.03.002. https://linkinghub.elsevier.com/retrieve/pii/S0306457309000259. Accessed 11 Sept 2023

21. Veličković, P., et al.: Graph Attention Networks (2017). arXiv Version Number: 3. https://doi.org/10.48550/ARXIV.1710.10903. https://arxiv.org/abs/1710.10903. Accessed 09 Feb 2023

22. Xiao, J., et al.: Robust anomaly-based intrusion detection system for in vehicle network by graph neural network framework. Appl. Intell. **53**(3), 3183–3206 (2023). ISSN 0924-669X, 1573-7497. https://doi.org/10.1007/s10489-022-03412-8. Accessed 24 Jan 2023

23. Zhang, S., et al.: Graph convolutional networks: a comprehensive review. Comput. Soc. Netw. **6**(1), 11 (2019). ISSN 2197-4314. https://doi.org/10.1186/s40649-019-0069-y. https://computationalsocialnetworks.springeropen.com/articles/10.1186/s40649-019-0069-y. Accessed 11 Sept 2023

24. Zhang, Y., et al.: Intrusion detection of industrial Internet-of-Things based on reconstructed graph neural networks. IEEE Trans. Netw. Sci. Eng. 1–12 (2022). ISSN 2327-4697, 2334-329X. https://doi.org/10.1109/TNSE.2022.3184975. https://ieeexplore.ieee.org/document/9802721/. Accessed 24 Jan 2023

25. Zhou, Y., Chiu, D.M., Lui, J.C.S.: A simple model for chunk-scheduling strategies in P2P streaming. IEEE/ACM Trans. Netw. **19**, 42–54 (2011). https://doi.org/10.1109/TNET.2010.2065237

Generating Synthetic Data to Improve Intrusion Detection in Smart City Network Systems

Pavel Čech⬤, Daniela Ponce⬤, Peter Mikulecký(✉)⬤, Karel Mls⬤, Andrea Žváčková⬤, Petr Tučník⬤, and Tereza Otčenášková⬤

University of Hradec Králové, Hradec Králové, Czech Republic
{pavel.cech,peter.mikulecky}@uhk.cz
http://www.uhk.cz

Abstract. Fast and reliable identification of cyber attacks in network systems of smart cities is currently a critical and demanding task. Machine learning algorithms have been used for intrusion detection, but the existing data sets intended for their training are often imbalanced, which can reduce the effectiveness of the proposed model. Oversampling and undersampling techniques can solve the problem but have limitations, such as the risk of overfitting and information loss. Furthermore, network data logs are noisy and inconsistent, making it challenging to capture essential patterns in the data accurately. To address these issues, this study proposes using Generative Adversarial Networks to generate synthetic network traffic data. The results offer new insight into developing more effective intrusion detection systems, especially in the context of smart cities' network infrastructure.

Keywords: smart cities · intrusion detection · imbalanced datasets · generative adversarial networks

1 Introduction

In the context of smart cities, cyber security plays an important role. A complex network infrastructure using the principles of the Internet of Things (IoT) is, like other network systems, under constant threat from various types of attacks. Smart cities collect and process vast amounts of data, including citizens' data. Securing this data is critical to prevent data breaches, identity theft, and other cyber attacks. In addition, smart cities include crucial infrastructure such as energy grids, water supply and transportation systems. Cyber attacks on this infrastructure can have catastrophic consequences. As mentioned above, smart cities increasingly have infrastructure based on IoT devices, such as sensors, cameras or traffic management devices. These devices can be the target of cyber-attacks if they are not adequately secured. It is, therefore, evident that cyber security must be an integral part of the planning, operation and development of smart cities.

S. Bouzefrane et al. (Eds.): MSPN 2023, LNCS 14482, pp. 40–51, 2024.
https://doi.org/10.1007/978-3-031-52426-4_3

The development and application of machine learning algorithms to detect various types of cyber attacks or intrusions has been an active area of research [13] in recent years. However, machine learning methods need training datasets of suitable composition to work effectively. Therefore, one of the main challenges in developing effective intrusion detection models is the presence of imbalanced data sets, where the number of examples in one class is much higher or lower than in another. In such cases, the performance of machine learning algorithms can be severely affected as they tend to be biased towards the majority class and produce poor predictions for the minority classes. The problem is further complicated when multiple subclasses exist in an imbalanced dataset, as this can make learning the algorithm in question even more difficult [7].

Several approaches have been proposed and are used to deal with the problem of imbalanced datasets in machine learning, including resampling, undersampling, or a combination of both. Oversampling techniques involve generating synthetic examples for minority classes, while undersampling techniques involve removing examples from the majority class. Both techniques aim to balance the number of examples in different classes and improve the performance of machine learning algorithms. However, these approaches have several limitations, including the risk of overfitting, loss of information, and the inability to capture the underlying distribution of the data accurately.

Intrusion detection in network systems often involves the analysis of large datasets of network data protocols, which can be challenging due to the high dimensionality and complexity of the data. In addition to the problems of imbalanced datasets and multiple subclasses, network data protocols also present specific challenges regarding their size, diversity, and quality. One of the common problems with network data protocols is their high noise and inconsistency, which can come from various sources such as network failures, software errors, and human error. The noisy and inconsistent nature of network data logs can make it challenging to train machine learning models that can accurately capture underlying patterns in the data.

Another challenge with network data protocols is obtaining high-quality labelled data for training and validation purposes. Manually tagging network data logs can be time-consuming and error-prone, and the tagging process may require expertise in network security and intrusion detection. This can result in a limited number of labelled samples, further exacerbating the problem of imbalanced datasets and multiple smaller classes.

Various methods for generating synthetic network data protocols, such as Monte Carlo simulation, generative models, and anomaly detection, have been proposed to address these issues. However, these methods have limitations in accurately capturing complex patterns and interactions in networked systems. Therefore, this study aims to generate synthetic network traffic data using Generative Adversarial Networks (GAN) to improve cyber attack detection in case of imbalanced data sets. The proposed approach attempts to overcome the limitations of existing methods and enhance the performance of intrusion detection classification models on network traffic data. The findings of this study can provide valuable insights into developing more efficient and robust intrusion detection systems for network security.

2   Imbalanced Dataset Problem

One of the biggest challenges in machine learning is dealing with dataset-related problems, which can lead to less accurate, unreliable, and fair models. Dataset-related issues can be related to imbalanced datasets [2], insufficient, noisy, biased, inconsistent or missing data. Dataset-related problems can have significant adverse effects on individuals and society as a whole. Addressing these issues requires careful attention to data collection, preprocessing, modelling techniques, and ongoing monitoring and evaluation of model performance [9]. In the following, we focus on one dataset-related problem: an imbalanced dataset.

Imbalanced datasets are common in real-world applications, such as fraud detection, medical diagnosis, and customer churn prediction, where the positive class (e.g., fraud, disease, churn) is rare. Therefore, it is essential to address the problem of imbalanced datasets to ensure that machine learning models can learn from all available data and produce accurate predictions for all classes. Few techniques to address the issue of imbalanced datasets exist, for example, resampling, cost-sensitive learning, one-class classification, ensemble methods, or synthetic data generation. The technique's choice depends on the dataset's specific characteristics and the problem being addressed. It may be necessary to combine different techniques to achieve the best performance.

2.1   Synthetic Data Generation

Synthetic data generation aims to create new instances for the minority class, which can augment the original dataset and balance the class distribution. Synthetic data generation techniques can be used to generate new examples for the minority class. The generated examples can improve the performance of the intrusion detection model.

One popular technique for synthetic data generation is GAN, a type of neural network architecture consisting of two parts: a generator network and a discriminator network. The generator network learns to generate new examples of the minority class by trying to fool the discriminator network, which is trained to distinguish between natural and synthetic data. The generator network is trained to produce synthetic data similar to the real data, while the discriminator network is trained to identify which examples are real and which are synthetic. Another technique for synthetic data generation is Variational Autoencoders (VAEs), a generative model that can learn a compact representation of the input data. VAEs can generate new examples of the minority class by sampling from the learned representation and decoding it to generate new examples.

In intrusion detection, GANs can generate new examples of attack data similar to real attack data. The synthetic data can be used to augment the original dataset and balance the class distribution, which can improve the performance of the intrusion detection model in detecting attacks.

Synthetic data generation techniques can suffer from some limitations. For example, if the synthetic data is not sufficiently diverse or does not capture the underlying distribution of the minority class, it may not be effective in improving the performance of the intrusion detection model. Additionally, synthetic data generation techniques may require many computational resources and may not always be feasible. Therefore, the choice of which technique to use depends on the specific problem being solved and the dataset's characteristics. A combination of techniques, such as resampling and synthetic data generation, may be required to effectively address the problem of imbalanced datasets in intrusion detection.

Coping with imbalanced datasets for network traffic attacks involves selecting appropriate sampling techniques and tools that can help balance the dataset and improve the performance of the classification model. The imbalance in the dataset hinders correct classification because when there is an imbalance between the class labels, the designed classifier may mispredict malicious data over benign data or vice versa [17]. Therefore, creating an effective model that correctly classifies attack instances when there is an imbalanced dataset is difficult.

The following section presents an overview of works related to our topic, mainly focusing on methods and tools for modifying imbalanced data to analyze potential security attacks on network traffic.

2.2   Related Works

A thorough analysis of the impact of various techniques for handling imbalanced data when machine learning approaches are applied to identifying encrypted traffic is provided in [14]. According to [12], several measures can be taken to improve classification accuracy in imbalanced data. One approach is to use resampling techniques, such as oversampling or undersampling, to balance the number of instances in each class. However, it is recommended to experiment with different techniques and evaluate their performance on the specific problem being addressed [12].

In the paper [1], a model fusion of deep neural networks for anomaly detection is discussed. As network security is crucial in today's digital age, network threat detection is essential to detect attacks and distinguish anomalous behaviours from regular traffic. Network anomaly detection (NAD) is a technique that facilitates network security with threat detection based on exceptional traffic patterns. The model fusion of deep neural networks (DNN) improves network anomaly detection by combining binary normal/attack DNN to detect the availability of any attack and multi-attack DNN to categorize the attacks. This approach addresses the problem of million-scale and highly imbalanced traffic data.

An excellent delineation of why it pays to use GAN in network intrusion detection is shown by [16]. Using GAN in malware detection is significant because it generates realistic malware adversarial samples with low attack costs and high attack success rates by exploiting the knowledge of adversarial samples. GANs have an advantage in sample generation, consisting of a generator and a discriminator. Through the game between the generator and the discriminator, the generator will learn the underlying patterns of the data and generate new data.

In [6], a GAN-based approach is proposed to identify malicious network behaviours even when hidden under a large amount of regular communication traffic. The technique used here is effective even when dealing with imbalanced data, which is challenging to label effectively. The whole training set of the minor class is adopted rather than some samples as a conventional oversampling method. The generator produces the expected well-structured data after the generative and discriminator models achieve equilibrium. This approach improves classification effectiveness by producing new data from the existing dataset, which helps identify malicious network behaviours even when hidden under a large amount of regular communication traffic.

The article [15] presents a new method for generating traffic data using a conditional GAN. The authors demonstrate that their approach can generate realistic traffic data that can be used for training machine learning models. A GAN is a machine-learning model usually consisting of two neural networks: a generator and a discriminator. The generator creates new data samples while the discriminator distinguishes between real and fake data. In contrast, a conditional GAN (cGAN) takes additional information as input to the generator and discriminator. This additional information can be used to control the characteristics of the generated data.

Various GAN-based approaches can be applied to different types of networks for detecting network attacks. These GAN-based techniques are designed to address the challenge of imbalanced data in network attack traffic detection, a common problem in this field. Several recent GAN-based approaches are described, e.g., in papers [3,4,8], or [18].

3   Materials

This section introduces the dataset used for the study and tools and techniques deployed for classification and synthetic data generation.

3.1   Data

This study used the UNSW-NB15 dataset provided by the Cyber Range Lab of UNSW Canberra to test the synthetic data generation [11]. The dataset is created by combining the regular network traffic with synthetic attack data. There are 49 features, including the binary label denoting the attack, organic data, and the attack category label. The dataset contains nine types of attacks. The complete dataset totals 2 540 044 records. To simplify the computation, only the first 700 001 records were utilized. Thus, the dataset comprises 677 786 (96.83%) records with organic network traffic and 22 215 (3.17%) records with attack signatures. The table 1 below details the counts and proportions of specific attack categories.

Table 1. Dataset categories with counts and proportions.

Attack	Analysis	Backdoors	DoS	Exploits	Fuzzers	Generic	Reconnaissance	Shellcode	Worms	None
count	526	534	1 167	5409	5 051	7 522	1 759	223	24	677 786
prop.	0.08%	0.08%	0.17%	0.77%	0.72%	1.07%	0.25%	0.03%	0.00%	96.83%

The dataset was transformed and cleaned to enable further processing. The features with constant values in any of the categories were removed. The nominal features were converted to factors with a corresponding number of levels. The records containing the NaN values in any of the features were removed. The binary label feature was removed. The organic traffic was labelled as the attack category with the value None. The cleaned dataset contains 699 934 records and 37 features, including the attack category label. The training of GAN was performed with standardized data that was rescaled to have zero mean and standard deviation 1. The classification was executed without standardization.

3.2 Tools and Techniques

The MATLAB 2022 computing platform with Statistics and Machine Learning Toolbox and Deep Learning Toolbox was deployed to conduct the data analyses and synthetic data generation. The classification of attacks was performed by fitting the classification tree on the network traffic feature data. The tree generation was restricted to 100 splits. The GINI index was used to measure the impurity of splits. The cost of misclassification was the same for all categories. The tree model applied a 5-fold cross-validation procedure during training. The performance of the classification is assessed using accuracy. The accuracy is the ratio of correctly classified samples and the total number of samples.

The synthetic data generation was executed with generative adversarial network architecture. The generator consists of 24 layers. The layers were arranged into 7 blocks of fully connected layer, batch normalization or drop out layer and rectified unit layer. The network's input was through the feature input layer of size given by the number of features. The last layer was the hyperbolic tangent activation layer. Figure 1 shows the layers of the generator. The other layer designs were also tested, but the introduced one was the most effective. The discriminator includes 12 layers. The design utilizes 3 blocks consisting of a fully connected layer, drop out layer and rectified unit layer. The feature input layer was used as an input layer, and the sigmoid layer of size one was used as an output layer. Figure 2 depicts the arrangement of layers used for the discriminator.

The training cycles of the generator and discriminator were treated separately. The discriminator was trained at the beginning of each training iteration of the generator. Thus, the discriminator was trained using the specified number of iterations and minibatches and then was used to train the generator. In particular, the generator was trained in 10 000 iterations. For each training iteration of the generator, there were 10 training cycles of the discriminator. The training was based on the Wasserstein loss function with gradient penalty [5].

Deploying the Wasserstein loss function with gradient penalty ensures excellent training stability and avoids convergence failures due to vanishing or exploding gradients.

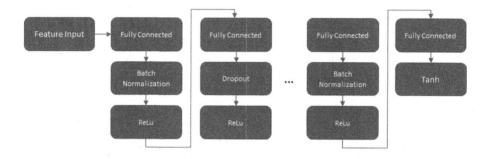

Fig. 1. The layers of the generator. The main layers are arranged into 7 blocks by 3 layers.

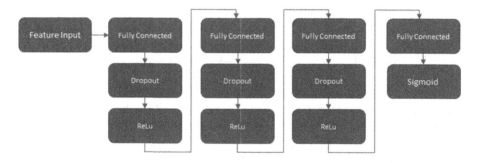

Fig. 2. The layers of the discriminator. The main layers are arranged into 3 blocks by 3 layers.

4   Results

In this section, the results of the study are presented. First, classification with the original dataset and detailed results are performed. Next, the results of the classifier trained on the extended dataset are compared with the former.

4.1   Classification with the Original Dataset

The classification tree was trained on the partially preprocessed UNSW-NB15 dataset. The trained classifier was used to predict the type of attack on the original dataset. The classifier achieved 99.05% accuracy. However, due to the low probability of the attack in the dataset, the classifier misclassified 6644 samples, out of which 2066 cases were attacks classified as organic traffic. The other cases were misclassified attack types. Figure 3 shows the confusion matrix for the classification with the original dataset.

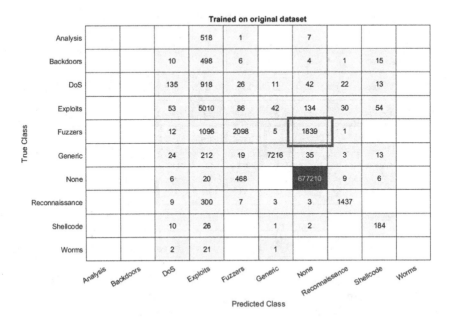

Trained on original dataset

True Class	Analysis	Backdoors	DoS	Exploits	Fuzzers	Generic	None	Reconnaissance	Shellcode	Worms
Analysis				518	1		7			
Backdoors			10	498	6		4	1	15	
DoS			135	918	26	11	42	22	13	
Exploits			53	5010	86	42	134	30	54	
Fuzzers			12	1096	2098	5	1839	1		
Generic			24	212	19	7216	35	3	13	
None			6	20	468		677210	9	6	
Reconnaissance			9	300	7	3	3	1437		
Shellcode			10	26		1	2		184	
Worms			2	21		1				

Predicted Class

Fig. 3. Confusion matrix showing the classifier's performance trained with the original dataset. The cell background reflects the frequency. The red rectangle points to a misclassification targeted in further study. (Color figure online)

The classification results with the original dataset reveal that the "Fuzzers" attack is misclassified as organic traffic in 1839 cases. There are also other categories being incorrectly classfied but the "Fuzzers" attack considered as an organic traffic is the most misclassfied category and accounts for 28% of all misclassfied cases. Therefore, the subsequent analyses will be focused on this type of attack.

4.2 Classification with the Extended Dataset

In reference to the previous section, the dataset was extended with 5 000 synthetically generated samples in the "Fuzzers" attack category using GAN architecture. The other categories remained the same. The extended dataset was fitted with the decision tree classifier. The confusion matrix for the classification is in Fig. 4. The figure shows that the "Fuzzers" attack was misclassified only in 1066 cases, that is 773 fewer samples as compared to the classification of the original dataset (i.e. improvement by approx. 42%). There is, however, a notable increase in misclassification of "Fuzzers" and "Exploits". The "Fuzzers" attack was considered an "Exploits" attack in 1096 cases with the original dataset. The misclassification increased to 1159 (by 63 cases, i.e. approx. 6%) after the classifier was trained on an extended dataset.

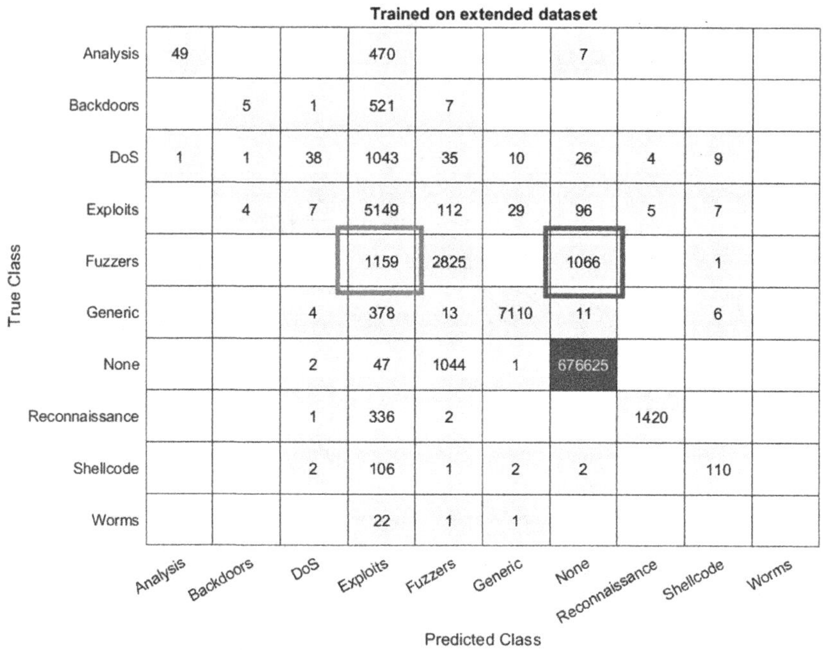

Trained on extended dataset

True Class	Analysis	Backdoors	DoS	Exploits	Fuzzers	Generic	None	Reconnaissance	Shellcode	Worms
Analysis	49			470			7			
Backdoors		5	1	521	7					
DoS	1	1	38	1043	35	10	26	4	9	
Exploits		4	7	5149	112	29	96	5	7	
Fuzzers				1159	2825		1066		1	
Generic			4	378	13	7110	11		6	
None			2	47	1044	1	676625			
Reconnaissance			1	336	2			1420		
Shellcode			2	106	1	2	2		110	
Worms				22	1	1				

Predicted Class

Fig. 4. Confusion matrix showing the classifier's performance trained with the dataset extended by the synthetic data. The cell background reflects the frequency. The red rectangle points to a misclassification targeted with synthetic data generation. The orange rectangle denotes the category notably worsened by the performed procedure. (Color figure online)

5   Discussion

The results show that the synthetic data generated using GAN architecture can be used in intrusion detection to improve the identification of some attacks. The results confirmed that the misclassification was reduced but only partly, and further study would be needed to improve the introduced synthetic data generation. These studies might focus, for instance, on the ratio between the original and the synthetic data. In the study, the dataset in the specified category of attacks was extended by the same number of samples as was in the original dataset. Thus, the category of attacks had twice the sample size. If more samples were added to the dataset, the performance deteriorates as the classifier learns more of the characteristics of the synthetic rather than the original samples. The generated samples were also in their characteristics close to another category of attacks, and the synthesized samples led to an increase in misclassification of that category. Generating synthetic data for other categories might help to avoid such misclassification. The loss function appeared to have a significant effect on learning. The log loss function performed worse under the given GAN architecture and sometimes failed to converge. The Wasserstein loss is a better choice for this type of task despite longer training time.

The results align with the study of Moualla et al. [10]. However, the study used SMOTE principle to extend the dataset and does not report improvements just by extending the dataset with synthetic data. Instead, the classification is also enhanced. The results are comparable to the study of Kumar and Sinha [8] in which the UNSW-NB15 is scrutinized. Still, the study down-sampled the organic traffic and over-sampled the other categories more significantly than this study.

There are several limitations to the present study. The study focused only on one dataset and one category of attacks. Further, studies must be conducted to verify the results on other datasets and several categories. The study used only one classificatory and did not attempt to improve the classification by different means, such as parametrization or different costs of misclassification. The results might have been different under different classificator configurations.

6   Conclusion

The currently popular and increasingly developing concept of smart cities cannot function without the trouble-free operation of extensive and sophisticated computer networks and their services, which form the basis of everything that smart cities provide. The implementation of the functionalities of smart cities in actual conditions often has a basis in the use of the Internet of Things (IoT) concept. However, it is unfortunate that the implementation of the Internet of Things and the networks enabling their operation is often the target of various types of intrusions, frequently making their correct use impossible. At the same time, valuable data and information are often leaked or destroyed.

Our article aimed to contribute to the issue of identifying attempts to disrupt the proper functioning of computer networks in the context of smart cities. However, approaches based on machine learning tools often encounter the problem of imbalanced datasets, which in their imbalanced form cannot be used to train the relevant machine learning tool seriously. In the article, we, therefore, deal with the possibility of removing the imbalance of datasets using Generative Adversarial Networks (GAN). The results of our experiments show that the synthetic data generated using GAN architecture can be used in intrusion detection to improve the identification of some attacks. Despite some limitations of our research, removing the imbalance of data sets by generating synthetic data sets using GANs appears helpful. It can help increase the security of the accurate functioning of the smart cities concept.

Acknowledgement. The financial support of the project "Application of Artificial Intelligence for Ensuring Cyber Security in Smart City", n. VJ02010016, granted by the Ministry of the Interior of the Czech Republic is gratefully acknowledged.

References

1. AlDahoul, N., Abdul Karim, H., Ba Wazir, A.S.: Model fusion of deep neural networks for anomaly detection. J. Big Data **8**, 1–18 (2021)
2. Buda, M., Maki, A., Mazurowski, M.A.: A systematic study of the class imbalance problem in convolutional neural networks. Neural Netw. **106**, 249–259 (2018)
3. Cao, X., Luo, Q., Wu, P.: Filter-GAN: imbalanced malicious traffic classification based on generative adversarial networks with filter. Mathematics **10**(19), 3482 (2022)
4. Chapaneri, R., Shah, S.: Enhanced detection of imbalanced malicious network traffic with regularized generative adversarial networks. J. Netw. Comput. Appl. **202**, 103368 (2022)
5. Gulrajani, I., Ahmed, F., Arjovsky, M., Dumoulin, V., Courville, A.: Improved training of wasserstein GANs. In: Proceedings of the 31st International Conference on Neural Information Processing Systems, NIPS 2017, pp. 5769–5779. Curran Associates Inc (2017)
6. Hao, X., et al.: Producing more with less: a gan-based network attack detection approach for imbalanced data. In: 2021 IEEE 24th International Conference on Computer Supported Cooperative Work in Design (CSCWD), pp. 384–390. IEEE (2021)
7. Johnson, J.M., Khoshgoftaar, T.M.: Survey on deep learning with class imbalance. J. Big Data **6**(1), 1–54 (2019)
8. Kumar, V., Sinha, D.: Synthetic attack data generation model applying generative adversarial network for intrusion detection. Comput. Secur. **125**, 103054 (2023)
9. Liu, W., Wang, Z., Liu, X., Zeng, N., Liu, Y., Alsaadi, F.E.: A survey of deep neural network architectures and their applications. Neurocomputing **234**, 11–26 (2017)
10. Moualla, S., Khorzom, K., Jafar, A.: Improving the performance of machine learning-based network intrusion detection systems on the UNSW-NB15 dataset. Comput. Intell. Neurosci. **2021**, e5557577 (2021)
11. Moustafa, N., Slay, J.: UNSW-NB15: a comprehensive data set for network intrusion detection systems (UNSW-NB15 network data set). In: 2015 Military Communications and Information Systems Conference (MilCIS), pp. 1–6 (2015)
12. Pulgar, F.J., Rivera, A.J., Charte, F., del Jesus, M.J.: On the impact of imbalanced data in convolutional neural networks performance. In: Martínez de Pisón, F.J., Urraca, R., Quintián, H., Corchado, E. (eds.) HAIS 2017. LNCS (LNAI), vol. 10334, pp. 220–232. Springer, Cham (2017). https://doi.org/10.1007/978-3-319-59650-1_19
13. Sommer, R., Paxson, V.: Outside the closed world: on using machine learning for network intrusion detection. In: 2010 IEEE Symposium on Security and Privacy, pp. 305–316. IEEE (2010)
14. Vu, L., Van Tra, D., Nguyen, Q.U.: Learning from imbalanced data for encrypted traffic identification problem. In: Proceedings of the 7th Symposium on Information and Communication Technology, pp. 147–152 (2016)
15. Wang, J., Yan, X., Liu, L., Li, L., Yu, Y.: CTTGAN: traffic data synthesizing scheme based on conditional GAN. Sensors **22**(14), 5243 (2022)

16. Xuan, B., Li, J., Song, Y.: SFCWGAN-BITCN with sequential features for malware detection. Appl. Sci. **13**(4), 2079 (2023)
17. Yilmaz, I., Masum, R., Siraj, A.: Addressing imbalanced data problem with generative adversarial network for intrusion detection. In: 2020 IEEE 21st International Conference on Information Reuse and Integration for Data Science (IRI), pp. 25–30. IEEE (2020)
18. Zekan, M., Tomičić, I., Schatten, M.: Low-sample classification in NIDS using the EC-GAN method. JUCS J. Univ. Comput. Sci. **28**(12), 1330–1346 (2022)

Building the Shortest Path Database in Urban Traffic Network Using RAO Algorithm

Le Vinh Thinh[1(✉)], Tran Thien Huan[2], and Nguyen Van Long[3]

[1] Faculty of Information Technology, HCM City University of Technology and Education,
Ho Chi Minh City, Vietnam
thinhlv@hcmute.edu.vn

[2] Faculty of Electronics and Telecommunication (FET), Saigon University (SGU),
Ho Chi Minh City, Vietnam
tthuan@sgu.edu.vn

[3] Department of Information and Technology, HCM City University of Technology and
Education, Ho Chi Minh City, Vietnam
longnv@hcmute.edu.vn

Abstract. In urban environments, traffic networks are characterized by fixed distances between nodes, representing intersections or landmarks. Efficiently identifying the shortest path between any two nodes is crucial for various applications, such as route optimization for emergency services, ride-sharing algorithms, and general traffic management. Traditional methods like Dijkstra's algorithm are computationally intensive, especially for large-scale networks. To address this challenge, we propose a novel approach that precomputes and stores the shortest paths in a dedicated database hosted on a server system. Our methodology leverages the RAO algorithm, an advanced optimization technique, to solve the shortest path problem. Unlike conventional methods, the RAO algorithm adapts to varying conditions and constraints, making it highly suitable for dynamic urban traffic networks. We construct a comprehensive database that contains pre-calculated shortest paths between any two nodes, thereby significantly reducing real-time computational load. To validate the effectiveness of our approach, we conducted experiments on networks of varying complexities: 6-node, 8-node, and 20-node configurations. These experiments serve to emulate different scales of urban traffic networks. We compared the performance of our RAO-based solution with the Particle Swarm Optimization (PSO) algorithm, using Dijkstra's algorithm as a baseline for evaluation. Our results indicate a marked improvement in computational efficiency and accuracy when using the RAO algorithm. Specifically, the RAO-based solution outperformed the PSO algorithm across all test cases, thereby confirming its suitability for real-world applications. Our research introduces a scalable and efficient solution for precomputing shortest paths in urban traffic networks using the RAO algorithm.

Keywords: Optimization · RAO · Dijkstra · Traffic

S. Bouzefrane et al. (Eds.): MSPN 2023, LNCS 14482, pp. 52–70, 2024.
https://doi.org/10.1007/978-3-031-52426-4_4

1   Introduction

Urban traffic management is a complex and challenging issue that has garnered significant attention in both academia and industry. With the rapid urbanization and population growth, cities worldwide are grappling with congested roads, increased travel times, and inefficiencies in transportation systems. The concept of finding the shortest path between two points in a network is a fundamental problem in graph theory and has extensive applications in various domains, including urban traffic management, logistics, telecommunications, and emergency response services.

Traditional algorithms like's algorithm [1] and A* [2] have been the cornerstone for solving shortest path problems. However, these algorithms often suffer from high computational complexity, particularly when applied to large, dynamic, and real-time systems. This limitation is a significant concern in the context of urban traffic networks, where real-time decision-making is crucial. Several alternative approaches have been explored to address these challenges. Genetic algorithms, for instance, have been applied to the shortest path problem with promising results. Gen et al. [3] utilized genetic algorithms to find optimal paths in static networks, while Ahn and Ramakrishna [4] extended this work by incorporating population sizing techniques. Learning algorithms have also been employed, [5] the authors using adaptive learning algorithms to find the shortest path in dynamic networks.

Particle Swarm Optimization (PSO) has been another avenue of research [6], but like genetic algorithms, it also requires significant computational resources. Recently, Rao introduced the RAO algorithm, a novel optimization technique devoid of metaphorical constructs, which has been applied successfully in various optimization scenarios [7]. Despite these advancements, there is a noticeable gap in the literature concerning the pre-computation and storage of shortest paths for real-time applications in urban traffic networks. Most existing solutions focus on real-time computation, which is often not feasible for large-scale, dynamic networks.

This research aims to fill this gap by proposing a novel approach that leverages the RAO algorithm to precompute and store the shortest paths between any two nodes in a dedicated server-side database. By doing so, we aim to significantly reduce the computational load for real-time applications, thereby offering a scalable and efficient solution. The database containing the best routes between any pair of nodes in the transportation network, generated via the RAO algorithm, will be hosted on cloud platforms. This enables users to quickly access the most efficient path between any two points within the network via the app, thereby obviating the necessity for on-the-spot optimization and consequently conserving time. The remainder of this paper is structured as follows: Sect. 2 delves into the related work, providing a comprehensive review of optimization algorithms applied to the shortest path problem. Section 3 outlines the methodology, detailing the RAO algorithm's implementation and the construction of the shortest path database. Section 4 presents the experimental setup, results, and a comparative analysis with existing algorithms like RAO, PSO and Dijkstra's algorithm for 6, 8 and 20-nodes cases. Finally, Sect. 5 concludes the paper, summarizing the key findings and contributions.

2 Related Work

The problem of efficiently solving the shortest path in urban traffic networks has been a subject of extensive research, given its critical importance in real-time traffic management systems. Traditional algorithms like Dijkstra's algorithm [1] have been foundational in this domain. Dijkstra's algorithm is known for its robustness and accuracy but suffers from computational limitations when applied to large, dynamic networks. This limitation becomes particularly significant in urban traffic systems, where the network is not only large but also highly dynamic, with traffic conditions changing rapidly.

The A* algorithm [2] offers a significant improvement over Dijkstra's algorithm by incorporating heuristics to estimate the cost of the path from the current node to the destination. This heuristic approach reduces the computational overhead, making it more suitable for real-time traffic management systems where quick decision-making is crucial. However, the effectiveness of the A* algorithm is highly dependent on the quality of the heuristic used, which can be a challenge in dynamic traffic scenarios.

Evolutionary algorithms have been another avenue of research for solving the shortest path problem. Gen et al. [3] were among the pioneers in applying genetic algorithms to this problem. Their work demonstrated the applicability of genetic algorithms in optimizing traffic flow and reducing congestion. The work by Goldberg and Voessner [8] on optimizing global-local search hybrids using genetic algorithms has implications for traffic management. Their approach can be adapted to manage complex traffic scenarios involving multiple objectives, such as minimizing both distance and travel time.

Learning algorithms have also shown promise in adapting to dynamic changes in traffic patterns. The authors in [5] applied adaptive learning algorithms to dynamically changing networks. Their approach is highly relevant for real-time traffic management, where the system needs to adapt to changing traffic conditions continually. The foundational work on reinforcement learning by Sutton and Barto [9] offers techniques that can be adapted for real-time traffic routing. Reinforcement learning algorithms can learn from the environment, making them highly adaptable to changing traffic conditions.

Particle Swarm Optimization (PSO) has been another focus of research. The work by Eberhart and [6] applied PSO to the Traveling Salesman Problem, a problem closely related to finding the shortest path in a network. Their work has been foundational in demonstrating the applicability of PSO in traffic management. Poli et al.'s comprehensive review discusses the adaptability of PSO in various scenarios, including dynamic traffic conditions. Their work provides insights into how PSO can be customized for specific traffic management problems.

The most recent advancement in this field is the RAO algorithm [7, 10]. The RAO algorithm is designed to adapt to varying conditions, making it an excellent candidate for managing dynamic traffic systems. The work of [11] and Suganthan [12] also discuss the application of nature-inspired algorithms, including RAO, for optimization problems. These algorithms offer innovative approaches to traffic optimization by mimicking natural processes, thereby providing robust and adaptable solutions.

Despite the plethora of algorithms and methods available, there remains a gap in the literature concerning the pre-computation and storage of shortest paths for real-time traffic management. This research aims to address this gap by employing the RAO algorithm to build a database of pre-computed shortest paths, thereby facilitating quicker and more efficient route optimization in real-time urban traffic scenarios.

3 RAO: Solving the Shortest Path Problem

3.1 Introduction to the RAO Algorithm

Professor Ravipudi Venkata Rao, from the Sardar Vallabhbhai National Institute of Technology, has developed a set of three unique optimization algorithms that are both straightforward and parameter-less. These algorithms are designed to provide efficient solutions to complex problems without relying on metaphorical inspirations or requiring specific tuning parameters.

The RAO algorithms have been successfully applied across various fields, including engineering and finance. More recently, they have been employed to solve the shortest path problem in urban traffic networks. Like the Teaching Learning Based Optimization (TLBO) algorithm [13] and the Jaya algorithm [14, 15] and [16], the RAO algorithms do not require any specific parameters, thus simplifying the task of algorithm tuning for designers. These algorithms are named Rao-1, Rao-2, and Rao-3.

Mathematical Model of the RAO Algorithm
The RAO algorithm is mathematically represented as

$$RAO = (C, E, Po, M, \Phi, T) \tag{1}$$

where:

C: Encoding method
E: Objective function
Po: Initial population
M: Population size
Φ: is the update operator.
T: Stopping condition

This mathematical model encapsulates the core components of the algorithm, providing a structured approach to solving optimization problems.

Basic Concepts about the RAO Algorithm

Encoding. To employ the RAO algorithm, feasible solutions must be encoded into vectors with a fixed structure. Each such vector is termed an "individual" or "candidate" within the population. Each element of the vector symbolizes a variable.

Population. The aggregate number of individuals in each iteration or generation is termed the population. A population encompasses a set of feasible solutions at the current iteration.

Objective Function. Each individual correlates with a feasible solution, and each solution corresponds to the value of the objective function. This value serves as a metric for gauging the adaptability of the individual to the environment.

Update. In the next generation, each individual in the population will have their variables adjusted. The goal is for the new individuals to strive to get closer to the best solution and to avoid moving towards the worst solution.

The RAO Algorithm Process. The following flowchart illustrates the process of the RAO algorithm (Fig. 1).

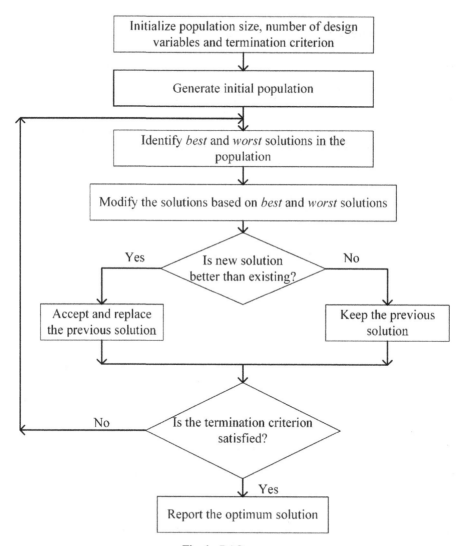

Fig. 1. RAO process

By applying the RAO algorithm to the problem of finding the shortest path in urban traffic networks, we aim to provide a robust and efficient solution that outperforms existing methods. The algorithm's adaptability and simplicity make it a promising tool for real-time traffic management systems.

3.2   RAO Algorithm to Solve the Shortest Path Problem

Problem Statement

In addressing the complexities of urban traffic networks, we employ a mathematical framework and define the optimization problem of finding the shortest path, which we intend to solve using the RAO algorithm. The traffic network is mathematically represented as a matrix A(n, n), where n signifies the total number of nodes in the network. The elements of this matrix, denoted by a(i, j), are established based on the following formula:

$$a(i,j) = \begin{cases} 0 & \text{if } i = j, \\ Inf & \text{if } i \text{ and } j \text{ are not connected}, \\ d(i,j > 0) & \text{if } i \text{ and } j \text{ are connected}, \end{cases} \quad (2)$$

Here, $i, j \in [1, n]$, , d(i, j) is a distant between node i and j and X is a positive real number representing the distance between nodes i and j. Within the urban traffic network, there are often multiple paths between any two nodes, S and T. The length of a specific path is the aggregate of the distances between the nodes constituting that path. The objective of the shortest path problem is to find a path from S to T that minimizes this aggregate distance. This is a classic optimization problem, and our proposed solution involves the application of the RAO algorithm. The RAO algorithm's inherent adaptability and computational efficiency make it an ideal candidate for solving this problem, especially in real-time urban traffic management systems that demand rapid and precise solutions. This problem statement serves as the foundation for our research, providing a clear mathematical representation of the traffic network and setting the stage for the application of the RAO algorithm, which will be explored in detail in the subsequent sections of this paper.

Encoding and Initial Population Initialization

In the context of solving the shortest path problem in urban traffic networks using the RAO algorithm, encoding and initial population initialization are crucial steps. These steps ensure that the algorithm starts with a diverse set of candidate solutions, thereby increasing the likelihood of finding an optimal or near-optimal solution.

In a specified traffic network, each node is represented as an element in a feasible solution vector, arranged according to the node number. The length of this vector is equal to the total number of nodes in the traffic network. The value of the first element in the vector signifies the starting node (S), while the value of the last element represents the ending node (T).

The values of the remaining elements in the vector are the sequential numbers of the nodes in the network, with the constraint that they must differ from the starting node (S). If any element's value matches the ending node (T), then all subsequent elements in the vector must also have the value of the ending node (T). In essence, the values of the elements in this vector delineate the sequence of nodes in a path from the starting node (S) to the ending node (T).

Object Function

Weight Matrix Construction. Initially, we need to construct a weight matrix A (also known as the adjacency matrix). This weight matrix reflects the distances between each pair of nodes in the network. Specifically, a_{ij} represents the distance $d(i, j)$ between node n_i and node n_j. Given that the traffic network is abstracted as an undirected graph, the weight matrix is symmetric. The diagonal elements of this matrix are set to zero, as exemplified in Table 1.

Definition of the Objective Function. Once the weight matrix of the graph is established, an adaptive objective function can be defined as follows:

$$f(X) = \sum_{n=1}^{D-1} a(X(n), X(n+1)) \tag{3}$$

In this equation, X represents the vector that contains the sequence of nodes along the path from S to T, as previously described. D stands for the length of the vector, which is also the total number of nodes in the traffic network. The function calculates the sum of the distances between adjacent nodes, as defined in weight matrix A.

Updating Individuals in the Population for the Next Generation

The RAO algorithm employs a straightforward approach for updating individuals in the population for the next generation. It does not rely on any control parameters but uses different vectors, which are obtained by subtracting the position of the worst individual from that of the best individual in the current iteration. This ensures that the population is always oriented towards an improved solution. The algorithm incorporates three distinct movements for position updates: the Best-Worst Movement, which is calculated based on the difference between the best and worst individuals; the Random Interaction Movement, generated through random interactions between candidate solutions; and the Adaptive Movement, which adapts based on the historical performance of the individuals. These movements simplify the optimization process while maintaining its effectiveness, as evidenced by the algorithm's performance in various applications [7].

RAO-1 Algorithm.

$$X_{i,j}^{new} = X_{i,j}^{Iter} + r_{1,j}\left(X_{best,j}^{Iter} - X_{worst,j}^{Iter}\right) \tag{4}$$

RAO-2 Algorithm.

$$\begin{cases} \text{if } f\left(X_i^{Iter}\right) < f\left(X_k^{Iter}\right) \\ X_{i,j}^{new} = X_{i,j}^{Iter} + r_{1,j}\left(X_{best,j}^{Iter} - X_{worst,j}^{Iter}\right) + r_{2,j}\left(\left|X_{i,j}^{Iter}\right| - \left|X_{k,j}^{Iter}\right|\right) \\ \text{else} \\ X_{i,j}^{new} = X_{i,j}^{Iter} + r_{1,j}\left(X_{best,j}^{Iter} - X_{worst,j}^{Iter}\right) + r_{2,j}\left(\left|X_{k,j}^{Iter}\right| - \left|X_{i,j}^{Iter}\right|\right) \end{cases} \tag{5}$$

RAO-3 Algorithm.

$$\begin{cases} \text{if } f\left(X_i^{Iter}\right) < f\left(X_k^{Iter}\right) \\ X_{i,j}^{new} = X_{i,j}^{Iter} + r_{1,j}\left(X_{best,j}^{Iter} - \left|X_{worst,j}^{Iter}\right|\right) + r_{2,j}\left(\left|X_{i,j}^{Iter}\right| - X_{k,j}^{Iter}\right) \\ \text{else} \\ X_{i,j}^{new} = X_{i,j}^{Iter} + r_{1,j}\left(X_{best,j}^{Iter} - \left|X_{worst,j}^{Iter}\right|\right) + r_{2,j}\left(\left|X_{k,j}^{Iter}\right| - X_{i,j}^{Iter}\right) \end{cases} \tag{6}$$

In the above equations, X is a vector that represents the sequence of nodes in the path from the starting node S to the ending node T, as previously elaborated; X_i^{Iter} represents the ith solution's location in the present iteration $Iter$; j (changing from 1 to D) represents the jth dimension of each solution; X_{best}^{Iter} and X_{worst}^{Iter} represent the position of the highest and lowest performing members of the population during the present iteration, in that order; r_1 and r_2 are two randomly selected values between 0 and 1 with the dimension of D; X_k^{Iter} represents the position of the kth solution, which is indiscriminately chosen; and $f(.)$ represents the numerical output of the function being optimized of the corresponding solution in the present iteration. The location of the ith solution in the next iteration is obtained using Eq. (7).

$$\begin{cases} \text{If } f\left(X_i^{new}\right) \leq f\left(X_i^{Iter}\right) \\ X_i^{Iter+1} = X_i^{new} \\ \text{else} \\ X_i^{Iter+1} = X_i^{Iter} \end{cases} \tag{7}$$

In this article, the RAO-3 algorithm is employed to solve the shortest path problem.

4 Experimental Work and Result Discussion

4.1 Experimental Work

In our study, we conducted experiments to find the shortest path between two arbitrary nodes in networks of varying sizes, 6-node, 8-node, and 20-node networks—using the RAO algorithm, the PSO algorithm, and the Dijkstra algorithm. For the 6-node network, we considered the source node $S = 1$ and the target node $T = 6$; for the 8-node network, $S = 1$ and $T = 8$; and for the 20-node network, $S = 1$ and $T = 20$.

Grid Schemes and Matrix Representation. The grid layouts and corresponding matrix representations for the three algorithms across the three different network sizes are detailed in Table 1. In this context, s and t are lists that contain the end nodes of each edge in the network. Specifically, s would contain the starting nodes, and t would contain the ending nodes for each edge. Additionally, w is a list that holds the weights or distances associated with each edge. This representation allows for a straightforward computation of the objective function and the evaluation of different paths in the network.

Table 1. Grid Schemes and Matrix Representation

6-Node Case [3]		
Grid Schemes		
Matrix Representation	PSO/RAO-3	A=[0 3 7 4 Inf Inf 3 0 2 Inf Inf 9 7 2 0 1 3 6 4 Inf 1 0 3 Inf Inf Inf 3 3 0 3 Inf 9 6 Inf 3 0];

	Dijkstra	s = [1 1 1 2 2 3 3 3 4 5];
		t = [2 3 4 3 6 4 5 6 5 6];
		w = [3 7 4 2 9 1 3 6 3 3];

8- Node Case [5]		
Grid Schemes		
Matrix Representation	PSO/RAO-3	A=[0 14 25 15 3 Inf Inf Inf 14 0 15 Inf 10 Inf 20 10 25 15 0 4 Inf 15 25 30 15 Inf 4 0 10 Inf Inf Inf 3 10 Inf 10 0 Inf Inf Inf Inf Inf 15 Inf Inf 0 Inf Inf Inf 20 25 Inf Inf Inf 0 5 Inf 10 30 Inf Inf Inf 5 0];

	Dijkstra	s = [1 1 1 1 2 2 2 2 3 3 3 3 4 7];
		t = [2 3 4 5 3 5 7 8 4 6 7 8 5 8];
		w = [14 25 15 3 15 10 20 10 4 15 25 30 10 5];

(continued)

Table 1. (*continued*)

20- Node Case [4]		
Grid Schemes		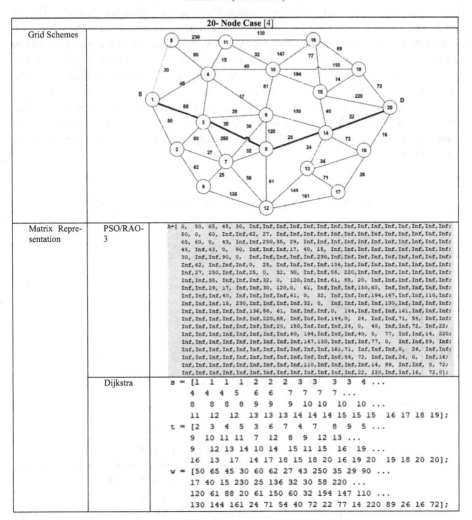
Matrix Repre-sentation	PSO/RAO-3	A=[0, 50, 65, 45, 30, Inf,Inf,Inf,Inf,Inf,Inf,Inf,Inf,Inf,Inf,Inf,Inf,Inf,Inf,Inf; 50, 0, 60, Inf,Inf,62, 27, Inf,Inf,Inf,Inf,Inf,Inf,Inf,Inf,Inf,Inf,Inf,Inf,Inf; 65, 60, 0, 43, Inf,Inf,250,35, 29, Inf,Inf,Inf,Inf,Inf,Inf,Inf,Inf,Inf,Inf,Inf; 45, Inf,43, 0, 90, Inf,Inf,Inf,17, 40, 15, Inf,Inf,Inf,Inf,Inf,Inf,Inf,Inf,Inf; 30, Inf,Inf,90, 0, Inf,Inf,Inf,Inf,Inf,230,Inf,Inf,Inf,Inf,Inf,Inf,Inf,Inf,Inf; Inf,62, Inf,Inf,Inf,0, 25, Inf,Inf,Inf,Inf,136,Inf,Inf,Inf,Inf,Inf,Inf,Inf,Inf; Inf,27, 250,Inf,Inf,25, 0, 32, 30, Inf,Inf,58, 220,Inf,Inf,Inf,Inf,Inf,Inf,Inf; Inf,Inf,35, Inf,Inf,Inf,32, 0, 120,Inf,Inf,61, 88, 20, Inf,Inf,Inf,Inf,Inf,Inf; Inf,Inf,29, 17, Inf,Inf,30, 120,0, 61, Inf,Inf,Inf,150,60, Inf,Inf,Inf,Inf,Inf; Inf,Inf,Inf,40, Inf,Inf,Inf,Inf,61, 0, 32, Inf,Inf,Inf,194,147,Inf,Inf,110,Inf; Inf,Inf,Inf,15, 230,Inf,Inf,Inf,Inf,32, 0, Inf,Inf,Inf,Inf,130,Inf,Inf,Inf,Inf; Inf,Inf,Inf,Inf,Inf,Inf,136,58, 61, Inf,Inf,Inf,0, 144,Inf,Inf,161,Inf,Inf,Inf; Inf,Inf,Inf,Inf,Inf,Inf,220,88, Inf,Inf,Inf,144,0, 24, Inf,Inf,71, 54, Inf,Inf; Inf,Inf,Inf,Inf,Inf,Inf,Inf,20, 150,Inf,Inf,Inf,24, 0, 40, Inf,Inf,72, Inf,22; Inf,Inf,Inf,Inf,Inf,Inf,Inf,Inf,60, 194,Inf,Inf,Inf,40, 0, 77, Inf,Inf,14, 220; Inf,Inf,Inf,Inf,Inf,Inf,Inf,Inf,147,130,Inf,Inf,Inf,77, 0, Inf,Inf,89, Inf; Inf,Inf,Inf,Inf,Inf,Inf,Inf,Inf,Inf,Inf,161,71, Inf,Inf,Inf,0, 26, Inf,Inf; Inf,Inf,Inf,Inf,Inf,Inf,Inf,Inf,Inf,Inf,Inf,54, 72, Inf,Inf,26, 0, Inf,16; Inf,Inf,Inf,Inf,Inf,Inf,Inf,Inf,Inf,Inf,Inf,Inf,110,Inf,Inf,Inf,14, 89, Inf, 0, 72; Inf,Inf,Inf,Inf,Inf,Inf,Inf,Inf,Inf,Inf,Inf,Inf,22, 220,Inf,Inf,16, 72,0];

	Dijkstra	s = [1 1 1 1 2 2 2 3 3 3 3 4 ...
		     4 4 4 5 6 6 7 7 7 7 ...
		     8 8 8 8 9 9 9 10 10 10 10 ...
		     11 12 12 13 13 13 14 14 14 15 15 15 16 17 18 19];
		t = [2 3 4 5 3 6 7 4 7 8 9 5 ...
		     9 10 11 11 7 12 8 9 12 13 ...
		     9 12 13 14 10 14 15 11 15 16 19 ...
		     16 13 17 14 17 18 15 18 20 16 19 20 19 18 20 20];
		w = [50 65 45 30 60 62 27 43 250 35 29 90 ...
		     17 40 15 230 25 136 32 30 58 220 ...
		     120 61 88 20 61 150 60 32 194 147 110 ...
		     130 144 161 24 71 54 40 72 22 77 14 220 89 26 16 72];

Parameter Values. Table 2 presents the parameter values used in both the PSO and RAO-3 algorithms for each of the three cases. These include the lower bound (LB) and upper bound (UB), which set the minimum and maximum allowable values for each element in the solution vector X. The population size dictates the number of individuals or solutions in the population, affecting both the diversity of the search and computational time. The mutation rate introduces variability by altering an individual's traits, helping the algorithm escape local minima. Additionally, there may be other algorithm-specific settings, such as crossover rate or inertia weight in PSO, that are unique to the specific optimization algorithm being used. These parameters are often fine-tuned to adapt the algorithm to specific problems, balancing the trade-off between exploration and exploitation.

Table 2. Values of Parameters in Both PSO and RAO Algorithms

Case	Algorithm	Parameter
6-node	PSO	LB = [1 1 1 1 1 1] UB = [6 6 6 6 6 6] NP = 10; D = 6; $C_1 = C_2 = 2$; W = 0.1; N = 200
	RAO-3	LB = [1 1 1 1 1 1] UB = [6 6 6 6 6 6] NP = 10; D = 6; N = 200
8-node	PSO	LB = [1 1 1 1 1 1 1 1] UB = [8 8 8 8 8 8 8 8] NP = 50; D = 8; $C_1 = C_2 = 2$; W = 0.1; N = 2000
	RAO-3	LB = [1 1 1 1 1 1 1 1] UB = [8 8 8 8 8 8 8 8] NP = 50; D = 8; N = 2000
20-node	PSO	LB = [1 1 1 1 1 1 1 1 1 1 1 1 1 1 1 1 1 1 1 1] UB = [20 20 20 20 20 20 20 20 20 20 20 20 20 20 20 20 20 20 20 20] NP = 50; D = 20; $C_1 = C_2 = 2$; W = 0.1; N = 2000
	RAO-3	LB = [1 1 1 1 1 1 1 1 1 1 1 1 1 1 1 1 1 1 1 1] UB = [20 20 20 20 20 20 20 20 20 20 20 20 20 20 20 20 20 20 20 20] NP = 50; D = 20; N = 2000

Optimization Process. Figures 2a, 2b, and 2c illustrate the optimization process for both the PSO and RAO algorithms in each of the three scenarios. Given the stochastic nature of the optimization mechanisms in both algorithms, we conducted 10 runs for each case to ensure objectivity in the comparison. We then averaged the objective function values across these runs.

Convergence and Performance. The results depicted in Figs. 2a, 2b, and 2c reveal that the RAO algorithm converges more quickly in all three cases compared to the PSO and Dijkstra algorithms.

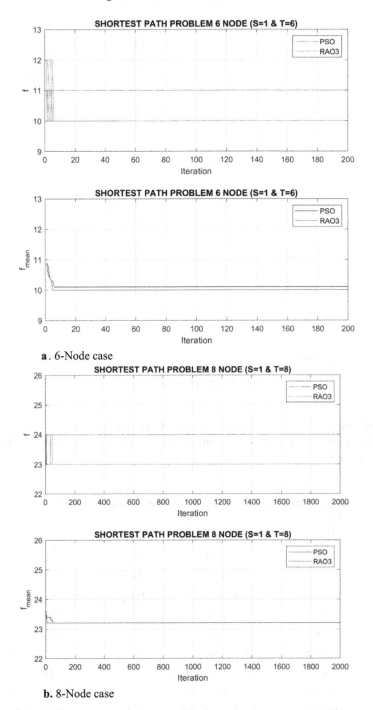

a. 6-Node case

b. 8-Node case

Fig. 2. Optimization Process of Both PSO and RAO-3 Algorithms for Finding the Shortest Path

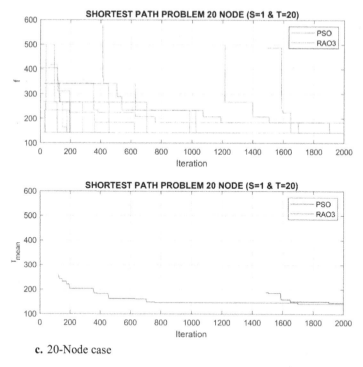

c. 20-Node case

Fig. 2. (*continued*)

Statistical Analysis. Table 3 provides a statistical summary of the optimal solutions and the computational time required for optimization by each of the three algorithms across the three scenarios.

Table 3. Comparison of Optimal Solutions and Optimal Execution Time

Case	Algorithm	Solution	Efficiency	Time (second)
6-node	*PSO*	[1, 4, 5, 6]	9/10	0.05678723
	RAO-3	[1, 4, 5, 6]	10/10	0.21841302
	Dijkstra	[1, 4, 5, 6]	10/10	0.03717860
8-node	*PSO*	[1, 5, 2, 8]	8/10	0.73226010
	RAO-3	[1, 5, 2, 8]	8/10	5.54644065
	Dijkstra	[1, 5, 2, 8]	10/10	0.05940060
20-node	*PSO*	[1, 3, 8, 14, 20]	9/10	1.18871753
	RAO-3	[1, 3, 8, 14, 20]	10/10	6.53339298
	Dijkstra	[1, 3, 8, 14, 20]	10/10	0.07070640

In general, by conducting these comprehensive experiments, we have been able to objectively evaluate the performance of the RAO algorithm in comparison with the PSO and Dijkstra algorithms. Our findings indicate that the RAO algorithm not only converges more quickly but also yields more efficient solutions, thereby validating its applicability for solving the shortest path problem in complex urban traffic networks.

4.2 Discussion

In this part, we discuss the outcomes of constructing the shortest path database in urban traffic networks using three distinct algorithms: Particle Swarm Optimization (PSO), Rao's Algorithm (RAO), and Dijkstra's Algorithm. We applied these algorithms to networks with varying complexities, specifically 6-node, 8-node, and 20-node networks.

Table 4. Parameter Settings for PSO and RAO Algorithms

Case	Algorithm	Parameters
6-node	PSO	LB = [1 1 1 1 1 1] UB = [6 6 6 6 6 6] NP = 50; D = 6; $C_1 = C_2 = 2$; W = 0.1; N = 2000
	RAO-3	LB = [1 1 1 1 1 1] UB = [6 6 6 6 6 6] NP = 50; D = 6; N = 2000
8-node	PSO	LB = [1 1 1 1 1 1 1 1] UB = [8 8 8 8 8 8 8 8] NP = 200; D = 8; $C_1 = C_2 = 2$; W = 0.1; N = 2000
	RAO-3	LB = [1 1 1 1 1 1 1 1] UB = [8 8 8 8 8 8 8 8] NP = 200; D = 8; N = 2000
20-node	PSO	LB = [1 1 1 1 1 1 1 1 1 1 1 1 1 1 1 1 1 1 1 1] UB = [20 20 20 20 20 20 20 20 20 20 20 20 20 20 20 20 20 20 20 20] NP = 500; D = 20; $C_1 = C_2 = 2$; W = 0.1; N = 5000
	RAO-3	LB = [1 1 1 1 1 1 1 1 1 1 1 1 1 1 1 1 1 1 1 1] UB = [20 20 20 20 20 20 20 20 20 20 20 20 20 20 20 20 20 20 20 20] NP = 500; D = 20; N = 5000

Table 4 presents the parameter values for both the PSO and RAO algorithms when applied to construct the shortest path database in networks with 6 nodes, 8 nodes, and 20 nodes.

Figure 3 demonstrates the shortest path database constructed for 6-node, 8-node, and 20-node networks. To this discussion, we take the 6-node network as a particular example to provide a detailed analysis.

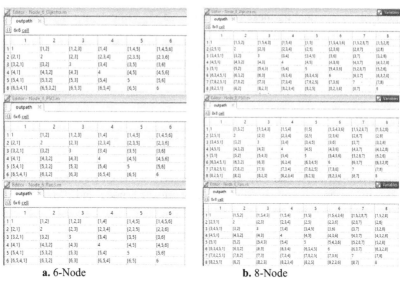

a. 6-Node   **b.** 8-Node

c. 20-Node

Fig. 3. Shortest Path Database in 6–8-20 Node Networks Constructed by PSO, RAO, and Dijkstra Algorithms

6-Node Network

- For the path from node 1 to node 3, there are two equivalent paths: 123 with a total distance of $3 + 2 = 53 + 2 = 5$ and 143 with a total distance of $4 + 1 = 54 + 1 = 5$.
- For the path from node 2 to node 6, there are two equivalent paths: 236 with a total distance of $2 + 6 = 82 + 6 = 8$ and 2356 with a total distance of $2 + 3 + 3 = 82 + 3 + 3 = 8$.
- For the path from node 3 to node 1, there are two equivalent paths: 321 with a total distance of $2 + 3 = 52 + 3 = 5$ and 341 with a total distance of $1 + 4 = 51 + 4 = 5$.
- For the path from node 3 to node 6, there are two equivalent paths: 6532 with a total distance of $3 + 3 + 2 = 83 + 3 + 2 = 8$ and 632 with a total distance of $6 + 2 = 86 + 2 = 8$.

These findings demonstrate the robustness and flexibility of the algorithms in identifying multiple optimal paths. This is particularly useful for dynamic urban traffic networks where conditions can change rapidly. We chose the 6-node network as a specific example to provide a detailed analysis. It's important to note that the 8-node and 20-node networks can be explained in a manner like the 6-node network, as illustrated in Fig. 3. The results for these larger networks are consistent with the findings for the 6-node network, reinforcing the effectiveness of the PSO, RAO, and Dijkstra algorithms in solving the shortest path problem in various network sizes.

Based on Fig. 3 and the previous observations, Table 5 and Fig. 4 presents the comparison of the shortest path database between any two points in the 6-node, 8-node, and 20-node networks using the PSO and RAO algorithms when benchmarked against the Dijkstra algorithm.

Table 5. Comparison of Optimal Solutions and Execution Time

Case	Algorithm	Efficiency (%)	Time (second)
6-node	*PSO*	100	29.823355
	RAO-3	100	253.4486
	Dijkstra	100	0.0887768
8-node	*PSO*	100	101.36823
	RAO-3	100	913.44416
	Dijkstra	100	0.1016713
20-node	*PSO*	95	6495.265
	RAO-3	96	49400.774
	Dijkstra	100	0.3497553

We clearly see that in terms of

Efficiency. All algorithms show 100% efficiency for the 6-node and 8-node networks. For the 20-node network, PSO and RAO-3 show slightly lower efficiency at 95% and 96%, respectively, compared to Dijkstra's 100%.

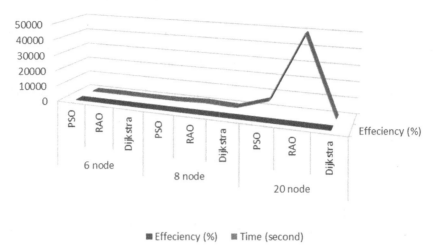

Fig. 4. Optimal Solutions and Execution Time

Execution Time. Dijkstra consistently has the lowest execution time across all network sizes. RAO-3 generally takes more time than PSO, especially noticeable in the 8-node and 20-node networks.

Scalability. While Dijkstra maintains high efficiency and low execution time, the scalability of PSO and RAO-3 is evident as they also maintain high efficiency but at the cost of increased execution time.

Benchmarking. When benchmarked against Dijkstra, both PSO and RAO-3 show competitive efficiency but lag in execution time, particularly in larger networks.

In short, the above evaluation substantiates the applicability and effectiveness of the PSO, RAO, and Dijkstra algorithms in addressing the shortest path problem across diverse network topologies.

The optimal path database between any two nodes in the traffic network, constructed using the RAO algorithm as depicted in Fig. 3, will be stored on cloud servers. This allows users to instantly retrieve the optimal path between any two nodes in the traffic network through the application, eliminating the need for real-time optimization and thus saving time.

4.3 Security concern in Vehicular Path Optimization

The optimization of vehicular routes in smart cities is not solely a matter of traffic efficiency and timesaving; it also has profound implications for urban security. This discussion aims to elucidate the integral role that path optimization algorithms, such as the Rao algorithm, play in bolstering security measures within the smart city framework.

Restricted Zones and Sensitive Locations. Smart cities often contain restricted areas that are inaccessible to unauthorized vehicles, such as government facilities or military bases. Algorithms for shortest path evaluation can be engineered to automatically exclude these zones from routing options, thereby mitigating the risk of unintentional or deliberate security violations [17, 18].

Real-time Threat Assessment. Shortest path algorithms can be synergized with real-time threat evaluation systems. For example, if a vehicle is flagged as a potential security hazard, the control system can dynamically reroute other vehicles to prevent intersection with the identified risk. This is especially relevant in vehicular ad-hoc networks (VANETs), where instantaneous data sharing can facilitate immediate action [17].

Data Integrity and Confidentiality. The integrity and confidentiality of data used in shortest path calculations are paramount for both individual privacy and collective security. Cryptographic methods can be utilized to safeguard data exchanges between vehicles and control centers, aligning with the Secure-by-Design principles [17].

Emergency Response Adaptability. In emergencies like natural calamities or terrorist attacks, shortest path algorithms can be modified to efficiently direct emergency vehicles while circumventing compromised or hazardous zones. This enhances response time and ensures the safety of emergency personnel [18].

In short, the optimization of vehicular routes in smart cities is intrinsically tied to the security of the entire urban ecosystem. By incorporating security considerations into the design and execution of path optimization algorithms, smart cities can augment their resilience against diverse threats, thereby fostering a safer and more secure habitat for their residents.

5 Conclusion

To sum up, in this research article, we have explored the feasibility of using the RAO algorithm for building the shortest path database in urban traffic network. Our proposed method has been rigorously tested on three different network sizes—6 nodes, 8 nodes, and 20 nodes. The simulation results are highly encouraging, showing that the Rao algorithm can accurately identify known optimal paths with a high degree of reliability. This indicates that the Rao algorithm shows potential as a novel method for addressing complex network optimization challenges. In our subsequent research, we plan to further validate the proposed construction of an optimal path database for larger networks exceeding 20 nodes, as well as explore the characteristics of traffic networks.

A limitation of this study is that the constructed database focuses only on distance and does not consider real-time factors. In future work, we plan to extend our shortest path calculations to include real-time objectives between any two nodes in an urban traffic network. These objectives would be influenced by variables such as weather and traffic density. By addressing these future research directions, we aim to make further contributions to the growing field of network optimization, especially in scenarios where real-time data is crucial.

References

1. Dijkstra, E. W.: A note on two problems in connexion with graphs. Numer. Math. **1**(1), 269–271 (1959). https://doi.org/10.1007/BF01386390

2. Hart, P., Nilsson, N., Raphael, B.: A formal basis for the heuristic determination of minimum cost paths. IEEE Trans. Syst. Sci. Cybern. **4**(2), 100–107 (1968). https://doi.org/10.1109/TSSC.1968.300136

3. Gen, M., Cheng, R., Wang, D.: Genetic algorithms for solving shortest path problems. In: Proceedings of 1997 IEEE International Conference on Evolutionary Computation (ICEC 1997), Indianapolis, IN, USA, pp. 401–406. IEEE (1997). https://doi.org/10.1109/ICEC.1997.592343

4. Ahn, C.W., Ramakrishna, R.S.: A genetic algorithm for shortest path routing problem and the sizing of populations. IEEE Trans. Evol. Comput. **6**(6), 566–579 (2002). https://doi.org/10.1109/TEVC.2002.804323

5. Bagheri, A., Akbarzadeh-T, M.-R., Saraee, M.-H.: Finding Shortest Path with Learning Algorithms, vol. 1 (2008)

6. Kennedy, J., Eberhart, R.: Particle swarm optimization. In: Proceedings of ICNN 1995 - International Conference on Neural Networks, Perth, WA, Australia, pp. 1942–1948. IEEE (1995). https://doi.org/10.1109/ICNN.1995.488968

7. Rao, R.V.: Rao algorithms: three metaphor-less simple algorithms for solving optimization problems. Int. J. Ind. Eng. Comput. 107–130 (2020). https://doi.org/10.5267/j.ijiec.2019.6.002

8. Goldberg, D.E., Voessner, S.: Optimizing Global-Local Search Hybrids

9. Sutton, R.S., Barto, A.G.: Reinforcement learning: an introduction. IEEE Trans. Neural Netw. **9**(5), 1054 (1998). https://doi.org/10.1109/TNN.1998.712192

10. Suyanto, S., Wibowo, A.T., Faraby, S.A., Saadah, S., Rismala, R.: Evolutionary Rao algorithm. J. Comput. Sci. **53**, 101368 (2021). https://doi.org/10.1016/j.jocs.2021.101368

11. Nanda, S.J., Panda, G.: A survey on nature inspired metaheuristic algorithms for partitional clustering. Swarm Evol. Comput. **16**, 1–18 (2014). https://doi.org/10.1016/j.swevo.2013.11.003

12. Das, S., Suganthan, P.N.: Differential evolution: a survey of the state-of-the-art. IEEE Trans. Evol. Comput. **15**(1), 4–31 (2011). https://doi.org/10.1109/TEVC.2010.2059031

13. Rao, R.V.: Teaching Learning Based Optimization Algorithm. Springer, Cham (2016). https://doi.org/10.1007/978-3-319-22732-0

14. Venkata Rao, R.: Jaya: a simple and new optimization algorithm for solving constrained and unconstrained optimization problems. Int. J. Ind. Eng. Comput. 19–34 (2016). https://doi.org/10.5267/j.ijiec.2015.8.004

15. Venkata Rao, R.: Jaya: An Advanced Optimization Algorithm and its Engineering Applications. Springer, Cham (2019). https://doi.org/10.1007/978-3-319-78922-4

16. Zhang, Y., Chi, A., Mirjalili, S.: Enhanced Jaya algorithm: a simple but efficient optimization method for constrained engineering design problems. Knowl.-Based Syst. **233**, 107555 (2021). https://doi.org/10.1016/j.knosys.2021.107555

17. Petho, Z., Khan, I., Torok, Á.: Analysis of security vulnerability levels of in-vehicle network topologies applying graph representations. J. Electron. Test. **37**(5–6), 613–621 (2021). https://doi.org/10.1007/s10836-021-05973-x

18. Wei, H., Zhang, S., He, X.: Shortest path algorithm in dynamic restricted area based on unidirectional road network model. Sensors **21**(1), 203 (2020). https://doi.org/10.3390/s21010203

Position Paper: Strengthening Applets on Legacy SIM Cards with Singularization, a New Moving Target Defense Strategy

Chrystel Gaber[1,2]([✉]), Gilles Macariot-Rat[1,2], Simona David[1,2], Jean-Philippe Wary[1,2], and Alain Cuaboz[3]

[1] Orange Innovation, Paris, France
chrystel.gaber@orange.com
[2] Orange Innovation, Bucharest, Romania
[3] Viaccess, Paris, France

Abstract. This article presents singularization, a new family of Moving Target Defense (MTD) strategy that we propose to strengthen the robustness of sensitive applets on SIMs without needing a full replacement of SIMs.

Keywords: SIM · Moving Target Defense strategy · legacy

1 Introduction

In opposition to the eSIM ecosystem, there is no mandatory process to certify the security of SIM cards. It is the responsibility of Mobile Network Operators to define the evaluation methodology and evaluate the SIM cards that they deploy. As a result, a fraction of SIMs deployed worldwide, for example legacy 2G/3G SIM cards which do not support NFC, are not certified up to EAL4+ Common Criteria. However, some emerging use cases such as identity management that require a SUBSTANTIAL or HIGH level of assurance (as per the EU CyberSecurity Act) are not compatible with these non-certified SIMs which can only reach the level of assurance BASIC, which would restrict the market reach of such use cases. The solution to replace these legacy SIMs by new ones is prohibitive in terms of cost considering that in some countries, such SIMs still represent a significant portion of the operators' SIM cards fleet, that the replacement of one card costs 15 €and that a natural roll-out is to be expected in the next 10 years with the adoption of eSIMs.

This paper presents a Moving Target Defense strategy based on the diversification of software logic (rather than remaining functionally equivalent as usual

We thank Olivier Vivolo and Jean-Marie Mele (Orange) for supporting this work. We thank Claire Loiseaux, Mohamad Hajj and Raphaël Bauduin for their insight on security certification.

© The Author(s), under exclusive license to Springer Nature Switzerland AG 2024
S. Bouzefrane et al. (Eds.): MSPN 2023, LNCS 14482, pp. 71–74, 2024.
https://doi.org/10.1007/978-3-031-52426-4_5

MTD strategy methodologies), its implementation in the context of SIM cards, as well as a return of experience by an expert from an accredited certification laboratory who performed a test session of our proof of concept. The paper is structured as follows. First, we position our proposal with regards to related works. Second, we present the main steps to achieve singularization. Then, we present our proof of concept implementation and preliminary evaluation results. Finally, we conclude our work.

2   Related Works

The main MTD techniques (IP shuffling, packet header reconfiguration, software/service reconfiguration, programming language diversity, software stack, code diversity) referenced by [3] are limited by the number of available alternatives (for example limited sets of instructions, number of ports available). Many of them are adapted to webservices and cannot be scaled down to target constrained embedded systems such as smartcards. The closest approach to ours consist in switching between multiple cryptosystems implementation by reconfiguring an embedded system firmware [2] and individualizing code at bytecode level [4]. Such techniques as well as software countermeasures routinely used by smartcard developers and are complementary to our approach. Encoding inputs and outputs are staple methods used in whitebox cryptography or code obfuscation. The difference with our work relies on the scale and granularity as in our solution, the diversification is done for each individual card or a small group of cards rather than the same input/output encoding for all cards. Also, the encoding is not performed within internal parts of the function to be protected but on its overall inputs and outputs.

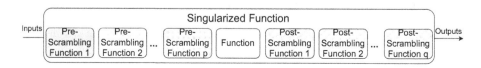

Fig. 1. Singularized Function

3   Singularization Principle

Singularization consists in creating a singular version of the function to be protected for each SIM card by adjoining scrambling functions on its outputs, as depicted in Fig. 1. Figure 2 illustrates a baseline architecture and process to initiate a singularized function. Three actors are involved, the Mobile Operator who owns the infrastructure used to manage SIM cards, the End User who owns a device in which a SIM card is deployed and a Service Provider who wishes to use a singularized security function provided by the SIM, typically to authenticate and grant an access to some resource provided by an online service. In addition

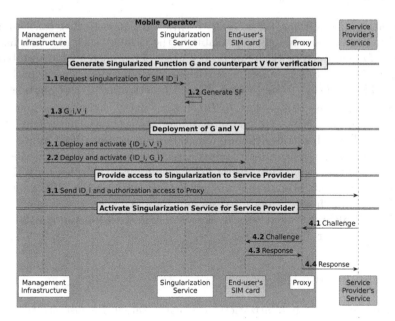

Fig. 2. Baseline instantiation

to its Management Infrastructure, the Mobile Operator puts in place a Singularization Service which generates a singularized function G for each deployed SIM and its counterpart V that can be used to verify the output produced by G as well as a Proxy server which provides a verification service to the Service Provider.

The process to initiate the use of a singularized function is divided in four steps. First, the security function G_i and its counterpart V_i are created for a given device ID_i. Second, G_i and V_i are respectively deployed in the SIM card and in a Proxy through secure channels managed by the mobile operator. The provisioning of G in the SIM card can be performed in factory during manufacturing, in shop at purchase time or on-demand by the end-user. Third, the verification service offered by the proxy is exposed to authorized Services through a secure channel. This can be achieved with access tokens for example. The Mobile Operator also provides to the Service Provider with some means to interact with G. For example, the Mobile Operator can provide to the Service Provider some APIs which allow him to deploy some code on the end-user device in order to consume the services exposed by the SF G. Fourth, a challenge/response sequence is initiated in order to verify that the service is effective before activating it.

4 Preliminary Evaluation - Unpredictability and Cost

The efficiency of MTD approaches relies on the number of variations available to achieve unpredictability. In our case, it is measured by the probability a specific combination among the total number $(n \cdot m)^k$ of sequences that can be formed by k functions chosen among n available in the catalog, each of which have an average of m parameters. Each function i and set of parameters j has a probability $p(x_{i,j})$ to be selected therefore a particular combination C has a probability $P(C) = \prod_i \prod_j p(x_{i,j})$ to be formed. If each function and set of parameter has the same probability to be selected, $P(C) = (n \cdot m)^{-k}$. In our experimentation, where $n = 40$, $k = 6$, $m = 2$, the probability to meet a specific combination is $P(C) = 80^{-6}$ which satisfies the unpredictability condition $P(C) << 0$.

Updating SIM applications requires a remote update campaign which cost can be estimating using the Aurora OTA evaluator [1]. Deploying a singularized function of 0.5 MB on 100 million devices with each 1 SIM would cost 10 m€instead of the 15 b€expected for full roll-out. Therefore, costs would be roughly equivalent if the operator deploys a singularized function on 100 million device twice a year during ten years.

5   Conclusion

This paper presents singularization, a Moving Target Defense strategy which consists in creating functional variants of a code that we propose to use to strengthen the robustness of legacy SIMs. When two parties deploy and use the same variant synchronously, they are able to trust each other while the attacker's effort to impersonate one of the parties is impacted by the unpredictability of the functional variant. We implemented several singular functions on smart cards and share a return of experience by an expert who tested our implementation. At first glance, this solution can achieve good levels of unpredictability and its cost is reasonable. Future works will concentrate on formally modelling and proving the security of the proposed scheme. We also plan to use game theoretic approach to determine the optimal size and replacement rate of functions to prevent attackers from learning the catalog of functions used for singularization.

References

1. AuroraLabs OTA cost simulator. https://www.auroralabs.com/ota-ccg-lp-1/
2. Casola, V., De Benedictis, A., Albanese, M.: A moving target defense approach for protecting resource-constrained distributed devices. In: 2013 IEEE 14th International Conference on Information Reuse & Integration (IRI), pp. 22–29 (2013). https://doi.org/10.1109/IRI.2013.6642449
3. Cho, J.H., et al.: Toward proactive, adaptive defense: a survey on moving target defense. IEEE Commun. Surv. Tutor. **22**(1), 709–745 (2020). https://doi.org/10.1109/COMST.2019.2963791
4. Jackson, T., Homescu, A., Crane, S., Larsen, P., Brunthaler, S., Franz, M.: Diversifying the software stack using randomized NOP insertion. In: Moving Target Defense II, pp. 151–173. Springer, New York (2013). https://doi.org/10.1007/978-1-4614-5416-8_8

A Smart Network Repository Based on Graph Database

Amar Abane[(✉)], Abdella Battou, Mheni Merzouki, and Tao Zhang

National Institute of Standards and Technology, Gaithersburg, MD, USA
{amar.abane,abdella.battou,mheni.merzouki,tao.zhang}@nist.gov

Abstract. To address the increasing complexity of network management and the limitations of data repositories in handling the various network operational data, this paper proposes a novel repository design that uniformly represents network operational data while allowing for a multiple abstractions access to the information. This smart repository simplifies network management functions by enabling network verification directly within the repository. The data is organized in a knowledge graph compatible with any general-purpose graph database, offering a comprehensive and extensible network repository. Performance evaluations confirm the feasibility of the proposed design. The repository's ability to natively support 'what-if' scenario evaluation is demonstrated by verifying Border Gateway Protocol (BGP) route policies and analyzing forwarding behavior with virtual Traceroute.

Keywords: network management · network data · repository · knowledge graph · SDN · Neo4j · control plane verification · data plane analysis · database-defined networks

1 Introduction

In the current era of rapidly growing network complexity and service diversity, preventing and detecting undesired behaviors is still a daunting task despite the increasing number of network management tools. One core challenge lies in the fragmented nature of network data. It is dispersed across various sources, management functions, and tools, which often lack a uniform representation for optimized usage. This scattering inevitably breeds inconsistency, reducing the utility of data and complicating its processing. Furthermore, when operators evaluate configuration changes using verification tools, it necessitates the transfer of network data from its original storage, such as databases or configuration file repositories, to the analytical tool. This approach further requires supplementary logic within the management software to process the data and integrate results, making conventional network repositories based on traditional databases [5] and distributed maps [1] inefficient.

To tackle these challenges, we present a novel repository to uniformly store and organize network data. This repository is grounded in a graph database

S. Bouzefrane et al. (Eds.): MSPN 2023, LNCS 14482, pp. 75–86, 2024.
https://doi.org/10.1007/978-3-031-52426-4_6

(GDB) which allows analysis of network data within the storage system. Creating a repository capable of addressing the intricate nuances of multi-technology network architectures, such as Beyond 5G (B5G) [6], necessitates a model that can represent these varied concepts uniformly. It's crucial for the model to align with various management scenarios by retaining the relationships in topology, connectivity, and configuration, bridging the gap between low-level network elements and high-level network intent [3]. In addition, the model must remain comprehensible and easily expendable to accommodate additional data, protocols, and technologies. Therefore, the proposed network repository is designed as a Knowledge Graph (KG) integrating semantics into the stored data. Its compatibility with general-purpose GDB allows for the construction of the KG with a systematic procedure developed in this paper. Performance assessments validate the KG's suitability as an effective network repository, underscoring its potential to enhance network management workflows.

By integrating *what-if?* scenario verification for control plane and data plane without additional code, the proposed repository simplifies the development logic of management functions, paving the way for a smart network repository. We showcase this ability through a proactive verification of route policies for Border Gateway Protocol (BGP) and an analysis of network forwarding behavior with a virtual Traceroute process. The smart repository code is publicly accessible and the features presented in this paper are reproducible[1].

This paper is organized as follows. Section 2 reports on recent approaches for storing and handling data for network management and discusses the differences with the repository proposed in this paper. Section 3 presents the design and construction of the proposed network repository and its knowledge graph schema. Section 4 provides an evaluation of the repository and discusses the implemented functionalities. Section 5 concludes the paper and discusses limitations.

2   Related Work

By using a KG to describe network data, it is possible to not only represent the network's physical and logical attributes but also uncover relationships across various dimensions within the network [4]. Many studies consider KGs to store different kinds of network data. Authors in [10] use a KG to represent network element attributes and topology of the physical network on which a ML-based technique is used to extract topology relationships between network elements. Our approach shares the same idea of representing network data using a KG. However, the proposed repository goes beyond network topology and includes device configuration, network services, routing behavior, and data plane. In [2], a solution is proposed to simplify network management workflow using a unified graph-based model for device, network, and service models. Data is represented through multiple graphs without detailing how the graphs are organized, making the model difficult to understand and reproduce. Our approach considers the same kinds of network data but uses a single graph to represent them, and

---

[1] https://github.com/usnistgov/smart-network-repository.

defines an understandable and reproducible method to build and extend the repository. KnowNet [4] builds a KG which captures and connects network data of a Software Defined Networking (SDN) controller. Applications exploit the KG to detect and respond to network issues, and derive new knowledge. Typical management applications are demonstrated, but the collection and organisation of the data is not specified and the KG is internally implemented in the tool without a standard interface to interact with it. SeaNet [9] proposes an autonomic network management solution for SDN driven by a KG and a telecommunication network ontology [8]. Our KG differs from SeaNet's as it supports the representation of configuration-based networks with a distributed control plane such as BGP, in addition to the network logical configuration and data plane. Nevertheless, the proposed KG and construction procedure consider general networking concepts and can be easily adapted to SDN networks.

The authors in [3] present a network repository design that enables an efficient representation of multiple network topology abstractions for various management purposes and share valuable insights from their experiences in curating a comprehensive and evolving topology taxonomy. They propose a Multi-Abstraction-Layer Topology (MALT) representation that supports all network management phases, including design, deployment, configuration, operation, measurement, and analysis. MALT is implemented as a specialized data processing layer on top of a SQL database, unlike our repository which is directly implemented in a native GDB.

Closest to our approach is [7] where the authors put forward the idea that SDN control is fundamentally about how data is represented. They introduce a straightforward data representation of the network that includes its topology, forwarding, and control aspects, all of which are accessible to applications via a single SQL interface. Their system represents the SDN network control infrastructure within a PostgreSQL database. Here, custom SQL queries are utilized to articulate various network abstractions. A significant hurdle in implementing this method was to coordinate on a relational database multiple abstractions that have a collective impact on the same network data.

Note that none of the network repository approaches described above provides a native support of *what-if* scenarios evaluation.

3 Proposed Repository

3.1 Overview

The repository's KG comprises three types of network information: operational, behavioral, and temporary. The operational information is the network state including devices and ports with physical and logical topology, connectivity, and configuration such as VLAN. It also includes data plane information such as routing information base (RIB) and forwarding information base (FIB), and access control list (ACL). Behavioral information is inserted to model the execution of routing protocols such as BGP, or the forwarding process such as Traceroute. Temporary information represents configuration changes not yet applied to the network. This makes verification and consistency checks easier to implement, by searching for particular data patterns in the knowledge graph such as two conflicting IP addresses attached to the same interface, or a BGP peer configured on an interface that is not longer enabled. This also makes it easy to extract configuration changes to apply to network elements.

We discuss in the following the repository design from the network data acquisition, to the KG schema and its systematic creation process. We then describe the design of *what-if* scenario evaluation for BGP and Traceroute.

3.2   Data Acquisition

The construction of the data repository is a multistage process that starts by collecting data from network elements in a non-structured vendor-dependent format.

In this design, we distinguish three categories of non-structured network data: (i) dynamic data representing topology and connectivity updates consisting on port/link status, device status, and BGP peer status changes. This information can be collected through NETCONF push notifications as they change frequently and must be collected as soon as they occur. (ii) static data representing device configuration that does not change frequently such as hostname, BGP router ID and ASN, and VLANs. This data is collected periodically (via NETCONF, RESTCONF, or CLI) and reinserted in the graph. (iii) semi-static data represents device configuration that may change during a day or over the week (see network data alterations measured in [2]), such as ACLs and BGP sessions and route policies. This data is also collected periodically, but more frequently than static data and only the changed/new attributes are updated in the graph.

Collected data is first converted to a vendor-neutral format, which is then processed to create the KG as described later.

3.3   Knowledge Graph Organizing Principle

For the construction of a KG flexible enough to accommodate a range of various networking concepts, it is imperative for its data to be easily queried and understood by users and developers. Consequently, the organization of data within the KG adheres to a set of intuitive principles, outlined below.

We first introduce basic graph database concepts used in this paper. A *node* refers to a graph vertex, which can have one or multiple labels identifying the node type. A *relationship* refers to the edge connecting two vertices. A *property* is a value pair representing an attribute of a node. Each node and relationship can have multiple properties. A *path* is a sequence of nodes and relationships going from one node to another. A *path-pattern* is a path containing node labels instead of specific nodes in the graph; it is used to express the shape of the requested data.

The graph is constructed from the physical layer up to the data plane. Each inserted node must be connected to an existing node to ensure that no dangling node exists. The network data is organized in the graph according to three main patterns defining an intuitive representation of the physical network and the logical protocol stack. First, devices and their interfaces, and the physical links that connect them are represented by the *Host-LTP-Link pattern*, where LTP stands for Link Termination Point. Second, protocol endpoints are represented in their respective layers according to their implementation. That is, link-layer protocols run on top of physical interfaces, and IP-layer protocols run on top of link layer. Endpoints of the same layer that are expected to interact can be connected with a relationship expressing the protocol information; for example, IP endpoints on top of two physically linked interfaces would be connected with a relationship corresponding to an ARP table entry. We refer to this pattern by *Layer-CTP-Connection*, where CTP stands for Connection Termination Point. Depending on the layer represented, the CTP has a type such as Ethernet, IPv4, TCP, etc. Third, device configurations and data plane information must be reachable from the device via a path of one or more hops. When a configuration or a data plane information is an independent fact, it is represented by a node connected to its parent node with a relationship. For example *"a FIB route in a host"* is represented with a FibRoute node connected with a "HAS_FIB" relationship to the Host node. When a configuration or a data plane information connects two independent configurations, it is represented by a relationship between the two nodes it refers to; for example, *"an interface is member of a VLAN"* should be represented "VLAN_MEMBER" relationship between the interface and the VLAN nodes.

Figure 1 shows the KG schema generated by the GDB. It represents the existing node labels and their relationships.

3.4   Knowledge Graph Construction

To illustrate the KG creation process, we consider a simple network from which the following data is collected: device properties (hostname, BGP router ID, etc.), ports properties (name, MTU, speed, etc.), VLAN configuration, LLDP neighbors, IPv4 addresses, BGP peers, and FIB routes.

Data collected from devices is converted to a vendor-neutral format grouped by device, which is then processed to produce facts. A fact is a map representing a network information to insert in the graph; either through a new node and new relationship(s), or only a new relationship between two existing nodes. Facts are organized according to their type and insertion order. For example, facts representing the network devices and their properties are to insert before facts representing interfaces, which are to be inserted before BGP peers configuration, and so on. The fact types are given in their insertion order as follows: devices, physical ports, Ethernet endpoints, IPv4 endpoints, VLAN L3 interfaces, physical links, IP neighbors connectivity, ACL rules, BGP peers, and FIB routes.

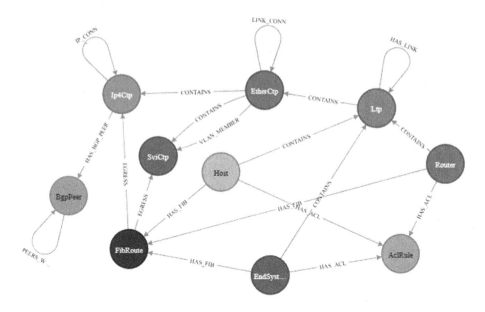

Fig. 1. KG schema visualization

Finally, the facts are converted to GDB queries. A query can insert one or multiple aggregated facts (see Sect. 4).

Figure 2 shows an example of parsing a BGP peer configuration from CLI output to the GDB query. The facts step is not shown since the fact is mapped directly to the GDB query.

The construction algorithm[2] creates a KG representing the network operational state, with topology, configuration and data plane information. Not all network data is discussed in this paper due to space limitation. However, information such as link aggregation and sub-interfaces can be easily represented in the KG using the organizing principles introduced above.

The complete graph creation process is executed only once. After that only portions of the graph are recreated periodically for static and semi-static network data as described above. Dynamic network state changes are received individually via notification, converted to a fact and inserted in the graph.

3.5   *What-if* support

The proposed repository natively supports *what-if* scenario evaluation through simple simulations. We selected BGP and Traceroute to showcase this capability. BGP route policies are known to be intricate and prone to errors, which is why some of the most significant internet outages are caused by misconfigured route policies that inadvertently leak or accept routes they shouldn't. Traceroute

---

[2] Not provided here due to space limitations. The reader can refer to the smart repository code for the complete KG creation process.

```
BGP neighbor is 172.0.1.0, remote AS 65199, local AS 65101, external link
  Description: spine01
Hostname: spine01
  Member of peer-group PEER_V4 for session parameters
  BGP version 4, remote router ID 10.255.255.101, local router ID 10.255.255.1
  BGP state = Established, up for 00:32:29
  Last read 00:00:02, Last write 00:00:02
  Hold time is 9, keepalive interval is 3 seconds
  Configured hold time is 9, keepalive interval is 3 seconds
```
1

```
BGP neighbor is 10.11.201.1, remote AS 200, local AS 100, external link
  BGP version 4, local router ID 192.168.0.2, remote router ID 0.0.0.0
  BGP state = Idle
  Last read Never, hold time is 90, keepalive interval is 30 seconds
```
2

```
"bgp": [...
   {
      "LOCALADDRESS": "172.0.1.1",
      "NEIGHBORADDRESS": "172.0.1.0",
      "LOCALAS": "65101",
      "REMOTEAS": "65199",
      "LOCALROUTERID": "10.255.255.1",
      "REMOTEROUTERID": "10.255.255.101",
      "HOLDTIME": "9",
      "KEEPALIVE": "3",
      "BGPSTATE": "Established"
   }
...]
```
3

```
MATCH
(r:Host {name:'spn10'})-[:CONTAINS*3]→(c:Ip4Ctp{ipAddr:'172.0.1.1'})
CREATE
(c)-[:HAS_CONFIG]→(b:Bgp
{lId: '10.255.255.1', lAsn: '65101', rAddr:'172.0.1.0',
rId:'10.255.255.101', rAsn:'65199', state: 'Established',
holdTime: '9', keepAlive: '3'});
```
4

Fig. 2. Simplified BGP configuration parsing example. 1: CLI output from a SONiC device, 2: CLI output from a OCNOS device, 3: Vendor-independent format, 4: GDP query

provides detailed information about the paths taken by a specified flow through the network, which is a powerful capability for exploring and testing network behavior.

The BGP process is a sequence of queries that modify the KG with nodes and relationships that describe BGP behavior. A BGP peer created on an interface of a router is represented by BgpPeer node connected to the corresponding IPv4 CTP node with a 'HAS_BGP_PEER' relationship. Two BGP peers that established a session are connected with a 'PEERS_WITH' relationship. A BGP route update is represented with BgpUpdate node and contains the announced prefix, origin Autonomous System (AS), next hop, AS path[3]. BgpUpdate is connected to the BGP peer through which it is sent (resp. received) via a 'BGP_UPDATE_TO_SEND' (resp. 'RECEIVED_BGP_UPDATE') relationships.

---

[3] Not all BGP features are included in this demonstration.

A clause of the route policy is represented with a Filter node connected to the device to which it belongs with a 'HAS_FILTER' relationship. A filter can be inbound or outbound, and contains a prefix and/or origin AS to match the route, a priority, a permit or deny action, and optional values for community and local preference to modify the route.

The Traceroute process is similar to that of BGP. The queries start by creating a Packet node connected to the source LTP from which it originates (Usually the loopback interface of a device). The packet contains flow information such as destination IP address, destination port, and protocol. The packet is virtually forwarded by finding the best matching route at each node, applying the inbound and outbound ACL rules, and sending the packet to the output LTP. Each forwarding step creates a relationship corresponding to the action between the packet and the corresponding node: LTP, ACL rule, and FIB route. This process continues until the destination is reached, no route is found for the packet, or the packet is blocked by an ACL rule.

4   Evaluation

The proposed repository is implemented on Neo4j, a popular GDB with an SQL-like query language.

To evaluate the feasibility of the proposed network repository, we measure its time and space efficiency, and we demonstrate two *what-if* scenarios by verifying BGP route policies and analyzing forwarding with a virtual Traceroute.

4.1   Performance Evaluation

When handling network data with a KG, the most critical evaluation criteria are the size of the graph on disk, the time to execute a query on the repository, and the graph creation time.

We emulate a leaf-spine network with 13 leaves, 10 spines, and 4 servers each connected on a different VLAN. The links between spines and leaves are Layer 3. The routing is realized with BGP. All nodes use SONiC as the network operating system.

The repository is implemented with Neo4j 4.4.25 Enterprise Edition, and the evaluation is performed on a server with a Core i5 8th generation CPU with 16 Gb of RAM.

The processing stage takes about 500 ms and includes the generations of facts and queries, with each fact mapped to one query. The graph creation takes about 106 s for a total number of 8466 queries representing 8466 facts, which corresponds to an average execution time of 13 ms per query. The execution time of queries is stable during the graph creation process because, as per the creation procedure, the queries do not need to process a large portion of the graph to insert a node/relationship. Consequently, the number of queries executed to create the graph can be reduced by aggregating multiple related facts and insert them in one query. Given the KG organizing principle (Sect. 3.3) and the creation process (Sect. 3.4), the more is known about the represented network concepts (e.g., topology, routing protocols, etc.) the more facts can be aggregated. After aggregating the facts of ports and Ethernet/IPv4 endpoints with each device creation query, the number of queries dropped by 39.6% (3359 queries) lowering the total graph creation time to 66 s while producing the same graph. Adding the BGP peers to this aggregation dropped the initial queries number by 42.6% (3610 queries) lowering the graph reaction time to 63 s. Finally, the aggregation of ACL rules facts belonging to the same ACL table, reduced the number of queries by 43.9% and the graph creation time to 61 s.

The KG of this network contains 7974 nodes and 17193 relationships, with a size on disk of around 3 MB. Therefore, on average, for each created node 3 relationships are created. Once the graph is established, the average query execution time is no more than 29 ms. This query execution time can represent the time to insert a notification about a dynamic network state change.

Note that a GDB system such as Neo4j is capable of supporting hundred millions of nodes and relationships.

4.2 *What-if* scenario with BGP

We consider an example leaf-spine network with 4 leaves, 4 spines, and 8 servers each connected on a different VLAN. The topology includes 2 border routers and 2 firewalls[4]. For simplicity, we assume route updates are allowed only between leaf01, leaf02, spine01, and spine02.

In the following, we run the simulated BGP behavior to analyse two examples of BGP route policies configuration, before applying them to the network. The filters in routes are configured in such a way that on only routes for prefix 10.11.200.0/24 are accepted and propagated.

In the first example, we mimic the advertisement of a route for the prefix 10.0.0.0/8 from leaf01 that will not be propagated. Figure 3 shows the queries that runs the *what-if* scenario and inspect the results to find where the route has been blocked.

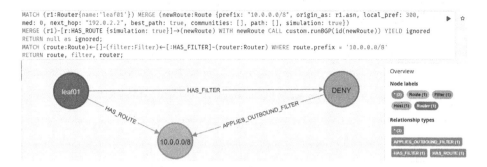

Fig. 3. Blocked route

---

[4] This network and "what-if" examples are available in the smart repository code.

In the second example, we mimic the advertisement of a route for the prefix "10.11.200.0/24 from leaf01 that will be propagated to all routers. Figure 4 shows the queries that runs the scenario and find the propagation path of the routes installed at leaf02.

```
MATCH (r1:Router{name:'leaf01'}) MERGE (newRoute:Route {prefix: "10.11.200.0/24", origin_as: r1.asn, local_pref:
300, med: 0, next_hop: "192.0.2.2", best_path: true, communities: [], path: [], simulation: true})
MERGE (r1)-[r:HAS_ROUTE {simulation: true}]→(newRoute) WITH newRoute CALL custom.runBGP(id(newRoute)) YIELD ignored
RETURN null as ignored;
MATCH path=(l02:Router{name:'leaf02'})-[:HAS_ROUTE]→(route:Route)-[:LEARNED_FROM]-(from_update:BgpUpdate)-
[:RECEIVES_UPDATE]-(p:BgpPeer)-[:PEERS_WITH]-(sp:BgpPeer)-[:HAS_BGP_PEER]-(:Ip4Ctp)-[:CONTAINS*2]-(:Ltp)-
[:CONTAINS]-(from_router:Router) WHERE route.prefix STARTS WITH '10.11.200.0' RETURN path;
```

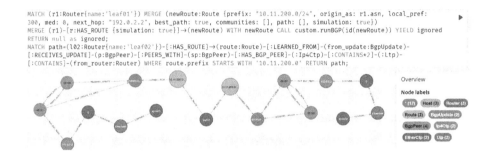

Fig. 4. Propagation path of a route

4.3   *What-if* scenario with Traceroute

In this example, we simulate the forwarding process to find the path taken by leaf01 router to reach the DNS Server 10.0.104.104 (server04). The following is the query that runs the *what-if* scenario and Fig. 5 shows the results.

```
CALL custom.traceroute('leaf01', '10.0.104.104', '10.0.104.0/24', 33434, 'UDP')
YIELD ignored RETURN ignored
```

```
MATCH (p:Packet)-[r]-(x)←[:CONTAINS|HAS_ACL|HAS_FIB*1..3]-(h:Host)
OPTIONAL MATCH (p)-[:REACHED]-(d)
WITH DISTINCT h,r,x ORDER BY r.hop, id(r)
RETURN h.name AS node, r AS action, x AS entity
```

node	action	entity
"leaf01"	[:IN_PACKET (hop: 0)]	(:Ltp {adminStatus: "up",name: "Loopback0",operStatus: "up"",type: "Other",speed: 0,mtu: 65536})
"leaf01"	[:FWD_WITH (hop: 0)]	(:FibRoute {cost: 1,to: "10.0.104.0/24",type: "B>*",via: "1
"leaf01"	[:APPLIES_OUT_ACL {hop: 0,action: "ACCEPT"}]	(:AclRule {protocol: "ANY",dPort: "ANY",aclTable: "default"ault",action: "ACCEPT",dIP: "ANY",sIP: "ANY",priority: 0,sP direction: "egress"})
"spine01"	[:IN_PACKET {simulation: true,hop: 1}]	(:Ltp {adminStatus: "up",name: "Ethernet0",operStatus: "up"",type: "Other",speed: 0,mtu: 9216})
"spine01"	[:APPLIES_IN_ACL {simulation: true,hop: 1,action: "ACCEPT"}]	(:AclRule {protocol: "ANY",dPort: "ANY",aclTable: "default"ault",action: "ACCEPT",dIP: "ANY",sIP: "ANY",priority: 0,sP direction: "ingress"})
"spine01"	[:FWD_WITH {simulation: true,hop: 1}]	(:FibRoute {cost: 1,to: "10.0.104.0/24",type: "B>*",via: "1
"spine01"	[:APPLIES_OUT_ACL {simulation: true,hop: 1,action: "ACCEPT"}]	(:AclRule {protocol: "ANY",dPort: "ANY",aclTable: "default"

Fig. 5. Traceroute results

5   Conclusion

This paper demonstrated a smart network repository based on a general-purpose native GDB. The repository can represent multiple levels of network abstraction, including topology, connectivity, configuration, and forwarding, in an organized and comprehensible manner. A systematic method is introduced to construct the repository's KG which contributes to the common understanding of network data, and creates a interoperable and extensible network repository, thus increasing the accessibility and usability of the network data.

The feasibility of a general-purpose GDB as a network repository was evaluated, establishing it as a viable solution for Network Management Systems (NMS) and SDN controllers.

The repository's potential extends beyond just storing and managing network data. We assessed its potential for running simple simulations to quickly evaluate what-if scenarios through queries. This capability, demonstrated for BGP route policy and Traceroute, opens up new avenues for smart network repositories that natively support analysis and verification.

Disclaimer

Any mention of commercial products or reference to commercial organizations is for information only; it does not imply recommendation or endorsement by NIST, nor does it imply that the products mentioned are necessarily the best available for the purpose.

References

1. Berde, P., et al.: Onos: Towards an open, distributed sdn os. In: Proceedings of the Third Workshop on Hot Topics in Software Defined Networking, HotSDN 2014, pp. 1–6. Association for Computing Machinery, New York (2014). https://doi.org/10.1145/2620728.2620744
2. Hong, H., et al.: Netgraph: an intelligent operated digital twin platform for data center networks. In: Proceedings of the ACM SIGCOMM 2021 Workshop on Network-Application Integration, NAI 2021, pp. 26–32. Association for Computing Machinery, New York (2021). https://doi.org/10.1145/3472727.3472802
3. Mogul, J.C., et al.: Experiences with modeling network topologies at multiple levels of abstraction. In: 17th Symposium on Networked Systems Design and Implementation (NSDI) (2020). https://www.usenix.org/conference/nsdi20/presentation/mogul
4. Quinn, R., et al.: Knownet: towards a knowledge plane for enterprise network management. In: NOMS 2016–2016 IEEE/IFIP Network Operations and Management Symposium, pp. 249–256 (2016). https://doi.org/10.1109/NOMS.2016.7502819
5. Sung, Y.W.E., Tie, X., Wong, S.H., Zeng, H.: Robotron: top-down network management at facebook scale. In: Proceedings of the 2016 ACM SIGCOMM Conference, SIGCOMM 2016, pp. 426–439. Association for Computing Machinery, New York (2016). https://doi.org/10.1145/2934872.2934874

6. Vilalta, R., et al.: Teraflow: secured autonomic traffic management for a tera of SDN flows. In: 2021 Joint European Conference on Networks and Communications & 6G Summit (EuCNC6G Summit), pp. 377–382 (2021). https://doi.org/10.1109/EuCNC/6GSummit51104.2021.9482469

7. Wang, A., Mei, X., Croft, J., Caesar, M., Godfrey, B.: Ravel: a database-defined network. In: Proceedings of the Symposium on SDN Research, SOSR 2016. Association for Computing Machinery, New York (2016). https://doi.org/10.1145/2890955.2890970

8. Zhou, Q., Gray, A.J.G., McLaughlin, S.: ToCo: an ontology for representing hybrid telecommunication networks. In: Hitzler, P., et al. (eds.) ESWC 2019. LNCS, vol. 11503, pp. 507–522. Springer, Cham (2019). https://doi.org/10.1007/978-3-030-21348-0_33

9. Zhou, Q., Gray, A.J.G., McLaughlin, S.: Towards a knowledge graph based autonomic management of software defined networks. CoRR abs/2106.13367 (2021). https://arxiv.org/abs/2106.13367

10. Zhu, Y., Chen, D., Zhou, C., Lu, L., Duan, X.: A knowledge graph based construction method for digital twin network. In: 2021 IEEE 1st International Conference on Digital Twins and Parallel Intelligence (DTPI), pp. 362–365 (2021). https://doi.org/10.1109/DTPI52967.2021.9540177

Enhancing Security in Connected Medical IoT Networks Through Deep Learning-Based Anomaly Detection

Ismaila Sy[1]([✉]) [iD], Birahime Diouf[1] [iD], Abdou Khadre Diop[1] [iD],
Cyril Drocourt[2] [iD], and David Durand[2] [iD]

[1] Université Alioune Diop de Bambey, Bambey, Senegal
ismaila.sy@uadb.edu.sn
[2] Université de Picardie Jules Verne, Amiens, France

Abstract. In recent years, there has been an alarming increase in cyber-attacks targeting connected medical devices. Distributed denial of service (DDoS) and botnet attacks are particularly common, and many vulnerabilities in IoT systems make these devices particularly vulnerable. Traditional intrusion detection techniques often fall short in addressing these threats. To overcome this challenge, we propose a deep learning-based intrusion detection system (IDS) for connected medical devices that utilizes four different architectures: multi-layer perceptron (MLP), long short-term memory (LSTM), convolutional neural network (CNN), and hybrid CNN-LSTM. We evaluated our system on the UNSW-NB15 and Edge-IIoTset datasets, and achieved a classification accuracy of 99.8% for binary classification and 96% for multiclass classification, with a false alarm rate of less than 2%. Our results show that deep learning can be an effective tool for detecting fraud attacks in connected medical devices. This research aims to enhance the security posture of medical IoT systems and mitigate potential risks.

Keywords: Cybersecurity · Deep learning · IDS · IoT · Medical Data

1 Introduction

Every second, 127 new devices connect to the Internet for the first time (McKinsey Digital). The number of connected devices is following an exponential curve, rising from 15 billion in 2015 to 30 billion in 2020 and 75 billion in 2025. This curve is likely to increase even faster with the arrival of 5G wireless technology, developed in part for the IOT world and enabling deployment in private networks. The business sectors concerned by IoT are wide-ranging: in 2018, they were mainly geared towards smart cities (23%), followed by connected industry (17%), with healthcare accounting for just 6% (iot-analytics.com), but growing fast. In 2019, 86% of companies in the healthcare sector were using connected objects (Comparitech, i-SCOOP). By 2020, according to Forbes, 646 million IoT devices will be in use in hospitals, clinics and doctors' surgeries. In the medical

S. Bouzefrane et al. (Eds.): MSPN 2023, LNCS 14482, pp. 87–99, 2024.
https://doi.org/10.1007/978-3-031-52426-4_7

IoT domain, connected networks enable real-time patient monitoring, seamless data collection, and enhanced healthcare delivery. However, this integration also expose inherent security risks that pose significant threats to patient confidentiality, data integrity, and overall network security. Implementing IoT security measures and finding suitable storage solutions will be the top priorities in the near future. To mitigate these risks, robust security measures are imperative [1]. Traditional intrusion detection methods, such as rule-based IDSs and signature-based IDSs, have shown their limitations in effectively detecting and adapting to new threats emerging in dynamic IoT environments. This inherent limitation prompts the exploration of more sophisticated and adaptive solutions, among which deep learning stands out. Deep learning, renowned for its exceptional capabilities in pattern recognition and anomaly detection tasks, emerges as a promising avenue to address the evolving challenges posed by the intricacies of IoT security.

In this paper, we make a significant contribution by employing a diverse set of deep learning methods for enhancing security in connected medical IoT networks. Specifically, we utilize three powerful deep learning models: Multi-Layer Perceptron (MLP), Convolutional Neural Network (CNN), and Long Short-Term Memory (LSTM) to implement our anomaly detection approach. This multi-model strategy allows us to leverage the strengths of different architectures, ensuring a comprehensive coverage of potential threats.

Our primary research objective is twofold: first, to achieve a high level of accuracy in identifying security threats in medical IoT networks, and second, to minimize the false positive rate. Through extensive experiments using real-world data (Edge-IIoTset), we have demonstrated high performance. The results display precision rates of 99.8% in binary classification and 96% in multi-class classification. This underscores the efficacy of our deep learning-based approach in accurately identifying and classifying security threats in the complex and dynamic medical IoT environment.

Moreover, our work stands out in its success in substantially reducing false alarm rates. By leveraging advanced deep learning techniques, we have significantly enhanced the precision of our intrusion detection system, ensuring that security alerts are more reliable and actionable. This reduction in false positives is critical in preventing unnecessary disruptions and resource wastage, making our approach not only accurate but also highly practical for real-world deployment.

In summary, our research contributes to advancing the state-of-the-art in connected medical IoT network security by employing a multi-model deep learning approach that not only achieves exceptional accuracy but also significantly reduces false alarm rates. This innovative methodology holds great promise for safeguarding patient data and improving the overall quality of healthcare delivery in the rapidly evolving digital landscape. In the upcoming sections, we conduct a comprehensive review of the security issues within connected medical IoT networks and the current methods for identifying anomalies. Ultimately, we summarize the primary outcomes and suggest potential paths for future research to bolster security in linked medical IoT networks.

2   Literature Review

Numerous researchers and experts have recognized the gravity of the situation and are actively studying the security aspects of IoMT. Johnson [2] emphasized the need to address security concerns in the context of the Internet of Things in healthcare. Uslu [3] delved into the specific security and privacy implications of the Internet of Medical Things, underscoring the urgency of robust protection measures. Zeadally et al. [4] provided an extensive survey on IoT security, encompassing IoMT as a critical domain. Additionally, Kocabas et al. [5] conducted a comprehensive review of recent advancements and future directions in IoMT, with a particular focus on security implications. Ferrag et al. [6] have conducted a deep learning investigation for intrusion detection. They evaluate the model's performances based on accuracy, false alarm rates, and detection rates. The CNNs showed more satisfactory performances than the FFN (Feedforward Neural Network) and RNN (Recurrent Neural Network). Odetola et al. [7] develop a multi-label classification method using a CNN on edge IoT devices. They also discuss recent research on IoT security, focusing on intrusion detection techniques based on neural network strategies. Idrissi et al. [8] carried out an extensive investigation to pinpoint vulnerabilities and security threats within IoT environments. Their research significantly adds to the comprehension of real-world threats and suggests strategies to strengthen security measures against emerging risks. Tian et al. [9] proposed a distributed approach to identify cyber threats via URLs using deep learning algorithms. Their framework can be practically effective due to its automated collection functions, ease of upgradeability and reliability in defending against attacks on distributed deep models. In a big data situation, Hassan et al. [10] have concocted a way to determine break-ins that involve a combination of a Weight-Dropped Long Short-Term Memory (WDLSTM) model and a CNN model. Liu et al. [11] proposed a hybrid approach that combines data sampling, cost-sensitive learning, ensemble learning, and deep learning for intrusion detection in imbalanced network traffic. In [12], the authors propose an approach based on Deep Transfer Learning (DTL) for IoT attacks detection. They have performed three series of experiments on recent datasets and the experimental results show that the DTL model brings an improvement on the accuracy of detection compared to classical approaches. Kandhro et al. [13] presents a generative adversarial network for detecting cyber threats in IoT-driven IIC networks. Their approach is evaluated with the KDDCup99, NSL-KDD and UNSW-NB15 datasets. The results show an increase in performance between 95% and 97% in terms of accuracy, reliability and efficiency in detecting numerous attacks. Wang et al. propose an anomaly detection model tailored for Industrial Control Systems (ICS), employing a deep residual Convolutional Neural Network (CNN). The model strategically incorporates transfer learning to identify unknown attacks, thereby minimizing training time [14]. Nevertheless, it is important to note that the model relies on a dataset containing known attacks for effective operation. In order to address the limitations of traditional machine learning techniques in detecting and classifying attacks in IoT networks, a novel anomaly-based intrusion detection model using deep learning, specifically convolutional neural networks (CNNs), is proposed by [15]. The model is implemented in 1D, 2D, and 3D, and is evaluated using four different IoT intrusion detection datasets. Transfer learning is also used to implement binary and multiclass classification using a pre-trained CNN model. The proposed model achieves high accuracy, precision, recall, and F1 score compared to existing deep learning implementations. To enhance the security of edge networks, L. Nie et al. [16] propose a deep learning-based intrusion detection algorithm based on the generative adversarial network (GAN). Their method includes three phases: feature selection, deep learning architecture design, and intrusion detection model combination. The proposed method achieves high accuracy in detecting multiple attacks, suggesting that GAN-based deep learning is a promising approach for intrusion detection in edge networks.

To identify IoT devices and/or IP addresses that are compromised by a Botnet attack, E. Gelenbe and M. Nakıp [17] propose a novel online Compromised Device Identification System (CDIS). CDIS uses an Auto-Associative Dense Random Dom Neural Network (AADRNN) to train itself online during normal operation, using traffic metrics measured as traffic arrives. Experimental evaluation on publicly available Mirai Botnet attack data shows that CDIS achieves high performance with Balanced Accuracy of 97%, despite its low on-line training and execution time. Y. K. Saheed et al. [18] propose a novel intrusion detection system (IDS) for the Internet of Medical Things (IoMT) using a deep recurrent neural network (DRNN) and supervised machine learning (SML) models. They first preprocess and normalize the network data, and then optimize the features using a bio-inspired particle swarm algorithm. Finally, they evaluate the proposed DRNN and SML models on a standard intrusion detection dataset. The results show that the proposed SML model outperforms existing approaches with an accuracy of 99.76%. While experiments have undoubtedly made great strides in developing intrusion detection systems, the ongoing challenge lies in finding a delicate balance of accuracy and reducing false positives. Striking the optimal balance of accurately identifying real threats and minimizing false positives is an ongoing pursuit in cybersecurity. This challenge highlights the importance of optimizing intrusion detection methods to minimize the impact of false alarms on system performance and to ensure strong protection against cyber threats.

3   Methodological Approach: Deep Learning-Based Anomaly Detection for Strengthening Security in Connected Medical IoT Networks

In this section, we discuss the datasets and methods we use. We will evaluate the performance of the proposed approaches by considering evaluation metrics commonly used for deep learning algorithms, such as recall, accuracy, F1 score, detection rate, and false alarm rate.

3.1 Datasets Selection

A good dataset is crucial for studying cyberattacks on IoT devices. By using diverse dataset, encompassing both hybrid traffic and specific IoT dataset, we can capture a wide range of attack vectors and scenarios, enhancing its robustness and generalizability. For our study, we utilized a hybrid dataset known as UNSW-NB15, which offers a comprehensive representation of various network traffic scenarios. This hybrid dataset incorporates both normal and attack data instances, making it a valuable resource for training and evaluating intrusion detection systems [19]. In addition to this, we employed the Edge-IIoTset dataset. This dataset focuses on IoT-specific network traffic, allowing us to investigate and enhance the security of connected IoT networks effectively.

3.2 Harnessing Deep Learning Algorithms to Safeguard Medical IoT Networks

In the exhilarating era of cyber infrastructure, where challenges in cybersecurity reach new heights, the exploration of vast data reservoirs in networks, operating systems, and information realms demands avant-garde solutions. Deep learning, a true catalyst of machine learning, emerges as the key for Intrusion Detection Systems (IDS), whether rooted in classical signatures or exploring anomalies. Plunging into the realms of classification and prediction, deep learning provides an immediate response by identifying unusual cybernetic patterns, anticipating not only ongoing attacks but also future threats, thereby redefining digital vigilance. With remarkable ingenuity, deep learning meets the escalating demands of Big Data, establishing a robust defense where high-performing IDS minimizes false alarms. In this captivating panorama, our approach highlights the use of deep learning in IDS, incorporating innovative approaches such as MLP, LSTM, CNN, and the hybrid CNN-LSTM, propelling proactive detection of malicious activities in an ever-evolving digital era. This wave of innovation holds crucial importance in the medical domain, accentuating the relevance of its applications and underscoring the critical necessity of resilient cybersecurity in this highly sensitive field.

Multi-layer Perceptrons (MLPs). Deep Neural Networks (DNNs) constitute a set of neurons organized into a sequence of multiple layers known as Multi-layer Perceptrons (MLPs). They distinguish themselves from traditional Artificial Neural Networks (ANNs) through their depth and the number of layers and nodes (neurons) comprising the network. When an ANN has two or more hidden layers, it is referred to as a deep neural network [20]. These networks aim to model data containing intricate architectures by combining various nonlinear transformations (Fig. 1). Rosenblatt[1] introduced the fundamental concept

---

[1] Frank Rosenblatt was an American psychologist who worked on artificial intelligence. As a prominent figure in the "neural network" movement, which aimed to construct artificial intelligence based on the design of the human neural network, he developed the perceptron in 1957 at Cornell University.

of the perceptron in 1958. The perceptron calculates a single output from multiple real-valued inputs (xi) by forming a linear combination based on its input weights (w) and then passing the output through a non-linear activation function. Mathematically, this can be expressed as follows:

$$y = \delta \left(\sum_{n=1}^{N} W_i x_i + b \right) = \delta(W^T X + b) \qquad (1)$$

With:

- W: the weight vector.
- X: the input vector.
- b: represents the bias.
- δ: denotes the activation function.

A multilayer perceptron network (MLP) consists of a set of source nodes forming an input layer, a hidden layer of one or more compute nodes, and an output layer of nodes. The input signal propagates through the network layer by layer. The signal flow in such a network with hidden layers is shown in Eq. (1). Deep neural networks (DNN) are often used for supervised learning problems. During model training (learning), all weights and biases are set to optimal values.

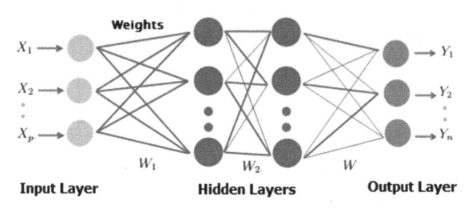

Fig. 1. The Layered Architecture of Deep Neural Networks (DNN)

Convolutional Neural Networks (CNNs). A Convolutional Neural Network (CNN) is an extension of traditional feed-forward neural networks (FFNs) inspired by biological factors. Initially designed for image processing, CNNs excel in tasks involving repetitive patterns, such as images with repeated edges and other patterns. CNNs outperform classical machine learning algorithms, achieving significant success in computer vision tasks. They find wide applications in image and video processing, natural language processing (NLP), recommendation systems, and more. Convolutional networks are particularly effective due to specialized layers, including convolutional layers, pooling layers, and fully connected layers (Fig. 2).

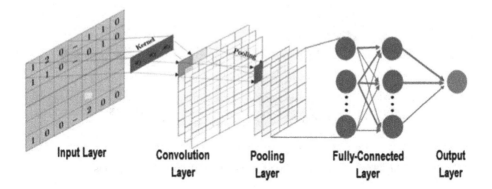

Fig. 2. Architectural of a Convolutional Neural Network

Long Short-Term Memory Units (LSTMs). The RNN has a long time step as it considers the previously stored state when updating the weights. However, as training progresses, gradients become smaller, and after a few steps, errors may fail to propagate to the end of the network. This result in a negligible difference in the outcome, preventing weight updates. This issue with RNN is known as vanishing gradients. To overcome this problem, a Long Short-Term Memory (LSTM) architecture was proposed in the mid-1990s by German researchers Sepp Hochreiter and Juergen Schmidhuber for recurrent neural networks. Additionally, Gated Recurrent Units (GRU) were introduced to further address the vanishing gradients problem (Fig. 3). Both LSTM and GRU architectures function similarly, but GRU uses fewer training parameters, requiring less memory and training faster than LSTMs. However, LSTMs tend to be more accurate on datasets with longer sequences [21].

Hybrid CNN-LSTM Network. A hybrid CNN-LSTM network is a combined architecture that integrates Convolutional Neural Network (CNN) layers for feature extraction with Long Short-Term Memory (LSTM) layers for sequence modeling and prediction (Fig. 4). This hybrid design is often employed in tasks such as visual time series prediction, where CNNs excel at capturing spatial features, and LSTMs handle temporal dependencies, offering a comprehensive approach to complex data patterns and activity recognition [22].

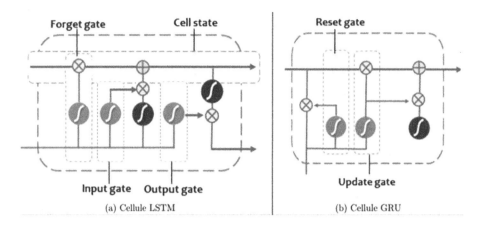

(b) Cellule GRU

Fig. 3. Architectural Overview of LSTM and GRU Models

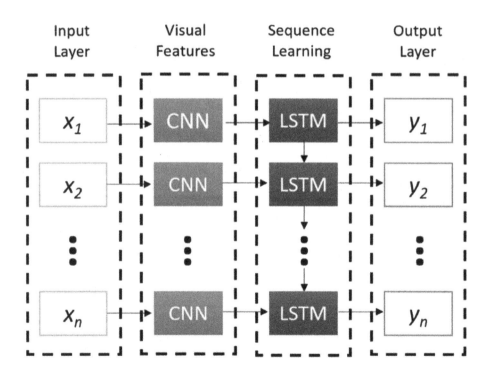

Fig. 4. Hybrid CNN-LSTM architecture

3.3   A Multi-architecture Approach to Intrusion Detection in Connected Medical Devices

In this study, we introduce four distinct models: a MLP, CNN, LSTM and a hybrid CNN-LSTM model. Initially, we conduct binary classification, which involves identifying whether the network traffic is normal or malicious. Additionally, we delve into multi-class classification, where we classify the traffic type into either normal or various attack categories, such as DOS, DDOS, or MITM (Man-In-The Middle) attacks (Fig. 5). This comprehensive approach allows us to accurately categorize and analyze the network traffic patterns for enhanced intrusion detection.

In summary, our methodology involved a dual-step classification process, first determining the normality of traffic versus maliciousness and then identifying the precise type of attack. Utilizing four models, including MLP, LSTM, CNN, and CNN-LSTM, we harnessed their strengths to discern between legitimate and malicious activities while achieving fine-grained attack categorization. This comprehensive approach not only enhances the detection accuracy but also equips cybersecurity practitioners with valuable insights for effective threat mitigation and network defense.

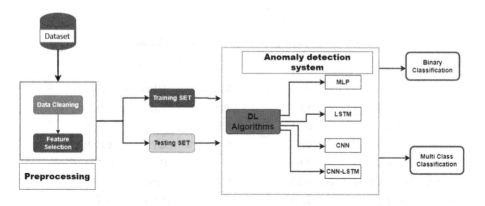

Fig. 5. Anomaly Detection Architecture

4   Results and Discussions

4.1   Binary Classification

This process involved training our selected classification models, namely the Multi-Layer Perceptron (MLP), Long Short-Term Memory (LSTM), Convolutional Neural Network (CNN), and a hybrid CNN-LSTM architecture.

Table 1. Binary Classification Models Performance

Models	Accuracy(%)	Validation accuracy(%)	Loss
LSTM_UNSW-NB15	93.00	94.00	0.13
MLP_Edge-IIoTset	99.99	99.80	2.67e−04
LSTM_Edge-IIoTset	99.99	99.99	9.98e−05
CNN_Edge-IIoTset	99.99	99.87	0,16
CNN-LSTM_Edge-IIoTset	99.98	99.97	1.13e−04

4.2 Multi-class Classification

In the Multi-Class Classification phase, we focused on the challenging task of classifying network traffic into multiple categories. By classifying the data into these six categories, we can gain a better understanding of the different types of attacks present in the dataset and develop more targeted and effective security measures to mitigate these threats. This reclassification provides a clearer and more concise representation of the diverse range of attacks encountered in real-world network traffic, enabling us to enhance the detection and prevention of cyber threats.

Table 2. Multi-Class Classification Performances

Multiclass classification			
Classes	Accuracy (%)	Recall (%)	F1-score	Support
---	---	---	---	---
Normal	1.00	1.00	1.00	409200
DDoS	0.91	0.99	0.95	86434
Code Injection	0.66	0.87	0.75	30810
Malware	0.94	0.49	0.65	25094
Information Theft	0.95	0.74	0.83	21257
MITM	1.00	1.00	1.00	107

In binary classification experiences (Table 1), we evaluated several classification models for binary network traffic analysis. The LSTM_UNSW-NB15 model demonstrated good performance with an accuracy of 93.98% on the test dataset, and an even higher accuracy of 94.99% during validation. The MLP_Edge-IIoTset model displayed remarkable accuracy, achieving a perfect 99.99% accuracy on the test dataset and maintaining a very high accuracy of 99.98% during validation. The model's exceptionally low loss value of 2.62×10^{-4} indicates its successful ability to distinguish between normal and malicious network traffic. Additionally, we observed outstanding performance from the LSTM_Edge-IIoTset model, which achieved high accuracy of 99.99% both on the test dataset and during validation. For the CNN_Edge-IIoTset model, an accuracy of 99.98% on the test dataset and a validation accuracy of 99.97% were achieved, with a relatively small loss value of 0.1676, demonstrating robust performance in classifying normal and malicious traffic. Lastly, the CNN_LSTM_Edge-IIoTset model attained a perfect accuracy of 99.98% on both the test dataset and during validation. The model's low loss value of 1.1334×10^{-4} further validates its effectiveness in accurately classifying network traffic.

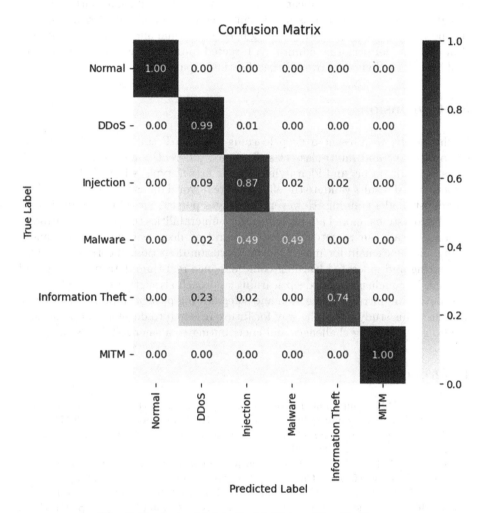

Fig. 6. Confusion Matrix for Multiclass Classification

The multiclass classification results (Table 2) underscore the model's commendable performance across various attack categories. Notably, the model achieves flawless identification of "Normal" traffic, demonstrating perfect accuracy, recall, and F1-score. The "DDoS" class also exhibits high accuracy and recall, indicative of the model's ability to effectively recognize instances, although the F1-score suggests some instances of misclassification. Challenges arise in the "Code Injection" class, where lower accuracy and F1-score suggest difficulty in precise identification, highlighting an area for potential improvement. In the "Malware" class, the model shows good accuracy but a lower recall, suggesting opportunities to enhance identification sensitivity. The "Information Theft" class demonstrates a balanced and robust performance across metrics. The "MITM" class achieves flawless classification. Importantly, the confusion matrix (Fig. 6) reveals no instances of attacks misclassified as normal and vice versa, affirming the model's reliability in distinguishing between normal and malicious activities. While the model performs admirably, targeted improvements in specific classes could further enhance its overall classification capabilities.

5   Conclusion

In this study, we present a deep learning based IoT traffic classification. We explore binary and multi-class classifications, differentiating normal and malicious network traffic, and identifying specific attack types within IoT networks. Experimental results validate the efficacy of real-world datasets like Edge-IIoTset for robust model training. However, challenges persist, including the intricacies of IoT ecosystems, model adaptability, and vulnerabilities to adversarial attacks. Looking ahead, our research suggests integrating deep learning with steganography and blockchain for more resilient intrusion detection. Incorporating edge computing and federated learning could enhance real-time data processing and privacy. In conclusion, our deep learning approach strengthens IoT cybersecurity, bolstering intrusion detection and safeguarding patient data and healthcare systems. This study paves the way for future research to develop comprehensive solutions, addressing challenges and contributing to a safer IoT landscape.

References

1. Tripathy, B.K., Anuradha, J. (eds.): Internet of Things (IoT): Technologies, Applications, Challenges and Solutions, 1st edn. CRC Press, Boca Raton (2017)
2. Johnson, M.E.: The Internet of Things in healthcare: prospects for the future. J. Law Med. **23**(4), 923–927 (2016)
3. Uslu, B., Akkaya, İ, Sirer, E.G.: Security and privacy aspects of the Internet of Medical Things (IoMT). Curr. Med. Res. Opin. **36**(5), 805–808 (2020)
4. Zeadally, S., Tounsi, M.A., Obaidat, M.S., Hassan, M.E.: Security of the Internet of Things: a review of the state of the art. ACM Comput. Surv. (CSUR) **47**(2), 1–54 (2014)
5. Kocabas, O.E., Gumussoy, M., Cetinkaya, M., Yildirim, S.: Internet of Medical Things (IoMT): a comprehensive survey on recent advancements and future directions. J. Med. Syst. **42**(11), 1–20 (2018)
6. Ferrag, M.A., Friha, O., Maglaras, L., Janicke, H., Shu, L.: Federated deep learning for cybersecurity in the internet of things: concepts, applications, and experimental analysis. IEEE Access **9**, 138509–138542 (2021)

7. Odetola, T.A., Oderhohwo, O., Hasan, S.R.: A scalable multi-label classification to deploy deep learning architectures for edge devices. arXiv preprint arXiv:1911.02098 (2019)

8. Idrissi, I., Azizi, M., Moussaoui, O.: IoT security with deep learning-based intrusion detection systems: a systematic literature review. In: 2020 Fourth International Conference on Intelligent Computing in Data Sciences (ICDS), pp. 1–10. IEEE (2020)

9. Tian, Z., Luo, C., Qiu, J., Du, X., Guizani, M.: A distributed deep learning system for web attack detection on edge devices. IEEE Trans. Ind. Inf. **16**(3), 1963–1971 (2019)

10. Hassan, M.M., Hossain, M.A., Uddin, M.S., Islam, M.R.: A hybrid deep learning model for efficient intrusion detection in big data environment. Comput. Secur. **87**, 101681 (2019)

11. Liu, L., Wang, P., Wang, W., Li, H., Wang, R.: Intrusion detection of imbalanced network traffic based on machine learning and deep learning. IEEE Access **9**, 7550–7563 (2021)

12. Vu, L., Nguyen, Q.U., Nguyen, D.N., Hoang, D.T., Dutkiewicz, E.: Deep transfer learning for IoT attack detection. IEEE Access **8**, 107335–107344 (2020)

13. Kandhro, I.A., et al.: Detection of real-time malicious intrusions and attacks in IoT empowered cybersecurity infrastructures. IEEE Access **11**, 9136–9148 (2023)

14. Wang, W., et al.: Anomaly detection of industrial control systems based on transfer learning. Tsinghua Sci. Technol. **26**(6), 821–832 (2021). https://doi.org/10.26599/TST.2020.9010041

15. Ullah, I., Mahmoud, Q.H.: Design and development of a deep learning-based model for anomaly detection in IoT networks. IEEE Access **9**, 103906–103926 (2021). https://doi.org/10.1109/ACCESS.2021.3094024

16. Nie, L., et al.: Intrusion detection for secure social Internet of Things based on collaborative edge computing: a generative adversarial network-based approach. IEEE Trans. Comput. Soc. Syst. **9**(1), 134–145 (2022). https://doi.org/10.1109/TCSS.2021.3063538

17. Gelenbe, E., Nakıp, M.: Traffic based sequential learning during botnet attacks to identify compromised IoT devices. IEEE Access **10**, 126536–126549 (2022). https://doi.org/10.1109/ACCESS.2022.3226700

18. Saheed, Y.K., Arowolo, M.O.: Efficient cyber attack detection on the Internet of Medical Things-smart environment based on deep recurrent neural network and machine learning algorithms. IEEE Access **9**, 161546–161554 (2021). https://doi.org/10.1109/ACCESS.2021.3128837

19. Canderra University. The UNSW-NB15 dataset. https://research.unsw.edu.au/projects/unsw-nb15-dataset, Sydney, Australia (2018)

20. Yin, Y., Jang-Jaccard, J., Xu, W., et al.: IGRF-RFE: a hybrid feature selection method for MLP-based network intrusion detection on UNSW-NB15 dataset. J. Big Data **10**(15), 1–10 (2023). https://doi.org/10.1186/s40537-023-00694-8

21. Laghrissi, F., Douzi, S., Douzi, K., et al.: Intrusion detection systems using long short-term memory (LSTM). J. Big Data **8**(65) (2021). https://doi.org/10.1186/s40537-021-00448-4

22. Tasdelen, A., Sen, B.: A hybrid CNN-LSTM model for pre-miRNA classification. Sci. Rep. **11**(1), 14125 (2021). https://doi.org/10.1038/s41598-021-93656-0

Blockchain-Driven Animal Healthcare: Leveraging NFTs, IPFS, and Smart Contracts for Comprehensive Animal Medical Record

T. L. Quy[1(✉)], N. D. P. Trong[1], H. V. Khanh[1], H. L. Huong[1], T. D. Khoa[1],
H. G. Khiem[1], N. T. Phuc[1], M. D. Hieu[1], V. C. P. Loc[1], N. H. Kha[1],
N. T. Anh[1], Q. N. Hien[1], L. K. Bang[1], Q. T. Bao[1], N. T. K. Ngan[2],
and M. N. Triet[1]

[1] FPT University, Can Tho, Vietnam
{quylt9,trietnm3}@fe.edu.vn
[2] FPT Polytechnic, Can Tho, Vietnam

Abstract. The domain of animal healthcare mandates robust mechanisms for maintaining the sanctity, reachability, and security of medical record. This paper delineates a cutting-edge methodology to overhaul traditional animal medical record handling by utilizing blockchain techniques. Through the strategic incorporation of Non-Fungible Tokens (NFTs), the InterPlanetary File System (IPFS), and Smart Contracts, we propose a versatile system that refines data retrieval and modification processes, bolstering both accountability and dependability. At the heart of our strategy lies a pioneering decentralized framework, empowering veterinary professionals with the tools to input, retrieve, and edit medical records, all the while being enveloped by rigorous access and identity validation measures. The inherent decentralized properties of IPFS furnish steadfast and immutable data retention capabilities, whilst the NFTs encapsulate the distinct medical trajectories of each animal. Through the symbiotic relationship of Smart Contracts, a fluid and unalterable lineage of medical logs is preserved. As a marked departure from traditional paradigms, our blueprint promises augmented safety, streamlined data operations, and unparalleled lucidity, marking the dawn of a transformative phase in animal healthcare.

Keywords: Animal Healthcare · Animal Medical Record (AMR) ·
Blockchain · Smart Contracts · NFT · IPFS · BNB Smart Chain ·
Celo · Fantom · Polygon

1 Introduction

The transformation from paper to digital records has revolutionized various aspects of healthcare, including veterinary care. In the realm of animal healthcare, Electronic Health Records (EHRs), often termed Animal Medical Records

(AMRs), have emerged as critical tools for streamlined clinical workflows, evidence-based decision-making, and in-depth scientific research. Studies such as [21] have illuminated how AMRs can offer a wealth of data for investigating the demographics and prevalent health conditions among domestic animals like dogs, cats, and rabbits. Similarly, research articles [20] and [6] exemplify how AMRs can be pivotal in addressing particular health issues, such as animal life stages and obesity rates, respectively.

The potential of AMRs transcends geographical and health-condition boundaries. Research efforts like [12] and [7] demonstrate the global relevance of AMRs, covering subjects ranging from common medical issues affecting dogs in Korea to ethical considerations surrounding animal euthanasia in the UK. Moreover, the scope of AMRs has also expanded to public health concerns, including syndromic surveillance as highlighted by [11] and [3]. Pharmaceutical trends are another domain where AMRs have proven invaluable, with studies such as [4] and [22] exploring veterinary prescribing behaviors based on AMR data.

However, the adoption of digital records comes with its own set of challenges, including data security, quality, and interoperability. Works like [19] and [16] shed light on these hurdles, exploring mechanisms for secure and quality-controlled data access in the context of AMRs. Existing EHR systems, centralized in nature, present certain vulnerabilities, including susceptibility to unauthorized access or data corruption [27,30]. The fragmentation of EHR platforms also poses challenges for seamless data sharing between different veterinary facilities [23]. Questions about data ownership and ethical considerations regarding data use persist [25].

This has spurred interest in alternative approaches to healthcare data management, including blockchain technologies [14]. The decentralized design inherent in blockchain addresses some of the core issues plaguing centralized systems, offering both robust security measures and improved data integrity [5,13,26]. Additionally, the adoption of smart contracts can standardize protocols for data sharing, making interoperability achievable [9]. Complementing the base capabilities of blockchain are ancillary techniques, such as off-chain storage for large datasets [15]. Tokenization methods can empower patients or, in the context of veterinary care, animal owners, by giving them agency over their data access and sharing permissions.

In the evolving world of blockchain, Non-Fungible Tokens (NFTs) stand out for their unique properties, allowing them to represent distinct digital assets. In the context of this work, NFTs can be employed to symbolize individual animal medical records. Each NFT can signify a animal's unique medical history, ensuring data indivisibility and establishing provenance. This ensures that each medical record remains distinct, verifiable, and tamper-proof. Parallelly, the InterPlanetary File System (IPFS) emerges as a potent decentralized system for data storage. Within our scope, IPFS provides a resilient platform to store and retrieve animal medical data. By transitioning away from centralized servers to a distributed file system, IPFS ensures that medical data is both available and persistent across multiple nodes. This serves to heighten data availability, even if parts of the network falter. When combined, NFTs and IPFS offer a revolutionary approach to animal medical data management, ensuring both the authenticity of the data (via NFTs) and its availability (through IPFS). Therefore, the primary endeavors of this paper can be encapsulated in the following salient contributions:

1. **Blockchain-based System for animal care:** We introduce a comprehensive blockchain-driven framework tailored for animal healthcare. This system not only captures, but also secures, and facilitates easy retrieval of animal medical records, ensuring streamlined animal care.
2. **Transparency through NFTs:** By leveraging NFTs, our approach tackles issues of data opacity. Each NFT representing a animal's medical record fosters transparency, enabling stakeholders to validate the origin and integrity of the records.
3. **IPFS for Public Medical Data Sharing:** Incorporating IPFS, we facilitate public sharing of animal medical data. This decentralized approach guarantees data availability across stakeholders, enhancing collaborative animal care efforts.
4. **Proof-of-Concept on Multiple Platforms:** Our system isn't merely theoretical. We have implemented a proof-of-concept, deploying it across four prominent EVM-supported platforms: BNB Smart Chain, Celo, Fantom, and Polygon. This demonstrates the versatility and adaptability of our solution across diverse blockchain infrastructures.
5. **Proof-of-Concept on Data Sharing via Pinata Platform:** Extending our commitment to enhanced data availability, we employ the IPFS-based approach (i.e., Pinata platform) for animal medical data sharing. This ensures that records are not only accessible but are stored persistently in a decentralized manner, mitigating risks associated with central points of failure.

2   Related Work

The existing body of literature on animal healthcare and electronic medical records provides a rich context within which our work resides. This section reviews existing research relevant to veterinary electronic health records, disease surveillance, medication prescriptions, and the more nascent field of blockchain technology in animal healthcare.

2.1   Veterinary Electronic Health Records

Sanchez et al. [21] explored the demographics of animals visiting veterinary practices in Great Britain and relied on electronic health records for their data. This work, although not utilizing blockchain, underscores the importance of robust electronic record-keeping systems. In a similar vein, Gray et al. [7] investigated the decision-making process around euthanasia for animals in the UK using electronic health records. Anholt's doctoral thesis [3] delved deep into the potential for syndromic surveillance in companion animals by using electronic medical records, which serves as a foundation for our approach to decentralized systems.

2.2 Disease and Health Status Surveillance

Kim et al. [12] scrutinized major medical causes affecting different breeds of dogs using electronic medical records, highlighting the need for comprehensive and easily accessible data. Kass et al. [11] extended the utility of electronic health records for syndromic surveillance in animals. Further, Anholt et al. [2] specifically mined free-text medical records for tracking enteric syndromes in companion animals. This indicates the need for data integrity and security, the core features of our blockchain-driven system.

2.3 Medication and Treatment

Burke et al. [4] and Singleton et al. [22] addressed the prescription patterns for specific treatments in cats and dogs, respectively. Their work points to the necessity of transparent, immutable, and easily retrievable records in animal healthcare, which our system aims to provide.

2.4 Fine-Grained Access Control

Romar's thesis [19] specifically delves into fine-grained access control in an animal health record, a feature our proposed system inherently supports through smart contracts.

2.5 Blockchain and Decentralization

While the incorporation of blockchain technology in animal healthcare is still in a nascent stage, Willner [32] and Aigner [1] have touched upon the requirements and prototypical implementation of Animal Health Records (AHR) which could potentially be built on blockchain.

2.6 Niche Studies

In terms of niche research, Tulloch et al. [31] used electronic health records for passive surveillance of ticks in companion animals. Menendez [16] tackled the issue of data quality in animal health records on dairy farms. These works point towards the broader applicability of health record data and the need for systems that can handle such diverse needs securely and efficiently.

Our work distinguishes itself by amalgamating the beneficial aspects of these individual efforts into a consolidated, decentralized framework. Leveraging blockchain, Non-Fungible Tokens (NFTs), and the InterPlanetary File System (IPFS), we offer a holistic solution that addresses not just secure and immutable record-keeping but also ensures enhanced accessibility, integrity, and privacy, thus marking a pioneering advancement in the realm of animal healthcare.

3   Approach

3.1   Traditional Model of Animal Care

Traditional animal care models are founded upon a complex nexus of interactions, intertwining veterinary expertise, comprehensive AMRs, the diverse range of animals, the commitment of animal caretakers, and the integral contributions of pharmaceutical outlets and diagnostic centers. A snapshot of this model is illustrated in Fig. 1.

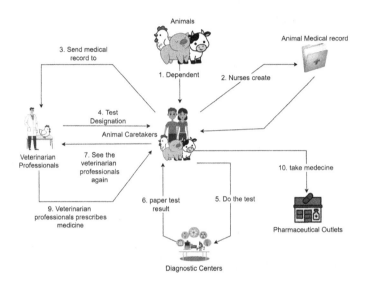

Fig. 1. Traditional framework for animal-care

Veterinary Professionals: Veterinary professionals, often referred to as vets, are the cornerstone of the conventional animal care model. Trained extensively both academically and clinically, they possess the skill set to address diverse animal health concerns, ranging from standard wellness checks to complex surgical interventions. These professionals curate and update AMRs, which chronicle various health-related events, ensuring a holistic approach to animal care.

Animal Medical Records (AMRs): AMRs serve as the central repository detailing an animal's health journey. Such records encapsulate essential events right from birth, highlighting vaccination schedules, any prior medical conditions, surgical histories, dietary specifics, and more. A well-maintained AMR is indispensable, ensuring a coherent and continuous treatment trajectory.

Animals: The diverse spectrum of animals, be it household pets, farm animals, or exotics, stands at the heart of this model. Their health and well-being drive the entire care paradigm. Each species, and often individual animals, present unique health considerations, mandating tailor-made care strategies.

Animal Caretakers: These individuals, whether they're pet owners, farm managers, or zookeepers, are more than mere guardians. Their active involvement, observations, and decision-making play a significant role in the healthcare journey, bridging the gap between veterinary advice and practical care implementation.

Pharmaceutical Outlets: Pharmacies and dispensaries form an essential cog in the wheel of animal care. Collaborating closely with veterinary professionals, they ensure timely provision of medications, supplements, and other vital therapeutic solutions. Their role extends beyond mere dispensing - they offer insights into medication usage, potential interactions, and safety protocols.

Diagnostic Centers: Whenever deeper medical insights are required, diagnostic centers come into play. Equipped with specialized apparatus and know-how, they conduct a range of tests from basic blood work to advanced genetic screenings, thus aiding vets in making informed treatment decisions.

Now, let's elucidate the sequence of events in a traditional animal care model, as illustrated in Fig. 1:

Initiating the Medical Record: Animal care begins with the caretaker reaching out to a veterinary professional. During this inaugural interaction, the vet collects foundational data about the animal, setting the stage for a structured health evaluation.

Presentation of Physical Medical Records: In this traditional setup, physical AMRs play a pivotal role. These records, safeguarded by caretakers, must be presented during consultations. Such a practice ensures that the vet possesses a holistic view of the animal's health, facilitating informed decision-making.

Examination and Diagnostic Recommendations: The core of any consultation is the health assessment. Vets carry out a thorough physical evaluation, covering critical physiological facets. Depending on the findings, and any exhibited symptoms, a battery of diagnostic tests might be proposed to derive deeper health insights.

Transmitting Diagnostic Test Orders to the Testing Facility. Following the decision to conduct diagnostic tests, the veterinarian issues formal test orders, typically on paper. These delineated instructions serve as a communication bridge between the vet and the diagnostic facility. Pet owners play an intermediary role, physically carrying these orders to the testing facility, ensuring that the right tests are conducted based on the veterinarian's evaluation.

Receiving Test Results from the Testing Facility. Upon completion of the ordered tests, the diagnostic facility prepares detailed reports outlining the results. Traditionally, these findings are shared with the pet owner in a paper format, containing all the pertinent data and observations made during the testing process. The responsibility falls upon the pet owner to retrieve these results in a timely manner, ensuring the continuity of the healthcare process.

Reviewing Test Results and Prescription of Medications. Armed with the diagnostic results, pet owners return to the veterinarian for a comprehensive review. The veterinarian meticulously evaluates the findings, cross-referencing them with the initial examination and the pet's historical medical data. Based on this holistic assessment, if a medical intervention is deemed necessary, medications are prescribed. The prescription contains specifics regarding the medication type, dosage, frequency, and potential side effects, ensuring the pet owner is well-informed about the treatment regimen.

Receiving and Administering Medications. The final step in this traditional model involves the procurement and administration of prescribed medications. Pet owners present the veterinarian's prescription to a pharmacy or drugstore. With accuracy and diligence, the pharmacy dispenses the appropriate medications, often complementing them with detailed instructions about administration, storage, and potential side effects. The pet owner, then, administers these medications to the pet, observing for therapeutic outcomes and any possible reactions.

We face several drawbacks of the traditional model for pet care (just mention a few below):

- **Dependency on Physical Documents:** The traditional model relies heavily on paper-based medical records. These can easily be lost, damaged, or even become outdated, causing potential lapses in a pet's healthcare journey.
- **Manual Transfer of Information:** Pet owners act as intermediaries, physically transferring documents and test orders between veterinarians and testing facilities. This can lead to delays, miscommunication, and potential loss of crucial information.
- **Limited Accessibility:** Paper records are not easily accessible by multiple parties simultaneously. If a pet owner decides to switch to a new veterinarian or consult a specialist, sharing the pet's entire health history becomes a cumbersome process.
- **Data Security Concerns:** Physical documents can be accessed by anyone who comes into contact with them, leading to potential privacy breaches.
- **Inefficiency and Delays:** The manual nature of ordering tests, receiving results, and then revisiting the veterinarian can cause delays in diagnosis and treatment.
- **Potential for Human Error:** Given the manual handling and transcription of data, there's a risk for human error, which can have critical implications for a pet's health.

3.2 Harnessing Blockchain for Advanced Animal Healthcare

In response to the shortcomings of conventional animal healthcare systems, our research introduces a cutting-edge blockchain-driven strategy. Central to our system are advanced technologies, such as smart contracts, NFTs, IPFS, and a meticulously designed blockchain framework. Figure 2 showcases the elements

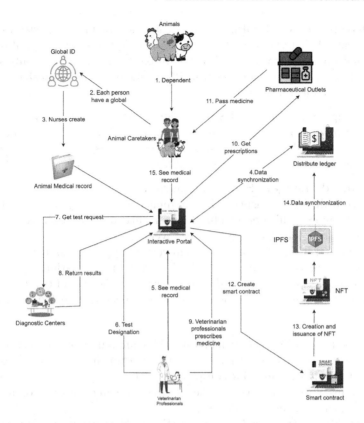

Fig. 2. Illustration of the blockchain-fueled model for advanced animal healthcare

that signify a transformative shift in animal healthcare, with specifics discussed subsequently.

Interactive Portal. The digital platform facilitates seamless interactions between veterinarians and the extensive database of animal medical histories. It's imperative for this portal to be intuitive, enriched with tools like graphical representations, AI-enabled diagnostic aids, and calendar features, considering the myriad of species and their diverse healthcare needs.

Animal ID Mechanism. To fortify data privacy, each animal is linked to a distinctive Animal Identification Code (AIC). This digital signature ensures that only authorized persons, whether it's the animal's caregiver or the vet, have the privilege to access and modify the records, safeguarding data confidentiality.

Smart Contract Integration. Though smart contracts are quintessential in blockchain models, they can also rejuvenate traditional systems. In our model, they function as auto-executable digital protocols, facilitating secure storage and management of animal health records. Their embedded rules and criteria ensure restricted and authentic access, fortifying data sanctity.

NFT-Driven Medical Profiles. Rather than viewing medical histories as mere files, conceptualizing them as NFTs imparts uniqueness and immutability to each animal's health record. This blockchain-backed approach not only solidifies its authenticity but also smoothes transitions like ownership transfers, ensuring continuity in medical histories.

Data Storage via IPFS. IPFS revolutionizes data storage, diverting from a single-point model to a decentralized one. For animal health, this means records on the IPFS are universally accessible, resilient against localized server issues, and are securely encrypted against unauthorized tampering.

Decentralized Ledger System. Imagine an extensive, consensus-based database recording every aspect of an animal's healthcare journey. Unlike conventional databases, this decentralized ledger authenticates each entry, assuring clarity and traceability for every medical event.

As visualized in Fig. 2, our blockchain-centric approach comprises a 14-step progression, emphasizing bolstered safety, clarity, and operational efficiency. In this discourse, we spotlight pivotal phases that form the core of this novel animal healthcare paradigm. For an encompassing perspective, the figure provides a detailed flow.

– **Universal Animal ID Initiation:** The animal caregiver establishes a unique ID, acting as the primary identifier within the blockchain ecosystem.
– **Digital Health Profile Development:** Veterinarians, migrating from age-old systems, engage with the blockchain to create an exhaustive digital health profile, encapsulating vital details.
– **Decentralized Ledger Documentation:** Information is recorded on the blockchain, ensuring unparalleled data veracity and safeguarding.
– **Health Data Retrieval and Augmentation:** Veterinarians, upon assessments, utilize blockchain to access and expand animal health profiles.
– **Specialized Test Requisitions:** Vets, via the blockchain platform, can direct specific diagnostic tests to affiliated labs.
– **Lab Procedures and Reporting:** Labs process diagnostic requests and record findings on the blockchain for vet accessibility.
– **Analytical Health Evaluations and Medication Allotment:** Analyzing data within the blockchain ecosystem, vets determine health outcomes and prescribe treatments, which are securely logged.
– **Medication Distribution:** Pharmacies, notified via blockchain, prepare and hand out the prescribed medicines.
– **Caregiver Engagement with the System:** Animal caregivers can transparently view health records, follow treatments, and manage their animal's health regimen through the blockchain interface.

Our blockchain-infused technique is a beacon in animal healthcare. Besides bolstering data safety and availability, it accentuates transparency, ensures record sanctity, and optimizes healthcare management. Contrasting with traditional systems, our methodology stands apart with seven distinct attributes:

- **Indelible Records:** The blockchain ensures permanence and unalterability of records, promising authentic and enduring animal medical histories.
- **Decentralized and Visible Operations:** With data distributed across nodes, the system negates single-point failures. Additionally, all entries are transparent, fostering trust among network participants.
- **Unique NFT-driven Profiles:** Each animal's health profile, tokenized as an NFT, stands unique, ensuring authenticity and simplifying data access and transfers.
- **IPFS-Powered Secure Archiving:** IPFS promises decentralized data archiving, diminishing risks and ensuring data continuity and accessibility.
- **Swift and Seamless Access:** Real-time sharing and retrieval of records are facilitated by the blockchain.
- **Superior Data Privacy and Safeguarding:** Advanced encryption techniques maintain data confidentiality, permitting access only to authorized entities.
- **Cost-Effectiveness:** The blockchain model, by sidestepping intermediaries, holds the potential to cut costs linked to data management and transactions.

4   Evaluation

The landscape of blockchain technology has evolved significantly, offering diverse platforms that are compatible with the Ethereum Virtual Machine (EVM). To rigorously assess the viability and effectiveness of our blockchain-centric approach to animal healthcare, we deployed the smart contracts integral to our system across four key EVM-compliant platforms: *Binance Smart Chain (BNB Smart Chain)*[1], *Polygon*[2], *Fantom*[3], and *Celo*[4]. The goal of this multi-platform deployment was to explore and capitalize on the distinct features and advantages that each ecosystem provides.

In parallel with these deployments, and in line with the rising popularity of decentralized storage and Non-Fungible Tokens (NFTs), we chose to store animal health records on the InterPlanetary File System (IPFS). To facilitate this, we utilized the *Pinata platform*[5] to securely and effectively host these critical datasets in a decentralized manner.

4.1   Decentralized Ecosystem Replication

In a decentralized network, nodes serve as the foundational elements that bolster data integrity, redundancy, and security measures. Our evaluation leveraged a simulated environment meticulously designed to emulate the intricacies typical of real-world decentralized blockchain systems. Figure 3 illustrates the 20 nodes implemented in our test environment, each uniquely identified by their public and private key pairs.

---

[1] https://github.com/bnb-chain/whitepaper/blob/master/WHITEPAPER.md.
[2] https://polygon.technology/lightpaper-polygon.pdf.
[3] https://whitepaper.io/document/438/fantom-whitepaper.
[4] https://celo.org/papers/whitepaper.
[5] Pinata: A leading developer API for IPFS https://www.pinata.cloud/.

Fig. 3. The simulation environment for test case with the first five nodes

Each node in our testing landscape potentially represents a different stake-holder in the blockchain-driven Animal Healthcare system. This includes veterinary facilities, pet owners, and research organizations. The public key acts as an open identifier for facilitating interactions between nodes, while the private key serves as a secure gateway for data encryption and access control. This dual-key architecture ensures that while authorized nodes can view records, only the node holding the corresponding private key can edit them.

To execute our evaluation, we employed a hybrid architecture combining both physical and virtual servers. This setup allowed for a broad assessment environment that closely mimics real-world configurations. The multi-faceted server setup enabled us to evaluate various performance metrics like system resilience, latency, and throughput under multiple conditions. It also highlighted potential vulnerabilities that might be more apparent in one type of environment over another.

In this simulated setting, we carried out various types of operations, including the execution of standard blockchain transactions, the generation and transfer of NFTs, and a comprehensive evaluation of our system's performance. Through iterative adjustments and improvements, our methodology was optimized to effectively function within the complex architecture of decentralized networks.

4.2   Four-Step Process on the IPFS Platform

The process of integrating animal medical records, such as those of a rabbit, into the IPFS platform can be articulated in four essential steps. Each step corresponds to a visual demonstration depicted in Figs. 4, 5, 6, and 7.

Animal Medical Record Representation. The initial step involves the creation of an animal medical record, denoted as Rabbit-AMR. This digital representation embodies all pertinent medical details such as medical history, and treatments. Figure 4 provides a visual snapshot of what such an animal medical record for a rabbit may look like.

```
const body = {
    veterinaryID: "veterinaryID 1",
    animalID: "animalID 1",
    kind : "Rabbit",
    name: "Blue Sky",
    Owner: "Kevin H. S.",
    Dianose: "Diagnose",
    treatmentHistory: "The past treatment of the rabbit",
    immunizations: 1,
    rabbitHealth: "pertinent health narratives",
};
const options = {
    pinataMetadata: {
        name: "Electronic Animal Medical Records.json",
    },
    pinataOptions: {
        cidVersion: 0,
    },
};
```

Fig. 4. A sample representation of a rabbit's medical record, termed Rabbit-AMR.

Hash Generation. Following the creation of Rabbit-AMR, the next step is to generate a unique hash for this record using IPFS. This hash acts as an identifier for the record within the decentralized network. Figure 5 illustrates the hash generation based on Rabbit-AMR.

```
You are using a version of Node.js that is not supported by Hardhat, and it may work incorrectly, or not work a
t all.

Please, make sure you are using a supported version of Node.js.

To learn more about which versions of Node.js are supported go to https://hardhat.org/nodejs-versions


  Lock
    Animal Care System
CID QmbzxM9sGijGDFFX6Q74yxuBwJu5FrjJdoRW2xLsXvuRtb
      ✓ Should set the right unlockTime (3715ms)


  1 passing (4s)
```

Fig. 5. Generation of a unique hash identifier for Rabbit-AMR.

IPFS Deployment via Pinata. Once the unique hash is generated, the Rabbit-AMR is uploaded onto the IPFS network via the Pinata platform, a developer API for IPFS. This secures the record within a decentralized file storage system. Figure 6 showcases the Rabbit-AMR being uploaded on the Pinata platform.

Fig. 6. Uploading Rabbit-AMR onto the IPFS network through the Pinata platform.

Hash ID Retrieval. The final step in this process is the retrieval of the hash ID generated for Rabbit-AMR, which confirms that the record has been successfully integrated into the IPFS network. This hash ID serves as a unique reference point for accessing the rabbit's medical record. Figure 7 displays the resulting hash ID generated for Rabbit-AMR.

```
     ⟳   🔒 https://maroon-wandering-fly-487.mypinata.cloud/ipfs/QmbzxM9sGijGDFFX6Q74yxuBwJu5FrjJdoRW2...   🔍

 1  {
 2      "veterinaryID": "veterinaryID 1",
 3      "animalID": "animalID 1",
 4      "kind": "Rabbit",
 5      "name": "Blue Sky",
 6      "Owner": "Kevin H. S.",
 7      "Dianose": "Diagnose",
 8      "treatmentHistory": "The past treatment of the rabbit",
 9      "immunizations": 1,
10      "rabbitHealth": "pertinent health narratives"
11  }
```

Fig. 7. Retrieval of the unique hash ID for Rabbit-AMR post-upload.

4.3   Assessment of Transaction Costs Across Select EVM-Compatible Platforms

The Ethereum Virtual Machine (EVM) serves as the underlying computational engine for a multitude of blockchain networks. To gauge the efficacy and cost-effectiveness of our animal healthcare system within this landscape, we opted for an evaluative lens focusing on four platforms compatible with EVM. These platforms are Binance Smart Chain, Polygon, Fantom, and Celo. Our assessment encompasses three fundamental aspects that are pivotal to our animal healthcare model:

1. **Record Insertion and Transaction Initiation:** This criterion gauges the facility and speed with which new medical records for pets can be instantiated within the blockchain architecture. The goal is to ascertain the latency and computational load associated with this fundamental operation.
2. **Tokenization via NFTs:** Because each animal's medical history is unique, translating these individual records into Non-Fungible Tokens (NFTs)

becomes critical. In this phase, we explore the resource consumption and responsiveness of NFT minting operations for medical records on each of the platforms under study.

3. **Ownership Transition for NFTs:** NFTs may change hands for a multitude of reasons-be it pet adoption, sale, or transitioning between different veterinary care providers. We scrutinize the mechanics, costs, and seamlessness of executing these ownership transfers across the selected blockchains (Table 1).

Our objective is to offer an exhaustive comparative analysis, elucidating the strengths and limitations of each platform when subjected to the particular requirements of animal healthcare data management, as well as the universal demands for blockchain efficiency[6]. Furthermore, a proof-of-concept implementation aligned with our proposed framework is available for public scrutiny on the test networks for each platform: BNB[7], MATIC[8], FTM[9], and CELO[10].

Table 1. Transaction fee

	Pet Medical Record/Transaction Creation	Mint NFT	Transfer NFT
BNB Smart Chain	0.0273134 BNB ($5.87)	0.00109162 BNB ($0.23)	0.00057003 BNB ($0.12)
Fantom	0.00957754 FTM ($0.001919)	0.000405167 FTM ($0.000081)	0.0002380105 FTM ($0.000048)
Polygon	0.006840710032835408 MATIC($0.00)	0.000289405001852192 MATIC($0.00)	0.000170007501088048 MATIC($0.00)
Celo	0.007097844 CELO ($0.003)	0.0002840812 CELO ($0.000)	0.0001554878 CELO ($0.000)

Transaction Fee. Certainly, in the context of animal healthcare, transaction fees for different blockchain platforms show considerable variation for operations related to medical records. The BNB Smart Chain has the most substantial fees for creating animal medical records, with a cost of 0.0273134 BNB, translating to approximately $5.87. Meanwhile, the Polygon platform is the most economical for this type of transaction, charging a fee of 0.006840710032835408 MATIC,

---

[6] The valuation of the tokens on the selected platforms is noted as of 9/09/2023, 4:00:00 PM UTC.

[7] https://testnet.bscscan.com/address/0xafa3888d1dfbfe957b1cd68c36ede4991e104a53.

[8] https://mumbai.polygonscan.com/address/0xd9ee80d850ef3c4978dd0b099a45a559fd7c5ef4.

[9] https://testnet.ftmscan.com/address/0x4a2573478c67a894e32d806c8dd23ee8e26f7847.

[10] https://explorer.celo.org/alfajores/address/0x4a2573478C67a894E32D806c8Dd23EE8E26f7847/transactions.

which is almost negligible in dollar terms. The platforms of Fantom and Celo offer moderate fees, at 0.00957754 FTM ($0.001919) and 0.007097844 CELO ($0.003) respectively, serving as affordable alternatives.

When it comes to minting Non-Fungible Tokens (NFTs) for unique animal medical records, BNB Smart Chain is again the priciest option, requiring a fee of 0.00109162 BNB or roughly $0.23. In contrast, Fantom, Polygon, and Celo charge significantly lower fees, specifically 0.000405167 FTM ($0.000081), 0.000289405001852192 MATIC ($0.00), and 0.0002840812 CELO ($0.000). These economical rates could make Fantom, Polygon, and Celo more attractive for projects focusing on the tokenization of animal healthcare data.

For the task of transferring ownership of the NFTs, which could represent vital animal medical records, BNB Smart Chain continues to be the most expensive option, costing 0.00057003 BNB or $0.12 per transaction. Fantom, Polygon, and Celo, on the other hand, offer budget-friendly solutions. Fantom charges 0.0002380105 FTM ($0.000048), Polygon's fee is 0.000170007501088048 MATIC ($0.00), and Celo's is 0.0001554878 CELO ($0.000). Therefore, while BNB Smart Chain has the highest transaction costs across all operations, the benefits it might provide in speed, security, or other attributes could potentially justify these costs. Fantom, Polygon, and Celo appear to offer a more cost-effective balance for operations related to animal medical records.

Table 2. Burn fee

	Pet Medical Record/Transaction Creation	Mint NFT	Transfer NFT
BNB Smart Chain	0.0050316262999993 BNB ($1.08)	0.0011175342 BNB ($0.24)	0.000849245 BNB ($0.18)
Fantom	not mention	not mention	not mention
Polygon	0.000000000032835408 MATIC	0.000000000001852192 MATIC	0.000000000001088048 MATIC
Celo	not mention	not mention	not mention

Burn Fee. The burn fee Table 2 presents a detailed comparison of the burn fees associated with three different operations: the creation of Animal Medical Records (AMRs), the minting of Non-Fungible Tokens (NFTs), and the transfer of these NFTs across four different blockchain platforms: BNB Smart Chain, Fantom, Polygon, and Celo.

The BNB Smart Chain shows a more considerable burn fee across all three operations. Specifically, the highest burn fee of $1.08 is observed in the creation of an animal medical record or transaction, followed by minting an NFT at $0.24, and transferring an NFT at $0.18. This suggests that, while BNB Smart Chain offers a robust infrastructure, its associated burn fees could be a limiting factor for users who are cost-sensitive.

Interestingly, Fantom and Celo did not provide information on burn fees for any of the three operations, which raises questions about their cost-effectiveness and transparency in this specific area. Polygon, on the other hand, reveals an exceptionally low burn fee for all three actions. The fees are almost negligible, indicating a high level of cost-effectiveness. This might make Polygon an attractive choice for users and organizations that prioritize low transaction costs.

In total, the analysis of burn fees highlights the potential trade-offs between different blockchain platforms. While BNB Smart Chain offers a versatile but costly solution, Polygon stands out for its minimal fees. Meanwhile, the absence of data for Fantom and Celo calls for further investigation into these platforms' cost structures.

5   Discussion

The evaluation phase of our study provides important insights into the effectiveness, efficiency, and practical implications of employing blockchain technology in the realm of animal healthcare. It reveals the strengths and weaknesses of various platforms supported by the Ethereum Virtual Machine (EVM) and offers a benchmark for transaction fees across them.

5.1   Platform Suitability and Trade-Offs

BNB Smart Chain stands out for its higher transaction fees but could potentially offer benefits in speed and security. On the other hand, Fantom, Polygon, and Celo pose as cost-effective platforms, making them favorable for smaller veterinary establishments or nonprofit animal care organizations. Hence, there exists a trade-off between operational costs and system capabilities, which stakeholders should consider based on their specific requirements.

5.2   Decentralized Ecosystem

The creation of a decentralized ecosystem offers stakeholders in animal healthcare—from veterinary clinics to research bodies—a robust framework for secure and transparent medical record-keeping. Our system's simulation emphasized the practicality and resilience of our architecture. However, transitioning from a traditional to a decentralized system would require overcoming adoption barriers, both technical and cultural.

5.3   Cost Implications

Our fee structure analysis highlights the need for cost-benefit considerations, particularly for veterinary establishments operating on a tight budget. While blockchain technology adds a layer of security and transparency, it does come with transactional costs that can add up over time, especially on platforms like BNB Smart Chain. Budget-conscious organizations may have to weigh the long-term benefits of such an immutable and transparent system against the operational costs incurred.

5.4   Limitation and Future Work

Although our simulated environment was designed to closely mimic real-world conditions, it remains a controlled setting and may not account for all potential challenges in a live blockchain network. Moreover, the economic analysis could be expanded to include not just transaction costs but also the costs of system setup, training, and maintenance.A By focusing on offering a detailed, empirical evaluation of our blockchain-driven approach, we aim to provide veterinary professionals and healthcare policymakers a comprehensive understanding of its utility and limitations. This work, therefore, paves the way for more informed and effective applications of blockchain technology in animal healthcare. Based on these limitations we will consider some ideas to extend the current work.

- An advanced analysis aimed at understanding the relationship between the assigned gas limit and the computational workload could shed light on how different blockchain platforms handle the complexity of animal medical records. This would aid in identifying the most resource-efficient solutions for storing and retrieving medical data [8].
- Investigating various scalability approaches, including layer-2 solutions, could offer strategies to lower transactional overheads or boost data processing speeds, which is critical when dealing with large datasets such as comprehensive animal medical records [18].
- The synergy between our blockchain-based animal medical record system and emerging technologies like Internet of Things (IoT) could open new dimensions in real-time health monitoring of animals. This could mean instantaneous updates to medical records when IoT devices detect changes in an animal's health, thereby enhancing both the accuracy and utility of the medical data [17,28,29].
- Future iterations of this blockchain-based system could benefit from comprehensive access control measures to address potential security and privacy concerns. By implementing dynamic policies for data access, we can ensure that the medical records are only available to authorized personnel, which is essential for maintaining both data integrity and compliance with privacy regulations [10,24,33].

6   Conclusion

The transition from traditional to digital mediums has revolutionized healthcare, extending its reach into the domain of animal medical care. Through Animal Medical Records (AMRs), powered by Electronic Health Records (EHRs), this work illuminates the diverse applications and myriad benefits of digitizing animal healthcare data. AMRs have proven to be instrumental in conducting targeted research, fostering evidence-based clinical practices, and addressing both local and global health concerns.

However, the shift to digital records is not without its hurdles, particularly in areas such as data security, integrity, and interoperability. Centralized systems, despite their widespread use, are fraught with vulnerabilities and limitations. In response, this paper offers a pioneering solution that leverages blockchain technology, coupled with Non-Fungible Tokens (NFTs) and the InterPlanetary File System (IPFS). Our comprehensive framework addresses critical issues in animal healthcare by ensuring data transparency, integrity, and availability. The use of NFTs adds an additional layer of data transparency, allowing for the verification of each unique animal health record. IPFS enhances this by ensuring that these records are accessible and persistently stored in a decentralized manner.

Significantly, the feasibility of our proposed framework is not confined to the theoretical domain. We have executed a proof-of-concept implementation across four different blockchain platforms underpinned by the Ethereum Virtual Machine (EVM), showcasing the system's adaptability and versatility. Furthermore, our approach harnesses the power of the Pinata platform, an IPFS-based solution, to fortify our commitment to data availability and decentralization. As we move toward a future where data integrity and availability are increasingly crucial, blockchain-driven systems like the one proposed here could well define the new standard for animal healthcare management.

Acknowledgements. We extend our deepest gratitude to Engineer Le Thanh Tuan and Dr. Ha Xuan Son, who have been invaluable assets throughout the conceptualization, practical execution, and assessment phases of this research project. Additionally, this endeavor received instrumental backing from FPT University's Cantho Campus in Vietnam, whose support facilitated the successful completion of this work.

References

1. Aigner, C.: Prototypical implementation of an animal health record (AHR) for livestock management. Ph.D. thesis (2014)
2. Anholt, R.M., Berezowski, J., Jamal, I., Ribble, C., Stephen, C.: Mining free-text medical records for companion animal enteric syndrome surveillance. Prev. Vet. Med. **113**(4), 417–422 (2014)
3. Anholt, R.: Informatics and the electronic medical record for syndromic surveillance in companion animals: development, application and utility. Ph.D. thesis, University of Calgary (2013)
4. Burke, S., Black, V., Sánchez-Vizcaíno, F., Radford, A., Hibbert, A., Tasker, S.: Use of cefovecin in a UK population of cats attending first-opinion practices as recorded in electronic health records. J. Feline Med. Surg. **19**(6), 687–692 (2017)
5. Duong-Trung, N., et al.: Multi-sessions mechanism for decentralized cash on delivery system. Int. J. Adv. Comput. Sci. Appl. **10**(9) (2019)
6. Gates, M., Zito, S., Harvey, L., Dale, A., Walker, J.: Assessing obesity in adult dogs and cats presenting for routine vaccination appointments in the north island of New Zealand using electronic medical records data. N. Z. Vet. J. **67**(3), 126–133 (2019)
7. Gray, C., Radford, A.: Using electronic health records to explore negotiations around euthanasia decision making for dogs and cats in the UK. Vet. Rec. 190(9), no-no (2022)

8. Ha, X.S., Le, H.T., Metoui, N., Duong-Trung, N.: Dem-cod: novel access-control-based cash on delivery mechanism for decentralized marketplace. In: 2020 IEEE 19th International Conference on Trust, Security and Privacy in Computing and Communications (TrustCom), pp. 71–78. IEEE (2020)

9. Ha, X.S., Le, T.H., Phan, T.T., Nguyen, H.H.D., Vo, H.K., Duong-Trung, N.: Scrutinizing trust and transparency in cash on delivery systems. In: Wang, G., Chen, B., Li, W., Di Pietro, R., Yan, X., Han, H. (eds.) SpaCCS 2020. LNCS, vol. 12382, pp. 214–227. Springer, Cham (2021). https://doi.org/10.1007/978-3-030-68851-6_15

10. Hoang, N.M., Son, H.X.: A dynamic solution for fine-grained policy conflict resolution. In: Proceedings of the 3rd International Conference on Cryptography, Security and Privacy, pp. 116–120 (2019)

11. Kass, P.H., et al.: Syndromic surveillance in companion animals utilizing electronic medical records data: development and proof of concept. PeerJ 4, e1940 (2016)

12. Kim, E., et al.: Major medical causes by breed and life stage for dogs presented at veterinary clinics in the republic of Korea: a survey of electronic medical records. PeerJ 6, e5161 (2018)

13. Le, H.T., et al.: Introducing multi shippers mechanism for decentralized cash on delivery system. Int. J. Adv. Comput. Sci. Appl. 10(6) (2019)

14. Le, H.T.: Patient-chain: patient-centered healthcare system a blockchain-based technology in dealing with emergencies. In: Shen, H., et al. (eds.) PDCAT 2021. LNCS, vol. 13148, pp. 576–583. Springer, Cham (2022). https://doi.org/10.1007/978-3-030-96772-7_54

15. Le, N.T.T., et al.: Assuring non-fraudulent transactions in cash on delivery by introducing double smart contracts. Int. J. Adv. Comput. Sci. Appl. 10(5), 677–684 (2019)

16. Menéndez, S., Steiner, A., Witschi, U., Danuser, J., Weber, U., Regula, G.: Data quality of animal health records on swiss dairy farms. Vet. Rec. 163(8), 241–246 (2008)

17. Nguyen, L.T.T., et al.: BMDD: a novel approach for IoT platform (broker-less and microservice architecture, decentralized identity, and dynamic transmission messages). PeerJ Comput. Sci. 8, e950 (2022)

18. Quoc, K.L., et al.: SSSB: an approach to insurance for cross-border exchange by using smart contracts. In: Awan, I., Younas, M., Poniszewska-Marańda, A. (eds.) MobiWIS 2022. LNCS, vol. 13475, pp. 179–192. Springer, Cham (2022). https://doi.org/10.1007/978-3-031-14391-5_14

19. Romar, A.: Fine-grained access control in an animal health record. Ph.D. thesis, Wien (2018)

20. Salt, C., Saito, E.K., O'Flynn, C., Allaway, D.: Stratification of companion animal life stages from electronic medical record diagnosis data. J. Gerontol. Ser. A 78(4), 579–586 (2023)

21. Sánchez-Vizcaíno, F., et al.: Demographics of dogs, cats, and rabbits attending veterinary practices in great Britain as recorded in their electronic health records. BMC Vet. Res. 13, 1–13 (2017)

22. Singleton, D.A., et al.: Pharmaceutical prescription in canine acute diarrhoea: a longitudinal electronic health record analysis of first opinion veterinary practices. Front. Vet. Sci. 218 (2019)

23. Son, H.X., Chen, E.: Towards a fine-grained access control mechanism for privacy protection and policy conflict resolution. Int. J. Adv. Comput. Sci. Appl. 10(2) (2019)

24. Son, H.X., Dang, T.K., Massacci, F.: REW-SMT: a new approach for rewriting XACML request with dynamic big data security policies. In: Wang, G., Atiquzzaman, M., Yan, Z., Choo, K.-K.R. (eds.) SpaCCS 2017. LNCS, vol. 10656, pp. 501–515. Springer, Cham (2017). https://doi.org/10.1007/978-3-319-72389-1_40

25. Son, H.X., Hoang, N.M.: A novel attribute-based access control system for fine-grained privacy protection. In: Proceedings of the 3rd International Conference on Cryptography, Security and Privacy, pp. 76–80 (2019)

26. Son, H.X., et al.: Towards a mechanism for protecting seller's interest of cash on delivery by using smart contract in hyperledger. Int. J. Adv. Comput. Sci. Appl. **10**(4) (2019)

27. Son, H.X., Nguyen, M.H., Vo, H.K., Nguyen, T.P.: Toward an privacy protection based on access control model in hybrid cloud for healthcare systems. In: Martínez Álvarez, F., Troncoso Lora, A., Sáez Muñoz, J.A., Quintián, H., Corchado, E. (eds.) CISIS/ICEUTE -2019. AISC, vol. 951, pp. 77–86. Springer, Cham (2020). https://doi.org/10.1007/978-3-030-20005-3_8

28. Thanh, L.N.T., et al.: Toward a security IoT platform with high rate transmission and low energy consumption. In: Gervasi, O., et al. (eds.) ICCSA 2021. LNCS, vol. 12949, pp. 647–662. Springer, Cham (2021). https://doi.org/10.1007/978-3-030-86653-2_47

29. Thanh, L.N.T., et al.: UIP2SOP: a unique IoT network applying single sign-on and message queue protocol. Int. J. Adv. Comput. Sci. Appl. **12**(6) (2021)

30. Thi, Q.N.T., Dang, T.K., Van, H.L., Son, H.X.: Using JSON to specify privacy preserving-enabled attribute-based access control policies. In: Wang, G., Atiquzzaman, M., Yan, Z., Choo, K.-K.R. (eds.) SpaCCS 2017. LNCS, vol. 10656, pp. 561–570. Springer, Cham (2017). https://doi.org/10.1007/978-3-319-72389-1_44

31. Tulloch, J., McGinley, L., Sánchez-Vizcaíno, F., Medlock, J., Radford, A.: The passive surveillance of ticks using companion animal electronic health records. Epidemiol. Infect. **145**(10), 2020–2029 (2017)

32. Willner, V.: Erhebung und Analyse der Anforderungen an einen Animal Health Record (AHR) für Kleintiere. Ph.D. thesis (2011)

33. Xuan, S.H., et al.: Rew-XAC: an approach to rewriting request for elastic ABAC enforcement with dynamic policies. In: 2016 International Conference on Advanced Computing and Applications (ACOMP), pp. 25–31. IEEE (2016)

Transforming Child Health Records: Integrating Blockchain, NFTs, and IPFS for Enhanced Medical Data Management

T. L. Quy[1($\boxtimes$)], N. D. P. Trong[1], H. V. Khanh[1], H. L. Huong[1], T. D. Khoa[1], H. G. Khiem[1], N. T. Phuc[1], M. D. Hieu[1], V. C. P. Loc[1], N. H. Kha[1], N. T. Anh[1], Q. N. Hien[1], L. K. Bang[1], Q. T. Bao[1], N. T. K. Ngan[2], and M. N. Triet[1($\boxtimes$)]

[1] FPT University, Can Tho, Vietnam
{quylt9,trietnm3}@fe.edu.vn
[2] FPT Polytechnic, Can Tho, Vietnam

Abstract. In the rapidly evolving landscape of medical record management, the traditional methods often grapple with issues related to data security, integrity, and accessibility. This paper introduces a groundbreaking approach to pediatric medical data management by leveraging the robust capabilities of blockchain, Non-Fungible Tokens (NFTs), InterPlanetary File System (IPFS), and distributed ledgers. Our proposed model meticulously addresses the limitations of the conventional systems by ensuring data immutability, transparency, and decentralized control. Starting with the creation of a unique Global ID for children, we outline a detailed 10-step approach to data storage, query, and update, emphasizing the pivotal roles of smart contracts and NFTs in guaranteeing data authenticity and uniqueness. The implementation section delves deeper into the intricacies of transaction creation, data query, and update mechanisms, underscoring the importance of secure interfaces, rigorous verification processes, and seamless synchronization with decentralized storage solutions. With the confluence of these advanced technologies, our approach promises a transformative shift in pediatric healthcare, simplifying processes for healthcare professionals and ensuring data security and privacy for patients.

Keywords: Pediatric Healthcare · Blockchain · Data Management · Electronic Health Records (EHRs) · Non-Fungible Tokens (NFTs) · InterPlanetary File System (IPFS) · Decentralized Storage · Smart Contracts

1 Introduction

The landscape of healthcare is undergoing a digital transformation, further emphasized by the nuanced requirements of pediatric care. Conventional medical data management approaches, although functional, present gaps in data security,

© The Author(s), under exclusive license to Springer Nature Switzerland AG 2024
S. Bouzefrane et al. (Eds.): MSPN 2023, LNCS 14482, pp. 120–138, 2024.
https://doi.org/10.1007/978-3-031-52426-4_9

interoperability, and accessibility, which are critical in pediatric settings [4, 25]. The emergence of innovative technologies like the Internet of Healthcare Things (IoHT), or decentralized architectures promises a sea change in the realm of healthcare data management [14, 23].

IoHT has been a pivotal addition to the healthcare ecosystem, offering microservice and brokerless architectures to streamline healthcare processes (e.g., [13]). Yet, despite the influx of technologies, challenges persist in pediatric healthcare, where data sensitivity is even more pronounced. For example, the application of Electronic Health Records (EHRs) has resulted in some improvements, like better screening for children with diabetes [2], but also demonstrated limitations, such as ineffective body mass index assessments [17].

While Electronic Health Records (EHRs) offer myriad benefits for pediatric care, existing systems confront a series of challenges [22, 24]. A centralized EHR infrastructure is susceptible to data security issues, unauthorized access, and potential alterations [19]. Moreover, inconsistent interoperability across EHR platforms complicates the fluid exchange of medical data, raising concerns about data accuracy and consistency [20]. To mitigate these shortcomings, emerging technologies like blockchain are being explored as transformative tools in healthcare data management [9]. Blockchain's decentralized nature eliminates single points of vulnerability and ensures data integrity through cryptographic mechanisms [5, 21]. Smart contracts enable standardized protocols for data exchange, enhancing the system's interoperability [7].

Beyond blockchain's foundational benefits, additional mechanisms like off-chain storage strategies can improve efficiency, allowing the bulk of child health records to be stored separately from the verification data [12]. Furthermore, the utilization of Non-Fungible Tokens (NFTs) allows for the unique representation of each child's medical history, empowering parents or guardians with greater control over data access and usage. Besides, the InterPlanetary File System (IPFS) augments this setup by providing a decentralized data storage system, enhancing both data availability and resilience [11]. In conjunction, NFTs and IPFS offer an unprecedented strategy for child medical data management, combining data authenticity with robust availability.

Among the significant contributions of our paper, the most prominent is the introduction of a comprehensive blockchain-based framework tailored to pediatric healthcare. This framework securely captures, stores, and facilitates the effortless retrieval of children's medical records, adding a new dimension to data management in pediatric care [10]. We also employ Non-Fungible Tokens (NFTs) to individualize each child's medical records, thereby enhancing transparency and allowing stakeholders to validate the origin and integrity of the data [15]. Our paper furthers the discourse by integrating the InterPlanetary File System (IPFS) to ensure consistent availability of these critical child health records, even in cases of network fragmentation. This innovation augments collaborative healthcare efforts by ensuring data availability across various stakeholders [6].

Importantly, our contributions are not merely theoretical constructs. We have implemented and rigorously tested the proposed framework across diverse blockchain platforms, establishing the system's flexibility and applicability across different infrastructures [18]. Lastly, we extend the functionality of our system by incorporating Pinata, an IPFS-based platform, for persistent decentralized data storage. This serves to fortify the data against risks associated with centralized points of failure, further substantiating the resilience of our approach [11].

2   Related Work

2.1   Electronic Health Records in Pediatric Healthcare

Advancements in digital health technology have had a transformative impact on pediatric care. Telehealth solutions, for instance, have become instrumental in overcoming geographical barriers to healthcare. Van Cleave et al. [25] emphasized the importance of telehealth, especially for children with special healthcare needs residing in isolated locations, which traditionally suffer from limited healthcare access.

Electronic Medical Records (EMRs) have also shown promise in enhancing the efficacy of pediatric healthcare systems. Choudhary et al. [2] demonstrated the role of EMRs in facilitating better adherence to diabetes screening guidelines, which is particularly crucial for childhood diabetes management. However, the use of EMRs is not devoid of challenges, particularly when it comes to vulnerable pediatric populations such as children in foster care. Deans et al. [4] cautioned against relying solely on EHRs, advocating instead for an integrated system that combines electronic health records with child welfare systems to capture a more holistic view of the child's health and well-being.

Strategic interventions using EMRs can lead to immediate and significant healthcare improvements. For example, Crosby et al. [3] employed EMRs to implement home pain management plans for children with sickle cell disease. Their approach led to a noticeable decrease in emergency department visits, underscoring the potential for EHR systems to bring about positive change in patient outcomes.

In the realm of data access and stakeholder experiences, Hagström et al. [8] delved into the nuanced dynamics of allowing adolescent and parental access to Pediatric Electronic Health Records (PAEHRs). They found a complex array of divergent opinions, emphasizing the need to balance transparency with the preservation of adolescent confidentiality.

2.2   Advancements and Challenges of EHRs in Pediatric Care

Electronic Health Records (EHRs) are gradually becoming the backbone of modern pediatric care, offering numerous advantages such as increased efficiency and enhanced patient care. Al-Shammari et al. [1] studied the implementation of an EHR system in a Pediatric Intensive Care Unit (PICU), revealing not only an increase in efficiency but also a positive attitude among healthcare providers towards adopting this technology.

However, it's not enough to simply integrate technology; it must also translate to effective clinical practices. For instance, Shaikh et al. [17] reported that merely incorporating automatic Body Mass Index (BMI) calculations into EHRs did not significantly improve weight assessments or nutritional counseling for children and adolescents. This observation points to the need for thoughtful design and implementation strategies that extend beyond simple technology adoption.

Promisingly, targeted modifications in EHR systems can have powerful effects. Saylam et al. [16] implemented an EHR alert for pediatric migraine patients to assess sleep quality using the Child and Adolescent Sleep Checklist (CASC). This change led to a marked improvement in identifying children with suboptimal sleep habits, showcasing the potential of intelligent EHR design to positively impact patient care.

3 Methodology

3.1 Traditional Model for Pediatric Healthcare

Traditional Model's Components. The classic model for the healthcare of children involves an intricate interplay of several key elements: physicians, comprehensive medical records, the children themselves, their parents or guardians, and auxiliary services like pharmacies and diagnostic centers. For an exhaustive visual representation, refer to Fig. 1.

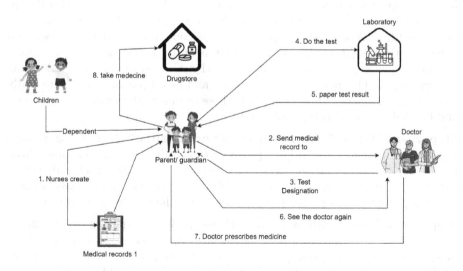

Fig. 1. Classic model for pediatric healthcare

1) **Doctor:** The doctor stands as an indispensable figure in the healthcare ecosystem, responsible for the initial examination, ongoing care, and medical record creation for children. 2) **Medical Records:** Acting as a vital repository,

medical records collate comprehensive information regarding a child's health history, diagnosis, test results, and prescribed treatments. These records are managed and updated by doctors to sustain the quality of child healthcare. **3) Children:** Within this framework, children are the primary care recipients, largely reliant on adults for navigation through medical procedures, from diagnosis to treatment. **4) Parents or Guardians:** These individuals are not merely custodians but active participants in the healthcare decisions concerning the child, often providing essential background medical history for more informed care. **5) Drugstore:** Pharmacies serve as the transaction point for medicinal needs, facilitating the dispensing of medications as per doctors' prescriptions to parents or guardians. **6) Laboratory:** Diagnostic centers or laboratories perform various tests as needed by the doctor, contributing crucial data that aids in comprehensive health evaluations for children.

Subsequently, we will delve into an in-depth discussion outlining the eight primary activities that define the traditional model of pediatric healthcare.

Traditional Model's Steps Step 1: Creating a Basic Medical Record. In this initial step, a nurse sets the stage for the child's medical evaluation by creating a basic paper-based medical record. This contains crucial data such as the child's name, birth date, and contact details. This completed record is then given to the parents or guardians of the child.

Step 2 and Step 3: Doctor's Visit and Examination. Upon receiving the basic medical record, parents or guardians take the child for a medical consultation. During this session, not only is the record presented, but any additional health information like symptoms or behavioral changes are shared. Subsequently, the doctor undertakes a detailed medical examination. This examination may include questioning to understand the child's health better, performing physical checks like measuring temperature and blood pressure, and potentially recommending further diagnostic tests. These recommendations are documented and handed to the parents or guardians.

Step 4 and Step 5: Laboratory Tests and Results. Following the doctor's suggestions, parents or guardians proceed to a medical laboratory. Specialized lab technicians carry out the prescribed tests. Once concluded, the laboratory assembles a complete report of the test findings, usually in a paper-based format, which is provided to the parents or guardians for the next steps in care.

Step 6 and Step 7: Follow-up and Prescriptions. Armed with lab results, the parents or guardians return to the doctor's office. After examining the findings, the doctor might issue prescriptions or recommend further care steps as needed. These prescriptions become a vital element in the child's healthcare and are handed to the parents or guardians.

Step 8: Medication Collection. Lastly, parents or guardians, prescription in hand, head to the pharmacy where the prescribed medications are dispensed by the pharmacy staff. This step completes the current healthcare process for the child, ensuring appropriate treatment is received.

Traditional Model's Limitation. The traditional model of child care has its roots deeply embedded in centralized systems and methodologies. One of its primary limitations is centralized data storage, which presents a single point of failure. If such a system encounters issues, crucial medical records risk being compromised or lost. Additionally, this centralization raises significant data privacy concerns. Unauthorized access or potential data breaches could lay bare sensitive medical records of children. Even if security isn't breached, the data within these systems might be spread across various healthcare providers, leading to potential inconsistencies and fragmentation. Such dispersion often leads to delays, especially when immediate access to medical histories is paramount in emergencies. Furthermore, the traditional model often requires the physical presence of parents or guardians for consultations, medicine collection, or accessing reports, contributing to operational inefficiencies. Lastly, a subtle yet significant concern is the limited ownership parents or guardians have over their child's medical records.

3.2 Innovative Blockchain Model for Child Care

In a bid to surpass the boundaries of conventional child care systems, our strategy employs an amalgamation of state-of-the-art blockchain technologies. As illustrated in Fig. 2, this comprehensive framework encompasses multiple trailblazing components such as the User Interface, Personal Identification Code, Smart Contract, NFT, IPFS, and the Distributed Ledger. These components collectively enhance the security, efficiency, and trustworthiness of child care practices.

Global ID. This unique identifier is assigned to each child's medical record and is closely linked with their parents or guardians, ensuring unparalleled security and privacy. It acts as a failsafe against data duplication or mishandling and facilitates streamlined data access.

System Interface. Designed to cater to medical professionals, this interactive platform serves as a conduit between the user and the blockchain architecture. It's designed for simplicity, allowing doctors to conveniently navigate, update, and engage with a child's medical data.

Smart Contract. Integrating Smart Contracts into our system revolutionizes the way data manipulation and automation are managed. These are automated contracts that govern the maintenance and alteration of medical records. These contracts activate specific actions when pre-defined conditions are met, thereby minimizing manual errors.

NFT (Non-Fungible Token). We utilize NFTs to establish the uniqueness and authentication of each child's medical data. Each record is tied to a specific NFT, ensuring data singularity and inviolability.

IPFS (InterPlanetary File System). To achieve robust data security and availability, our framework leverages IPFS for decentralized storage. It distributes encrypted data blocks across multiple nodes, offering resilience against node failures and unauthorized access.

Distributed Ledger. This serves as the mainstay for data recovery in our system, linking with decentralized platforms like IPFS to guarantee rapid and accurate data access. This ledger acts as a navigator, guiding users to the precise location of a child's medical records within the complex decentralized network.

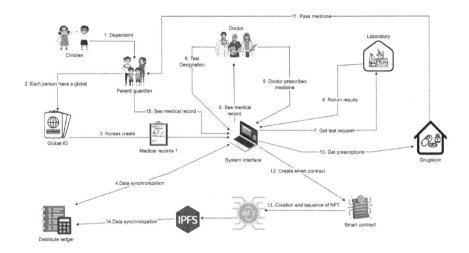

Fig. 2. Innovative Blockchain Model for Child Care

Our groundbreaking methodology for child healthcare is based on a meticulously designed ten-step sequence. This journey starts with the creation of a unique Global ID by the parents or guardians and concludes with them reviewing their child's medical history. It effectively weaves in the roles of nurses, physicians, labs, and pharmacies, all under the aegis of blockchain technology, smart contracts, and IPFS. Our framework's cornerstone is the transparency, integrity, and security of data.

Initialization of Access step: Parents or guardians initialize the process by creating a unique Global ID for their child, serving as the cornerstone for all subsequent system interactions. Upon establishing the Global ID, nurses employ the System Interface to draft the preliminary medical record, documenting key details like the child's name, birth date, and essential contact information (i.e., **Medical Record Initiation**). Once the initial medical record is compiled, smart contracts autonomously incorporate this data into the distributed ledger, which acts as a bulwark against unauthorized access and data alteration - **Integration with Distributed Ledger**.

Doctor's Interface Interaction. Doctors, utilizing the System Interface, not only consult the initial data but also supplement the medical records with diagnostic information, enriching the healthcare narrative for each child.

Diagnostic Recommendations. Where further medical scrutiny is required, doctors can recommend additional tests, which are documented within the dynamic medical record.

Laboratory Involvement. Laboratories interpret the diagnostic requests and, post-examination, update the findings in the system, possibly utilizing IPFS for secure data storage.

Review and Prescription. After evaluating the lab outcomes, doctors prescribe necessary medications or treatment, and this information is securely embedded within the child's healthcare dossier.

Drugstore Engagement. Pharmacies decipher the digital prescriptions, ensuring the exact medications are provided, thereby meeting the child's therapeutic requirements effectively.

Parental Access and Monitoring. Parents or guardians maintain an active role by using a specialized user interface to monitor and manage their child's healthcare journey, thereby ensuring compliance with medical guidelines.

4   Realization of the Framework

The practical deployment of our state-of-the-art child healthcare system rests on the robust execution of three pivotal operations—*transaction origination*, *data retrieval*, and *data modification*. The ensuing discussion provides an in-depth examination of each function's technical architecture, practical implications, and their collective role in enhancing the system's overall efficacy. Through this discussion, we aim to bridge the gap between theoretical excellence and actual benefits realized in a real-world setting.

4.1   Initial Data Entry

The journey commences with a medical doctor, whose expertise sets the groundwork for the child's digital medical portfolio. After conducting a comprehensive evaluation, which includes not only clinical findings but also health history reported by the parents, the doctor decides on the parameters and scope of the medical record to be established.

Next, the System Interface comes into play, serving as an intuitive, user-friendly digital environment engineered specifically for healthcare practitioners. This is where physicians interact with the blockchain, entering, reviewing, and handling medical data in a manner that minimizes the scope for errors and ensures smooth operations.

At this juncture, parents or guardians step in as the key contributors of their child's initial health metrics. This information spans a wide array—from prior

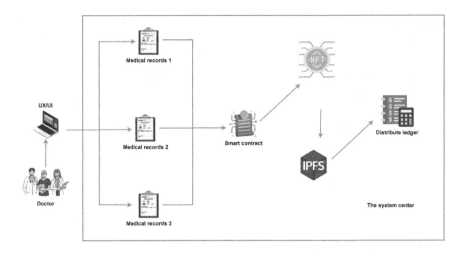

Fig. 3. Initializing Transactions and Data

medical conditions to allergies and genetic factors. After doctor verification, this crucial information is integrated into the blockchain-based system, laying the groundwork for advanced data handling mechanisms (Fig. 3).

This is where Smart Contracts make their entrance. Triggered by the new data entries, they govern the handling, access, and potential modifications of the child's medical data. Programmed to follow explicit rules and guidelines, these contracts add an extra layer of security and operational precision.

Simultaneously, a unique NFT is generated, serving as the cryptographic avatar of the child's health data. Its uniqueness precludes any chance of data collision or unauthorized duplication, thereby elevating the system's data integrity standards.

Moreover, this NFT contains an embedded link that points to the data hosted on the IPFS. Known for its robustness and decentralization, IPFS ensures that the child's medical data remains secure and perpetually accessible, regardless of network conditions or localized technical glitches.

Completing the data management circle is the Distributed Ledger. This blockchain-based ledger works in tandem with IPFS to offer an exhaustive, tamper-proof log of all transactions related to the child's healthcare. Accessible only to verified users, it offers transparency and accountability, enriching the decision-making process at every step of the child's healthcare journey.

4.2   Procedure for Data Retrieval

Data retrieval is a cornerstone activity in our healthcare model, ensuring that healthcare providers can securely and efficiently access a child's medical records. The orchestrated coordination among the user interfaces, smart contracts, and the decentralized IPFS storage forms the backbone of this crucial operation. We

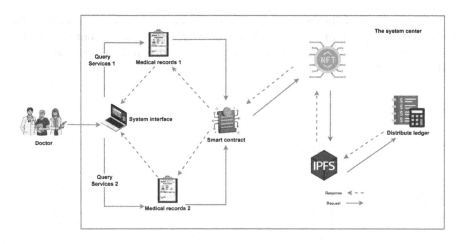

Fig. 4. Process for Data Retrieval

will explore the functioning of the key components involved in this process in the following discussion (Fig. 4).

The initial step for data retrieval takes place through a specialized system interface for medical professionals. This user-friendly platform serves as the nexus where physicians can initiate requests for specific medical records, communicating these requests to the embedded smart contracts. Physicians engage with this interface, equipped with a toolkit designed to facilitate interaction with smart contracts. The pivotal element in this interaction is the child-specific NFT. Physicians utilize this unique cryptographic identifier as the access key for requesting the child's medical details.

The crux of data retrieval lies in the system's processing of the query. Here, smart contracts play an essential role in validating the provided NFT to confirm a physician's authorization to access the specified records. Upon successful verification, the smart contract interfaces with the IPFS storage system. Exploiting IPFS's decentralized architecture, the contract identifies and retrieves the medical data relevant to the physician's request.

The query process reaches its conclusion as the system directs the obtained information back to the requesting physician and updates the distributed ledger. The physician receives the sought-after medical data via the system interface. Simultaneously, to maintain transparency and ensure system robustness, each data retrieval action is meticulously recorded on the distributed ledger. This creates an immutable history, thereby fortifying the system's overall integrity and the security of the child's medical data.

4.3   Data Modification Mechanism

The ongoing management of children's healthcare information necessitates routine updates to the stored records. Whether due to shifts in the child's health status, new medical findings, or supplemental diagnostic tests, ensuring that medical records remain current is critical. This discussion elaborates on the integral components and operations that drive a secure and efficient data modification procedure (Fig. 5).

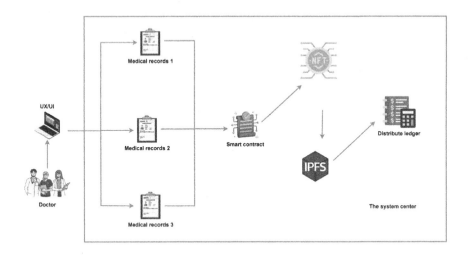

Fig. 5. Procedure for Data Modification

Initiating changes to a child's medical record begins with the physician's engagement with the system interface. The specialized interface, designed for healthcare providers, includes features that facilitate the doctor's ability to adjust or supplement the information within the child's record. Upon confirming the necessary amendments, physicians activate the update instruction, targeting the embedded smart contract and triggering the next steps in the data modification workflow.

Following the issuance of the update command, the system engages in a phase of verification, principally guided by the interactions between the smart contract, NFT, and the IPFS storage. The smart contract, at this juncture, rigorously validates the provided NFT to ascertain the physician's right to modify the data. Once the NFT receives clearance, the smart contract collaborates with the IPFS to fetch the existing version of the medical record set for amendment.

To ensure that the process is both transparent and immutable, a complete log of every update to a child's medical record is maintained. These transaction logs are permanently stored within the distributed ledger, providing an unalterable historical account that upholds both the integrity and the transparency of the modification process.

Beyond simply amending data, the system is ardently designed to safeguard the integrity of the stored medical information. The cornerstone of this protective strategy is a stringent access control, powered by the smart contract, that restricts medical record interactions to only authorized individuals, such as physicians and relevant stakeholders. This multi-layered security architecture serves as an impregnable barrier against unauthorized access or unintended alterations to the records.

This scrupulous data modification scheme is underpinned by the key pillars of blockchain technology, NFTs, IPFS, and the distributed ledger. With blockchain ensuring transaction tracking and authentication, NFTs validating the uniqueness of each record, IPFS supporting decentralized data storage, and the distributed ledger documenting every transaction event, the system guarantees an unmatched level of security, integrity, and efficiency in updating children's medical records.

5   Comprehensive Assessment Methodology

In the rapidly evolving domain of blockchain solutions, multiple platforms with unique attributes and capabilities have come to the forefront. For an exhaustive appraisal of our envisioned model, we elected to implement our smart contracts across four EVM-compatible platforms. Specifically, our selected platforms encompass Binance Smart Chain, Polygon, Fantom, and Celo[1]. These platforms were chosen due to their established reputation, robust underpinnings, and EVM compatibility, which facilitate effortless smart contract deployment. Additionally, given the significance of NFTs in our framework, we also scrutinize their performance on IPFS using the Pinata platform[2], renowned for its efficient and secure NFT storage solutions.

5.1   Scenario-Based Evaluation

To conduct a rigorous analysis of our system's efficacy, we engineered a simulation reflective of likely real-world applications and hurdles.

Fundamental to any distributed system are its nodes. As depicted in Fig. 6, we generated a 20-node sample for our evaluation. Each node was carefully set up with a dual-key system, consisting of a public key for network identification and a private key for encrypted communications, thereby ensuring data privacy and integrity. The arrangement of nodes was designed to mimic a realistic decentralized network, thus providing an environment that accounts for potential challenges like latency, data loss, and node breakdowns. Upon establishing the network, fabricated yet realistic children's medical data was introduced into the nodes. This dataset was diverse, simulating various health indicators, past medical events, and possible health conditions, providing a comprehensive backdrop for evaluating our system's capabilities. The next step involved simulating diverse transaction types, such as the initiation of new medical records, amending existing data, NFT transactions between nodes, and data queries. These simulations offered us insights into system performance parameters like speed, resilience, and security.

---

[1] References for the platforms can be added here.

[2] Pinata is a noted IPFS developer API https://www.pinata.cloud/.

```
PS E:\Document\viet-bao\Thang 8\medical children\code\medical-record-Blockchain-NFT> npx hardhat node
Started HTTP and WebSocket JSON-RPC server at http://127.0.0.1:8545/

Accounts
========

WARNING: These accounts, and their private keys, are publicly known.
Any funds sent to them on Mainnet or any other live network WILL BE LOST.

Account #0: 0xf39Fd6e51aad88F6F4ce6aB8827279cfffFb92266 (10000 ETH)
Private Key: 0xac0974bec39a17e36ba4a6b4d238ff944bacb478cbed5efcae784d7bf4f2ff80

Account #1: 0x70997970C51812dc3A010C7d01b50e0d17dc79C8 (10000 ETH)
Private Key: 0x59c6995e998f97a5a0044966f0945389dc9e86dae88c7a8412f4603b6b78690d

Account #2: 0x3C44CdDdB6a900fa2b585dd299e03d12FA4293BC (10000 ETH)
Private Key: 0x5de4111afa1a4b94908f83103eb1f1706367c2e68ca870fc3fb9a804cdab365a

Account #3: 0x90F79bf6EB2c4f870365E785982E1f101E93b906 (10000 ETH)
Private Key: 0x7c852118294e51e653712a81e05800f419141751be58f605c371e15141b007a6

Account #4: 0x15d34AAf54267DB7D7c367839AAf71A00a2C6A65 (10000 ETH)
Private Key: 0x47e179ec197488593b187f80a00eb0da91f1b9d0b13f8733639f19c30a34926a

Account #5: 0x9965507D1a55bcC2695C58ba16FB37d819B0A4dc (10000 ETH)
Private Key: 0x8b3a350cf5c34c9194ca85829a2df0ec3153be0318b5e2d3348e872092edffba

Account #6: 0x976EA74026E726554dB657fA54763abd0C3a0aa9 (10000 ETH)
Private Key: 0x92db14e403b83dfe3df233f83dfa3a0d7096f21ca9b0d6d6b8d88b2b4ec1564e

Account #7: 0x14dC79964da2C08b23698B3D3cc7Ca32193d9955 (10000 ETH)
Private Key: 0x4bbbf85ce3377467afe5d46f804f221813b2bb87f24d81f60f1fcdbf7cbf4356

Account #8: 0x23618e81E3f5cdF7f54C3d65f7FBc0aBf5B21E8f (10000 ETH)
Private Key: 0xdbda1821b80551c9d65939329250298aa3472ba22feea921c0cf5d620ea67b97

Account #9: 0xa0Ee7A142d267C1f36714E4a8F75612F20a79720 (10000 ETH)
Private Key: 0x2a871d0798f97d79848a013d4936a73bf4cc922c825d33c1cf7073dff6d409c6

Account #10: 0xBcd4042DE499D14e55001CcbB24a551F3b954096 (10000 ETH)
Private Key: 0xf214f2b2cd398c806f84e317254e0f0b801d0643303237d97a22a48e01628897
```

Fig. 6. Example of 20 nodes with respective public and private keys

Vital performance metrics were culled from these simulations to gauge both efficiency and dependability. Metrics examined included transaction validation times, speed of data access, computational overhead, and resistance to security threats.

5.2   Utilizing IPFS for Secure Storage of Pediatric Health Records

In the contemporary digital age, the safekeeping, accessibility, and swift recovery of health data are crucial. With its decentralized architecture, the InterPlanetary File System (IPFS) offers an innovative solution that is resilient against data failure and enhances data security. When it comes to sensitive pediatric health information, storing these records via IPFS becomes particularly relevant.

As illustrated in Fig. 7, a typical pediatric health record is highlighted, containing essential health metrics and past medical data. These records are transformed into a distinct digital hash to maintain data genuineness and integrity.

```
44
45        const body = {
46            testType: "testType 1",
47            testingResults: "testingResults 1",
48            testingTime: "testingTime 1",
49            testingPlace: "testingPlace 1",
50            doctorName: "doctorName 1",
51            nurseID: "nurseID 1",
52            childrenName: "children name 1",
53            parentsName: "parents name",
54            treatmentHistory: "Children treatment History 1",
55            result: "result 1",
56        };
57        const options = {
58            pinataMetadata: {
59                name: "Children medical records.json",
60            },
```

Fig. 7. Example Pediatric Health Record

```
PS E:\Document\viet-bao\Thang 8\medical children\code\medical-record-Blockchain-NFT> npx hardhat test


  Lock
    Deployment
CID QmZbzkyAoMvPa1J8txgspyifUMqdGKFuKitHZErwYTNrAa
      ✓ Should set the right unlockTime (3919ms)


  1 passing (4s)
```

Fig. 8. Generation of Unique Hash Link for Pediatric Records on IPFS

Figure 8 presents the unique hash link generation process for a pediatric record on IPFS. This hash functions as a unique pointer for the stored record. Leveraging the capabilities of the Pinata platform, a known IPFS developer API, these records find their secure home on IPFS. Pinata's advantages include user-friendly features and strong encryption protocols, ensuring data privacy and controlled accessibility.

IPFS's decentralized nature provides insulation from system failures that affect a single point in the network, adding a layer of redundancy vital for maintaining the perpetual availability of health records. Figure 9 displays a pediatric health record identifier as it appears on the Pinata platform, highlighting the harmonious collaboration between IPFS and Pinata.

Fig. 9. Pediatric Record Identifier on Pinata Interface

As demonstrated in Fig. 10, upon querying the specific identifier linked to a child's health record, the comprehensive medical information can be recovered. The integration of IPFS and Pinata in our approach assures all involved parties—from parents to healthcare providers—that pediatric medical information remains secure, transparent, and promptly retrievable.

5.3   Assessment Across Platforms Compatible with the Ethereum Virtual Machine

To comprehensively gauge the reliability, scalability, and flexibility of our proposed system, we conducted tests for our smart contracts across four leading platforms compatible with the Ethereum Virtual Machine (EVM): Binance Smart Chain, Polygon, Fantom, and Celo. These platforms offer unique characteristics in terms of infrastructure, transaction fees, and performance, serving as excellent benchmarks to evaluate the adaptability of our framework.

Initial Data and Transaction Setup. The first step in our multi-platform evaluation was to look into the creation of data and transactions. We deployed our smart contracts across the chosen platforms to assess the ease of initiating transactions, the duration required for transaction confirmations, and the fees involved. Metrics like these are essential for assessing the real-world applicability of our system, especially when quick and cost-efficient data setup is crucial.

Creating Non-Fungible Tokens (NFTs). The subsequent phase of our evaluation was devoted to NFT creation. Within our framework, NFTs act as individualized digital signatures for each child's medical data. Employing the token standards provided by the EVM, we were able to create NFTs across the platforms, measuring the efficiency, related expenses, and required time for the procedure (see Fig. 11). The ability to produce NFTs quickly and at a low cost is vital for securely and promptly converting medical records into unique digital assets.

Secure Transfer of NFTs. The final component of our evaluation involved the process of transferring NFTs. Given the sensitive nature of healthcare data, it's essential that NFTs can be safely transferred between different parties, such as

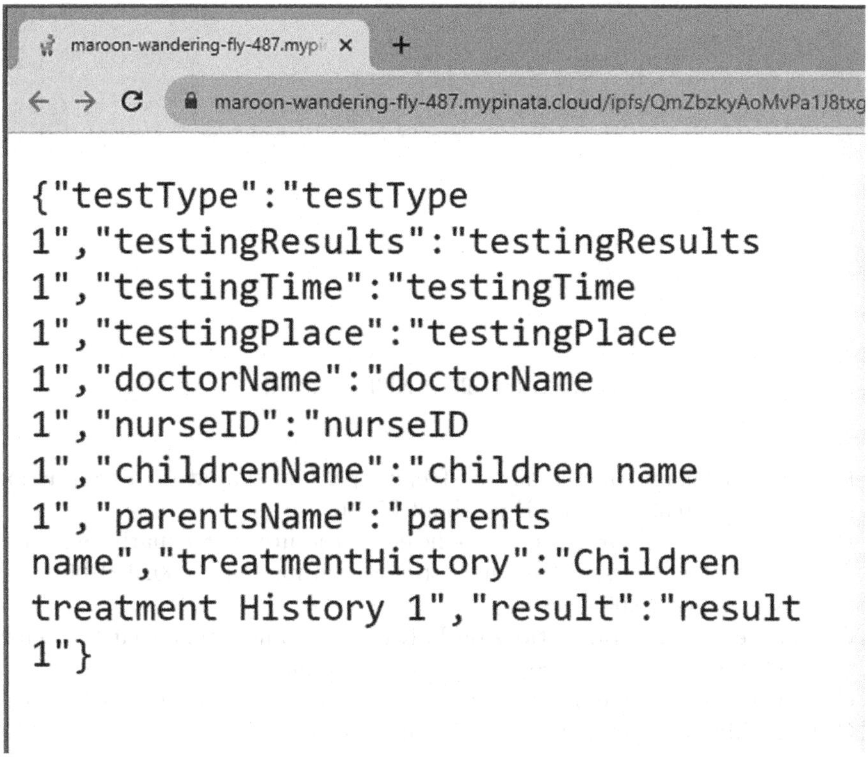
maroon-wandering-fly-487.myp
maroon-wandering-fly-487.mypinata.cloud/ipfs/QmZbzkyAoMvPa1J8txg
{"testType":"testType 1","testingResults":"testingResults 1","testingTime":"testingTime 1","testingPlace":"testingPlace 1","doctorName":"doctorName 1","nurseID":"nurseID 1","childrenName":"children name 1","parentsName":"parents name","treatmentHistory":"Children treatment History 1","result":"result 1"}

Fig. 10. Retrieval of Pediatric Medical Data Using Identifier

between healthcare providers and specialized medical facilities. We analyzed the transfer rates, security measures, and associated fees on each platform.

5.4 Transaction Fee Across EVM-Supported Platforms

Table 1. Transaction fees across EVM-supported platforms

Platform	Transaction Creation	Create NFT	Transfer NFT
BNB Smart Chain	0.0273134 BNB ($5.74)	0.00109162 BNB ($0.23)	0.00057003 BNB ($0.12)
Fantom	0.00957754 FTM ($0.001823)	0.000405167 FTM ($0.000077)	0.0002380105 FTM ($0.000045)
Polygon	0.006840710032835408 MATIC($0.00)	0.000289405001852192 MATIC($0.00)	0.000170007501088048 MATIC($0.00)
Celo	0.007097844 CELO ($0.003)	0.0002840812 CELO ($0.000)	0.0001554878 CELO ($0.000)

As illustrated in Table 1, the costs associated with three key operations—Initiating Transactions, NFT Generation, and NFT Transmission—are compared across the platforms discussed earlier[3]. The expenses are expressed in the native currency of each respective platform. Noteworthy points include:

[3] We deploy the smart contract and collect the price in Sept 24th 2023.

Fig. 11. Details of NFT Creation

- BNB Smart Chain commands the steepest price for initiating a transaction, tallying up to 0.0273134 BNB or about $5.74.
- Fantom displays a far more cost-efficient structure, particularly evidenced by its NFT Transmission fee which stands at a meager 0.0002380105 FTM, roughly equal to $0.000045.
- Costs for executing transactions on Polygon are so negligible that they effectively round to zero when converted to U.S. dollars.
- Celo offers competitive pricing, with an NFT Generation fee of 0.0002840812 CELO, which is practically negligible in dollar terms.

These varying fee structures highlight the crucial role of selecting a suitable platform based on economic aspects for a given application. It becomes essential for both developers and enterprises to take these operational costs into account, especially for applications that are expected to experience heavy transactional activity.

6 Conclusion

In this paper, we've taken significant strides in this direction by introducing a comprehensive framework based on blockchain technology, tailored specifically for the nuanced realm of pediatric care. Our approach not only addresses gaps in conventional systems but also adds new layers of security, accessibility, and transparency through the use of Non-Fungible Tokens (NFTs) and the Inter-Planetary File System (IPFS).

We've demonstrated how our framework eliminates the vulnerability inherent in centralized data storage and management systems, reinforcing data integrity and security. Through the integration of NFTs, each child's medical record becomes a unique, immutable asset on the blockchain, granting parents and guardians more control over their child's data. Coupling this with the decentralized data storage capabilities of IPFS ensures that these critical medical records are consistently available, enhancing the resilience of the entire system.

Our work isn't confined to theoretical propositions; we've validated our framework by implementing it across multiple blockchain platforms. The diverse tests reaffirm the system's adaptability and readiness for real-world application. Moreover, by leveraging the Pinata platform, an IPFS-based data storage solution, we have further fortified the system against single points of failure.

Acknowledgement. We extend our heartfelt gratitude to Engineer Le Thanh Tuan and Dr. Ha Xuan Son for their invaluable guidance throughout the conceptualization, execution, and assessment phases of this project. Additionally, we are grateful for the support provided by FPT University Cantho Campus in Vietnam.

References

1. Al-Shammari, M.A.G., Yasir, A.A., Al-Doori, N.M.: Application of electronic medical record at intensive care unit in maternity and children hospital (2009)
2. Choudhary, D., Brown, B., Khawar, N., Narula, P., Agdere, L.: Implementation of electronic medical record template improves screening for complications in children with type 1 diabetes mellitus, pp. 219–223. Pediatric Health, Medicine and Therapeutics pp (2020)
3. Crosby, L.E., et al.: Using quality improvement methods to implement an electronic medical record (EMR) supported individualized home pain management plan for children with sickle cell disease. J. Clin. Outcomes Manag. JCOM **21**(5), 210 (2014)
4. Deans, K., et al.: Health care quality measures for children and adolescents in foster care: feasibility testing in electronic records. BMC Pediatr. **18**, 1–11 (2018)
5. Duong-Trung, N., et al.: Multi-sessions mechanism for decentralized cash on delivery system. Int. J. Adv. Comput. Sci. Appl **10**(9) (2019)
6. Duong-Trung, N., et al.: Smart care: integrating blockchain technology into the design of patient-centered healthcare systems. In: Proceedings of the 2020 4th International Conference on Cryptography, Security and Privacy, pp. 105–109 (2020)
7. Ha, X.S., Le, T.H., Phan, T.T., Nguyen, H.H.D., Vo, H.K., Duong-Trung, N.: Scrutinizing trust and transparency in cash on delivery systems. In: Wang, G., Chen, B., Li, W., Di Pietro, R., Yan, X., Han, H. (eds.) SpaCCS 2020. LNCS, vol. 12382, pp. 214–227. Springer, Cham (2021). https://doi.org/10.1007/978-3-030-68851-6_15
8. Hagström, J., Blease, C., Haage, B., Scandurra, I., Hansson, S., Hägglund, M.: Views, use, and experiences of web-based access to pediatric electronic health records for children, adolescents, and parents: scoping review. J. Med. Internet Res. **24**(11), e40328 (2022)
9. Le, H.T.: Patient-chain: patient-centered healthcare system a blockchain-based technology in dealing with emergencies. In: Shen, H., et al. (eds.) PDCAT 2021. LNCS, vol. 13148, pp. 576–583. Springer, Cham (2022). https://doi.org/10.1007/978-3-030-96772-7_54
10. Le, H.T., et al.: Bloodchain: a blood donation network managed by blockchain technologies. Network **2**(1), 21–35 (2022)
11. Le, H.T., et al.: Medical-waste chain: a medical waste collection, classification and treatment management by blockchain technology. Computers **11**(7), 113 (2022)
12. Le, N.T.T., et al.: Assuring non-fraudulent transactions in cash on delivery by introducing double smart contracts. Int. J. Adv. Comput. Sci. Appl. **10**(5), 677–684 (2019)

13. Nguyen, L.T.T., et al.: BMDD: a novel approach for IoT platform (broker-less and microservice architecture, decentralized identity, and dynamic transmission messages). PeerJ Comput. Sci. **8**, e950 (2022)

14. Nguyen, T.T.L., et al.: Toward a unique IoT network via single sign-on protocol and message queue. In: Saeed, K., Dvorský, J. (eds.) CISIM 2021. LNCS, vol. 12883, pp. 270–284. Springer, Cham (2021). https://doi.org/10.1007/978-3-030-84340-3_22

15. Quynh, N.T.T.: Toward a design of blood donation management by blockchain technologies. In: Gervasi, O., et al. (eds.) ICCSA 2021. LNCS, vol. 12956, pp. 78–90. Springer, Cham (2021). https://doi.org/10.1007/978-3-030-87010-2_6

16. Saylam, E., Ramani, P., James, B., Savage, M., Jambhekar, S., Veerapandiyan, A.: Assessing sleep quality in children with migraines: implementation of electronic health record cue (s4. 005) (2022)

17. Shaikh, U., Nelson, R., Tancredi, D., Byrd, R.S.: Presentation of body mass index within an electronic health record to improve weight assessment and counselling in children and adolescents. Inform. Primary Care **18**(4) (2010)

18. Son, H.X., Carminati, B., Ferrari, E.: A risk assessment mechanism for android apps. In: 2021 IEEE International Conference on Smart Internet of Things (SmartIoT), pp. 237–244. IEEE (2021)

19. Son, H.X., Chen, E.: Towards a fine-grained access control mechanism for privacy protection and policy conflict resolution. Int. J. Adv. Comput. Sci. Appl. **10**(2) (2019)

20. Son, H.X., Hoang, N.M.: A novel attribute-based access control system for fine-grained privacy protection. In: Proceedings of the 3rd International Conference on Cryptography, Security and Privacy, pp. 76–80 (2019)

21. Son, H.X., et al.: Towards a mechanism for protecting seller's interest of cash on delivery by using smart contract in hyperledger. Int. J. Adv. Comput. Sci. Appl. **10**(4) (2019)

22. Son, H.X., Nguyen, M.H., Vo, H.K., Nguyen, T.P.: Toward an privacy protection based on access control model in hybrid cloud for healthcare systems. In: Martínez Álvarez, F., Troncoso Lora, A., Sáez Muñoz, J.A., Quintián, H., Corchado, E. (eds.) CISIS/ICEUTE -2019. AISC, vol. 951, pp. 77–86. Springer, Cham (2020). https://doi.org/10.1007/978-3-030-20005-3_8

23. Thanh, L.N.T., et al.: IoHT-MBA: an internet of healthcare things (IoHT) platform based on microservice and brokerless architecture. Int. J. Adv. Comput. Sci. Appl. **12**(7) (2021)

24. Thi, Q.N.T., Dang, T.K., Van, H.L., Son, H.X.: Using JSON to specify privacy preserving-enabled attribute-based access control policies. In: Wang, G., Atiquzzaman, M., Yan, Z., Choo, K.-K.R. (eds.) SpaCCS 2017. LNCS, vol. 10656, pp. 561–570. Springer, Cham (2017). https://doi.org/10.1007/978-3-319-72389-1_44

25. Van Cleave, J., Stille, C., Hall, D.E.: Child health, vulnerability, and complexity: use of telehealth to enhance care for children and youth with special health care needs. Acad. Pediatr. **22**(2), S34–S40 (2022)

Privacy-Preserving Tree-Based Inference with TFHE

Jordan Frery[(✉)], Andrei Stoian, Roman Bredehoft, Luis Montero,
Celia Kherfallah, Benoit Chevallier-Mames, and Arthur Meyre

Zama, Hong Kong, China
hello@zama.ai
http://zama.ai

Abstract. Fully Homomorphic Encryption is a powerful tool for processing encrypted data and is particularly adapted to the type of programs that are common in machine learning (ML). On tabular data, tree-based ML models obtain state-of-the-art results, are more robust, and are easier to use and deploy than neural networks. We introduce an implementation of privacy-preserving decision tree evaluation based on the TFHE scheme, leveraging optimized representations for encrypted integer and TFHE's powerful programmable bootstrapping mechanism. Our technique is applicable to decision trees, random forests, and gradient boosted trees. We demonstrate our approach on popular datasets and show that accuracy on encrypted data is very close the one obtained by the same models applied to clear data, while latency is competitive with the state of the art.

1 Introduction

Over the past decade, machine learning has become a powerful tool in many applications such as image classification, automatic translation, speech-to-text, voice synthesis, image and text generation. The rise of ML is owed to advancements in hardware and to higher data availability, which have allowed training of increasingly complex models. Additionally, the development of deep learning techniques, such as convolutional neural networks, has played a significant role in the success of ML in various domains.

Tree-based models are a popular choice for both classification and regression, and they are particularly adapted for tabular data. Indeed, studies have shown that tree-based models are still the best solution for this type of data, which contains categorical features that are usually expressed with highly sparse one-hot encodings [GOV22]. Furthermore, tree-based models are scale-invariant and, thus, are easy to train as they obviate specific feature engineering or preprocessing.

Machine learning models are often applied to sensitive data in use-cases such as facial recognition, biometrics, finance, advertising and healthcare. Due to data confidentiality issues, processing health data to gain insights or to diagnose

S. Bouzefrane et al. (Eds.): MSPN 2023, LNCS 14482, pp. 139–156, 2024.
https://doi.org/10.1007/978-3-031-52426-4_10

diseases using artificial intelligence lags behind, in terms of adoption. For example, most hospitals have restrictions on sharing patient data with third parties, which often prevents them from using state-of-the-art data-driven algorithms. Privacy-preserving machine learning (PPML) inference on encrypted data would be a powerful tool to protect the privacy of data while still allowing for accurate predictions [ARC19]. Several types of approaches exist, including multi-party computation (MPC) [Gol98], secure enclaves, and fully homomorphic encryption (FHE) [Gen09b].

The first realization of FHE was introduced by Gentry [Gen09b, Gen09a], through the *bootstrapping* mechanism that is vital for the wide applicability of FHE. Most FHE schemes rely on noise to ensure the security of the data, but the noise accumulates when homomorphic operations are applied. Bootstrapping reduces the noise of a ciphertext, therefore it allows more operations to be performed. Boostrapping can be applied whenever the noise increases in a manner that may corrupt the message bits. Thus, applying boostrapping as often as needed, frees the application developer to increase the size of encrypted programs.

1.1 Our Contribution

Our approach is based on FHE, which is designed to enable complex processing to be carried out on ciphertexts, without the need for any secret information. Therefore, untrusted servers can process private data.

In this paper, we present a new method for Private Decision-Tree Evaluation (PDTE) with FHE. We restrict ourselves to secure *inference*. While secure *training*, using techniques such as Differential Privacy [Dwo06] or Federated Learning [BEG+19], is also an interesting challenge in the PPML space, it is beyond the scope of our work. Our technique can easily be used with any tree-based model, and works for both regression and classification[1]. We demonstrate our method on decision trees, random forests, and gradient boosted trees.

Our contributions are the following:

1. We use ciphertexts that store multi-bit integers and parameterize the cryptosystem to allow for correct leveled accumulation of ciphertexts.
2. We apply quantization on individual data features to control the message space required in the ciphertexts and, by leveraging tensorized computation on integers and programmable boostrapping (PBS), we implement PDTE in TFHE.
3. Crypto-system parameters are determined using an automated method relying on optimization. Thus it is possible to easily vary the size of the message space size, by adjusting the quantization of the input data, to find the best operating point that maximizes FHE inference speed while preserving accuracy.

---

[1] We implemented our method in CONCRETE-ML library [MCMF+2].

The plan of our paper is as follows: We first give an overview of FHE, TFHE and tree-based models. We then describe our method for PDTE with FHE. Next, we show our experimental results on a variety of datasets. We conclude with a discussion.

1.2   Existing Works

Boostrapping is a central feature of FHE, but not all implementations of machine learning in FHE make use of it in practice. For example, schemes such as CKKS [CKKS17] uses approximate arithmetic, managing the noise budget in a way that avoids costly boostrapping by making the encrypted program contain only few multiplications. Similarly BGV [BGV12] or BFV use the same approach. Using only additions and multiplications for ML model inference has the drawback that models which use non-linear functions such as sign or ReLU have to rely on polynomial approximations of these functions.

A number of methods have been proposed for PDTE with FHE. [ALR+22] relies on the polynomial approximation of the sign function to compute the decisions in the trees. Since the degree of the polynomials must be kept low to stay within the noise budget, the approximation may have large error. To combat this issue, [Huy20] expresses the decision tree as a neural network and fine-tunes it to adjust the decision thresholds. However, this adds complexity to the training process. [TBK20a] uses the BFV scheme which supports both an addition and a multiplication operation. They show an approach using bit-string representations and another with integer ciphertexts. Comparison is implemented using BFV multiplication between bits and decisions along a path are stored in a path vector. Finally, the decision for a leaf node is taken based on the multiplication of the decision bits along the path that leads to the leaf and the leaf's value.

In the TFHE scheme [CGGI16, CGGI17, CGGI20], that is used in this work, any non-linear univariate function can be computed on ciphertexts by the *programmable bootstrapping (PBS)* [CJP21] mechanism. A notable contribution to private decision tree evaluation, [CDPP22] is based on TFHE, coupled with transciphering which helps bring down the ciphertext size. Their work represents inputs as strings of encrypted bits, corresponding to integers obtained by quantizing floating point data points using 11 bits of precision. This is in contrast to our approach that uses multi-bit ciphertexts. To perform classification [CDPP22] uses homomorphic tree traversal computed using encrypted multiplication expressed through binary AND gates on individual bits. In our work we use parallel computation to evaluate all tree nodes using PBS, and to identify the decision path using a path code also using PBS. In their work, as in ours, the result of tree traversal is a one-hot vector containing a single value of one in the cell corresponding to the leaf that is chosen for a certain input.

Other attempts, such as [MF20], rely on additive homomorphic encryption [Pai99] and on order-preserving encryption [BCLO09] which allows them to compare encrypted data with the same cost as comparing clear data. On the downside, using order-preserving encryption only satisfies a weaker security model than TFHE [BCO11] in the context where the server is not trusted.

2 Preliminaries

2.1 Fully Homomorphic Encryption

An encryption scheme f is said to have *homomorphic* properties when there exist two operations $\cdot$ and $\bullet$ such that

$$f(a \cdot b) = f(a) \bullet f(b),$$

for all valid messages a and b. Often $\cdot$ and $\bullet$ are the same operations. Homomorphic schemes have been known since the introduction of public-key cryptography. Indeed RSA has the multiplicative homomorphic property [RSA78]. Additive homomorphic schemes, such as Paillier, are also known [Pai99] and have been widely used, for example in voting schemes.

Fully homomorphic encryption schemes are homomorphic for an universal set of operations. The field of cryptography had to wait until Gentry's breakthrough [Gen09b, Gen09a] to have a first construction of FHE. One key ingredient of his construction (and of those which followed) is the *bootstrapping* mechanism, which allows to reduce the noise in a ciphertext. Several FHE schemes have since been introduced, which are both secure and practical, notably BFV [Bra12, FV12], GSW [GSW13], BGV [BGV12, BGV14], FHEW [DM15], CKKS [CKKS17], and TFHE [CGGI16, CGGI17, CGGI20].

2.2 Integer Computations with TFHE and Corresponding Constraints

Encoding Multi-bit Numbers. TFHE supports both leveled operations, i.e. operations that increase noise, but also comes with fast boostrapping that is programmable.

We use the approach from [BMMP18], to represent integers with TFHE. To represent values that require p bits, the torus is split into at least $2^p + 1$ slices, one for each possible message. To ensure leveled operations are always correct, p must be the maximum bit-width obtained anywhere in the computation and the noise must be configured to take into account the clear constants that are multiplied with encrypted values. To correctly compute a dot-product such as $x \cdot w$ the standard deviation of the noise added during encryption of the plaintexts must be at most equal to the output noise standard deviation divided by $|w|_2$.

The PBS can perform a table look-up operation (TLU) on the input ciphertext, all the while reducing noise in the ciphertext. Furthermore, TFHE can be easily parameterized to ensure that noise accumulation due to leveled operations does not overwrite the message bits.

Depending on crypto-system parameters, the PBS might have a probability of failure p_{error} (usually chosen to be very small). The table look-up operation implemented with PBS can thus be defined as follows:

$$TLU[x] = \begin{cases} T[x], \text{ with probability } (1 - p_{\text{error}}) \\ T[x + k], \text{ with probability } < p_{\text{error}}, k = \{\pm 1, \pm 2, ...\} \end{cases} \tag{1}$$

However, these properties come with some constraints [Joy21], and we summarize here those that impact our design for PDTE:

1. Every input value and intermediate value within the model must be an integer type. To eliminate the possibility of noise corrupting the message during accumulation, our approach is to select crypto-system parameters that provision enough message and padding space to perform accumulation[2]. Therefore, we cannot use sufficiently high precision to support floating point inputs and, thus, the training and test data must be quantized.
2. Control-flow (i.e. branching) is not possible in any FHE scheme. We explain in Sect. 3.2 how to circumvent this limitation by leveraging the PBS, which is so far a tool only available in **TFHE**. In general, the PBS is well adapted to computing arbitrary univariate non-linear functions of encrypted inputs[3].

2.3 Decision Tree, Random Forest and XGBoost

Tree-based models are a popular class of machine learning models that can perform both classification and regression. They are attractive as they are relatively interpretable [GBY+18], easy to use (thanks to popular libraries such as SCIKIT-LEARN), and remain to this day the state-of-the-art models when it comes to accuracy on tabular datasets [SZA22]. Decision trees can be easily trained using a variety of algorithms, including the popular CART algorithm [BFOS17] which may train decision trees or ensembles of trees, such as Random Forests (RF) or Gradient Boosted Trees (XGBoost) [CG16].

Once trained, tree-based models can be used for inference by traversing the trees from the root node to a leaf node which predicts a class or a regression value. Each internal node of the tree represents a test on an input feature and branches are followed according to the outcome of such tests. For ensembles one then applies a weighted sum of the individual tree outputs.

2.4 Quantization

Quantization is the process of converting a continuous value into a discrete value. A common example of quantization is converting a signal from an analog domain to a digital domain. In the context of machine learning, quantization refers to the process of converting the learned parameters of a model but also to performing model inference using only quantized intermediary values. This can be achieved using a variety of methods, in particular uniform quantization [JKC+18]. Quantization is often used to improve the efficiency of neural networks, both in terms of memory usage and computational speed. It can also be used to reduce the amount of data that needs to be stored and transmitted, which is important for applications such as mobile devices or embedded systems.

---

[2] Accumulating without noise corruption is detailed in [Zam22].
[3] The computational complexity of a PBS grows rapidly with the input bit-width and some implementations limit this bit-width to 16-bits.

Symmetric Quantization. The straightforward approach is to use uniform quantization as follows:

$$q(x) = \text{round}\left(\frac{x}{\Delta}\right) \tag{2}$$

where x is a real number, $q(x)$ is the *quantized value* and Δ is the step size also called the *scale*.

An appropriate step size takes the possible max and min of x in consideration can be computed as follows:

$$\Delta = \frac{\text{max}(x) - \text{min}(x)}{2^p - 1} \tag{3}$$

where p is the number of bits that will be used to represent the quantized values. In this case, the quantized values will be integers between -2^{p-1} and $2^{p-1} - 1$. In this equation, we assume $\text{max}(x)$ and $\text{min}(x)$ are computed independently on a representative set of values of x. The value of Δ is used during the inference stage of the model through Eq. 2.

Asymmetric Quantization. Symmetric quantization works well as long as the distribution of the floating point values is symmetric around zero. In some cases, the distribution does not satisfy this property and it is more useful to use asymmetric quantization with a *zero point* value z, defined as follows:

$$q_a(x) = \text{round}\left(\frac{x}{\Delta}\right) + z \tag{4}$$

The zero point is typically chosen such that the minimum of x becomes the integer 0 after quantization, i.e., $q_a(\text{min}(x)) = 0$. Asymmetric quantization allows better use of the available representation bit-width.

3   Private Decision Tree Evaluation with TFHE

In this section, we present our technique for PDTE using FHE. As outlined in Sect. 2.1, TFHE imposes certain limitations and constraints, particularly in regard to condition and flow-operations.

Our method can be decomposed in three parts:

- training an integer tree-based model on quantized data, as detailed in Sect. 3.1.
- implementing integer tree-based models by replacing conditions with an evaluation of all branches and then retrieving the leaf node by looking up the decision path. Both steps are performed using both leveled operations and PBS
- selecting crypto-system parameters based on analysis of the sequences of leveled operations and PBSs. The parameters are chosen so that leveled operations are always exact. PBS error level is configured by experimentation.

3.1   Quantizing Tree-Based Models

In this section, we describe how we transform a floating-point model to an FHE-compatible integer one using quantization.

Let $T = (V, E, L, \tau)$ be a decision tree with V the set of nodes, E the edges, L the values in the tree leaves and τ the thresholds associated to the nodes. Let N be the number of such trees in an ensemble. The following steps are applied to quantize a tree-based model:

1. The training data X is fully quantized and the model is trained in this new representation space with the classical training algorithms
2. The decision thresholds are quantized. The training algorithms for tree-based models (e.g. GINIGAIN, ENTROPY or XGBOOST) choose decision thresholds between discrete feature values in the training data.
3. We apply either ceil or floor to the thresholds to obtain quantized thresholds.
4. The values stored in the leaves (either class weights or regression values) are quantized with asymmetric quantization.

Algorithm 1. Quantization strategy

Require

- X: training dataset (in floating point)
- p: the number of quantization bits

Step 1: $(X_q, Q_X) \leftarrow$ `train_quantizer`(X, p)
Step 2: $(V, E, \tau, L) \leftarrow$ `train`(X_q)
Step 3: $\tau' \leftarrow$ `floor`(τ)
Step 4: $(L_q, Q_L) \leftarrow$ `train_quantizer`(L, p)
Return: $T = (V, E, L_q, \tau', Q_X, Q_L)$

Asymmetric quantization is preferred for its greater precision, as it does not assume a symmetrical distribution of values around zero. In the first step it is used for quantizing input features. Let the `train_quantizer`(X, p) function be defined as the computation of Δ as in Eq. 3 while setting $z = -\lfloor \frac{\min(x)}{\Delta} \rfloor$

Since a tree-based model does not perform linear combinations of the inputs, we can safely quantize every single feature independently of each other. This allows us to have a scale and zero point for each feature which is a great advantage when the input dimensions follow different distributions. In the case described here, the quantization zero-point can be ignored. Indeed the decision thresholds are learned over the quantized integer values representing the features.

On the other hand, the quantization of the values stored in the leaves of the tree is applied globally for the entire vector of values. Thus, a single scale and zero-point are used for all of the leaf values. For ensemble models the leaf values will be represented by a matrix with of size $N \times m$ with N being the number of trees in the ensemble and m the number of leaf nodes.

At this point, our FHE tree-based model is fully quantized. However, as we mentioned previously, control-flow operations are not directly possible in FHE, and require a different approach, which is explained in next section.

3.2   Evaluating Decision Nodes in FHE

We evaluate all the decision nodes in the tree using PBS which can implement any univariate function, including comparison and equality test.

Consider a two-dimensional integer input space where each data point $x \in X$ belongs to the set $[0, 2^p)^2$. Here, p represents the number of bits used to encode the features of x. Let the first feature of x be denoted as $x^{(1)}$ and the second feature as $x^{(2)}$, with $p = 3$ in this example. Our goal is to classify each data point $x \in X$ into one of two classes, C_0 and C_1, by finding a function f such that x is assigned to $C_{f(x)}$ by our algorithm.

A simple boundary such as $x^{(2)} > 3$ can be represented by the decision stump (tree depth of 1) and expressed as follows:

$$f(x) = \begin{cases} 0, & \text{if } x^{(2)} > 3 \\ 1, & \text{otherwise} \end{cases}$$

This function can be implemented using a TLU as follows:

$$f(x) = T[x], \text{ with } T = [1, 1, 1, 1, 0, 0, 0, 0]$$

3.3   Tree Traversal Conversion to Tensor Operations

The tree traversal approach is a common way to perform tree model inference. However, in FHE, tree traversal is not possible since control-flow operations are not supported. To overcome this, we compute all branching decisions simultaneously by converting the tree traversal into tensor operations. Transforming a program that contains control-flow operations into one without branches is a common approach to accelerate computation over specific hardware (e.g. GPU). We follow the implementation of [Mic22].

Algorithm 2 lists the tensors used in the conversion process as well as the process itself.

Algorithm 2. GEMM Strategy for Tree Inference

Require

- x_q: quantized input example
- A: feature-node selection matrix
- B: threshold value
- C: relationship between leaf nodes and internal nodes
- D: count of internal nodes in the path from a leaf node to the tree root
- L_q: mapping between leaf nodes and class labels

Step 1: $P \leftarrow x_q \cdot A$
Step 2: $Q \leftarrow P < B$
Step 3: $R \leftarrow Q \cdot C$
Step 4: $S \leftarrow R == D$
Step 5: $T \leftarrow S \cdot L_q$
Return: T

Q and S are matrices of 1-bit integers, while P, R and T are matrices of multi-bit integers. A, B, C, D, L_q are obtained by converting the model's tree structure. The matrices are created as follows.

1. Tensor A maps features to thresholds. For tree-ensembles A is a 3-dimensional tensor and the mapping of different trees are stored along the 3rd dimension of A:

$$A_{kij} = \begin{cases} 1, & \text{if threshold } \tau_i \text{ is compared to feature } P_j \text{ in tree k} \\ 0, & \text{otherwise} \end{cases}$$

2. Matrix B contains the quantized thresholds:

$$B_{ki} = \tau'_i, \forall k$$

3. Tensor C is the tree-hierarchy encoder tensor.

$$C_{kij} = \begin{cases} \begin{cases} 1, & \text{if node } i \text{ is the left child} \\ -1, & \text{otherwise} \end{cases} & \text{if node } i \text{ is a child of } j \\ 0, & \text{otherwise} \end{cases}$$

4. Tensor D is used to identify the selected leaf node. Each leaf node in the graph can be reached by a decision path which can be encoded with a sequence of $[-1, 1]$ values, such as those in matrix C. Summing up those values along each decision path gives the path identification matrix R in **Step 3**. Comparing R with D will uniquely identify the decision path, and thus the predicted leaf node, resulting in one-hot vectors for each tree.

5. Tensor L_q encodes the values in the leaf nodes, as detailed in Algorithm 1. The matrix S contains multiple one-hot vectors representing the predicted leaf nodes for each tree in the ensemble. The predicted output is obtained in **Step 5** as a dot product.

3.4   Crypto-System Parameter Optimization

The computation described in Algorithm 2 can be represented as a directed acyclic graph (DAG) containing accumulation operations and PBSs. We use the approach detailed in [BBB+22] to find crypto-system parameters, depending on the quantization bit-widths of the input values X and of the constants in the A, C and L_q matrices. The A constant matrix contains only 0/1 values so it is represented with single bits. Multiplying it with the X vector produces a result Q with the same bit-width as X. Next, matrix R contains values that are at most equal to the tree depth d, which is usually quite low (5–10), requiring at most $\log_2(d) + 1$ bits. The final step is a dot product between two-dimensional matrices S and L_q (Fig. 1).

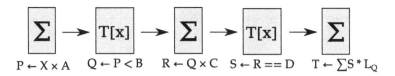

$$P \leftarrow X \times A \qquad Q \leftarrow P < B \qquad R \leftarrow Q \times C \qquad S \leftarrow R == D \qquad T \leftarrow \sum S * L_Q$$

Fig. 1. TFHE operations representing Algorithm 2. The Σ nodes represent leveled accumulation and $T[x]$ nodes represent table look-up operations implemented with PBS

The final step, $S \leftarrow R \cdot L_q$ can be split in two. Indeed the leaf values for each tree are quantized to the same bit-width as the input. However, when multiple trees are present in the ensemble, their predictions need to be summed as well. This second sum can be performed in the clear, to avoid accumulating a large bit-width value that would exceed the bit-width of the input.

- **Step 5.1 (encrypted):** $T_k \leftarrow \sum_i S \times L_q$
- **Step 5.2 (clear):** $T \leftarrow \sum_k T_k$

Applying this modification to Algorithm 2 upper bounds the bit-widths of the integers in the entire computation graph to the input bit-width p plus one. The additional bit is required to represent signed values in matrix R, since the input features are quantized to unsigned integers on p bits.

When a tree-ensemble model is used, the vector of results of the individual trees must be aggregated over the trees. Next, for classification, the argmax will need to be computed over the decisions. We perform the aggregation as shown in **Step 5.1 and 5.2**, and the argmax is computed on the client side, after decryption. Moreover, the client will apply the inverse operation to quantization, dequantization, to get back the values that would have been predicted by the floating point algorithms without encryption.

An optimization algorithm divides the graph into subgraphs containing leveled operations (addition of encrypted values, multiplication of encrypted values with clear values) and ending with a PBS. Since the clear values are known (the matrices A, B, C, D, L_q are constant), the maximal bit-width of accumulated values can be computed. In our case the maximum bit-width will be $p + 1$. It is therefore possible to generate crypto-parameters that provision sufficient message-space for any input x_q, such that leveled operations are always correct. The values of x_q are assumed to always be bounded by the input bit-width p chosen during model training.

4   Experimental Results

In this section we describe the experiments we performed to evaluate our method and we discuss the results. We first test the accuracy of quantized models, as defined in Sect. 3.1, and we compare it with the one of floating point (FP32) models.

PDTE has the drawback of having a significantly longer inference time than the clear model inference. This execution time depends mainly on two factors: the crypto-system parameters and the complexity of the FHE circuit. As the security level is constant - 128 bits -, cryptographic parameters depend mainly on the precision we use (i.e., the upper value of the bit width of intermediate values) while the complexity of the FHE circuit is directly correlated to the model hyper-parameters. For tree models these are: the total number of nodes, the maximum depth d and the number of trees in an ensemble, N.

We performed experiments with three different types of tree-based model for classification, as they are the most common [BRAN19]:

- DecisionTreeClassifier from SCIKIT-LEARN library.
- RandomForestClassifier from SCIKIT-LEARN library.
- XGBoostClassifier from the XGBOOST library [CG16].

4.1   Quantization Precision and FHE Inference Time

First we study the impact of quantization on model accuracy. In Fig. 2, we compute the f1 score and average precision (AP) for different quantization bit-widths and we plot them along with the metrics from the floating point value model. For the three different tree-based models, we can observe a convergence of the quantized model toward the full precision model. In the case of decision trees the accuracy with quantized data can sometimes exceed the one obtained by training on floating point data since quantization regularizes the training procedure, avoiding over-fit. Ensemble models are more robust to over-fit and do not show this behavior.

Such a behavior is expected and the natural choice would be obviously to select the highest bit width. However, FHE execution time is impacted by the bit-width. To have a better understanding of the impact of quantization, we run an experiment in Fig. 3 where we compute the FHE inference time for the three models at different quantization bit-widths. This figure shows that computation time for a single decision node (one PBS) increases exponentially for $p > 4$.

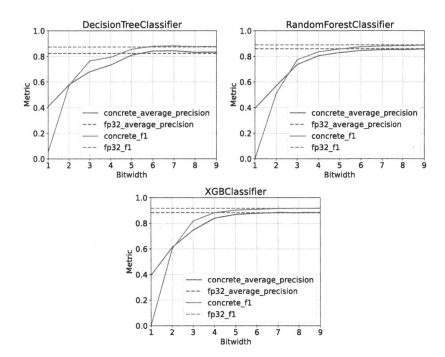

Fig. 2. Experiment reporting the f1-score and average precision with varying precision on the spambase dataset.

Figures 2 and 3 provide a good overview of the trade-off between model accuracy vs. FHE inference time. We can see that a large increase in FHE inference time is found to be between starting at 7 bits. On the other hand, 5 and 6 bits give results close to those of the FP32 model: a less than 2% point drop in the metrics reported for 6 bits precision. In the following section, we use $p = 6$ bits as our quantization precision for both the input features and output tree values.

4.2   Experiments on Various Datasets

Table 1 presents the mean results of 5-fold cross validation repeated 3 times (or 15 runs in total per model per dataset).

Hyper-parameters used for both the FHE and sklearn models are:

- N, the number of estimators, is set to 50 and defines the number of trees in the ensemble for both Random Forest (RF) and Gradient Boosting (XGB).
- maximum depth d is set to 5 for both the decision tree (DT) and XGB. Random forest is bounded at a max depth of 4. This parameter defines the maximum depth a tree can have once fully trained.
- the maximum number of nodes #nodes is left unbounded and is measured once the tree is trained

Table 1. FHE vs FP32 tree-based experiments. The accuracy, f1-score and average precision (AP) are averaged over 15 runs. The inference time per model is reported in the Latency column and the execution time ratio between FHE and FP32 model is computed. The PBS probability of error is set to $p_{error} = 2^{-40}$. We do not report f1-score and AP for multi-class datasets.

		accuracy	f1	AP	#nodes	Time (s)	FHE/Clear
spambase	FHE-DT	91.0%	88.0%	84.3%	23	1.313	825x
	FP32-DT	90.3%	87.4%	82.4%	-	0.002	-
	FHE-XGB	93.1%	90.9%	87.7%	350	7.020	4617x
	FP32-XGB	93.6%	91.7%	88.3%	-	0.002	-
	FHE-RF	90.9%	87.5%	84.6%	750	16.248	8520x
	FP32-RF	91.8%	89.0%	86.0%	-	0.002	-
wine	FHE-DT	90.8%	-	-	7	0.420	463x
	FP32-DT	90.5%	-	-	-	0.001	-
	FHE-XGB	96.4%	-	-	900	15.394	16740x
	FP32-XGB	95.9%	-	-	-	0.001	-
	FHE-RF	98.5%	-	-	500	9.803	11421x
	FP32-RF	98.1%	-	-	-	0.001	-
heart-h	FHE-DT	61.0%	-	-	21	0.691	815x
	FP32-DT	60.0%	-	-	-	0.001	-
	FHE-XGB	66.8%	-	-	1750	33.472	34101x
	FP32-XGB	65.5%	-	-	-	0.001	-
	FHE-RF	66.8%	-	-	750	15.619	18559x
	FP32-RF	66.4%	-	-	-	0.001	-
wdbc	FHE-DT	94.2%	92.0%	88.4%	15	0.451	395x
	FP32-DT	93.9%	91.7%	87.3%	-	0.001	-
	FHE-XGB	96.5%	95.1%	92.8%	350	6.975	6119x
	FP32-XGB	96.4%	94.9%	92.6%	-	0.001	-
	FHE-RF	95.6%	93.9%	91.2%	700	13.999	12809x
	FP32-RF	95.3%	93.4%	90.4%	-	0.001	-
adult	FHE-DT	83.6%	60.4%	50.3%	30	0.794	1004x
	FP32-DT	83.6%	60.4%	50.3%	-	0.001	-
	FHE-XGB	84.8%	64.9%	53.8%	350	7.372	7151x
	FP32-XGB	84.8%	65.2%	53.9%	-	0.001	-
	FHE-RF	83.4%	57.6%	49.2%	750	16.297	18993x
	FP32-RF	83.4%	57.6%	49.2%	-	0.001	-
steel	FHE-DT	97.2%	96.1%	92.5%	5	0.400	369x
	FP32-DT	97.2%	96.1%	92.5%	-	0.001	-
	FHE-XGB	100.0%	100.0%	100.0%	150	3.361	2856x
	FP32-XGB	100.0%	100.0%	100.0%	-	0.001	-
	FHE-RF	96.9%	95.4%	93.6%	700	12.658	8744x
	FP32-RF	95.9%	93.9%	91.4%	-	0.001	-

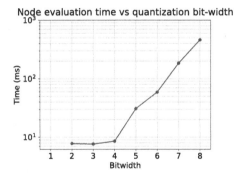

Fig. 3. FHE node evaluation latency for decision nodes with $p_{\mathtt{error}} = 2^{-40}$. Decisions are batched and computed in parallel on 8 CPU cores.

The experiment shows interesting properties of the tree-based models. Decision trees, trained with a limited depth $d = 5$, have the fastest average FHE execution time. However, due to their lower capacity, their accuracy is lower than the one of ensemble methods. The ratio of latency in FHE versus FP32 is roughly 10–20000x on average for ensemble methods which show the closest accuracy with respect to the FP32 models.

Next, we performed experiments on the impact of the p_{error} probability of error of the PBS. Figure 4 shows a grid-search for the best p_{error} value that maintains accuracy while minimizing latency. A value as high as $p_{error} = 0.05$ maintains accuracy while providing an 8x speed-up.

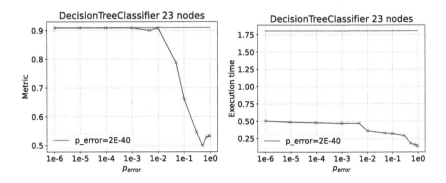

Fig. 4. Varying the probability of PBS error

Based on the experiments above, we configured decision tree models with 6 bits of precision and a $p_{error} = 0.05$. We performed experiments on trees with the same structure as those in [TBK20a] and, in Table 2 we compare results.

Table 2. Comparison with a BFV-scheme based implementation of PDTE.

Dataset	sklearn acc	Ours acc	d	#nodes	Latency (s) $p_{error} = 2^{-40}$	Latency (s) $p_{error} = 0.05$	[TBK20a] latency (s)
spam	93,0%	95,0%	13	57	3.36	0.62	3.66
heart	61,0%	56,0%	3	4	0.84	0.22	0.94

5   Conclusion

The present study offers a method for the conversion of tree-based models into their fully homomorphic encryption (FHE) equivalent, thus providing a secure mechanism for the deployment of machine learning models by service providers.

Our solution offers numerous advantages. To the best of our knowledge, it is the first tree-based solution to offer (i) easy customization that can obtain an optimal quantization/inference speed trade-off, (ii) compatibility with ensemble methods, and (iii) accuracy equivalent to execution in the clear.

Security is directly handled under the hood: crypto-system parameters are determined automatically and are optimal for a specific tree model, ensuring correctness of the leveled computations.

We believe this method represents a significant advancement in the field and the method, as implemented in the open-source library CONCRETE-ML, is a step forward to democratizing privacy-preserving machine learning.

References

[ALR+22] Akavia, A., Leibovich, M., Resheff, Y.S., Ron, R., Shahar, M., Vald, M.: Privacy-preserving decision trees training and prediction. ACM Transactions on Privacy and Security **25**(3), 1–30 (2022)

[ARC19] Al-Rubaie, M., Chang, J.M.: Privacy-preserving machine learning: threats and solutions. IEEE Secur. Priv. **17**(2), 49–58 (2019)

[BBB+22] Bergerat, L., et al.: Parameter optimization & larger precision for (T)FHE. Cryptology ePrint Archive, Paper 2022/704 (2022). https://eprint.iacr.org/2022/704

[BCLO09] Boldyreva, A., Chenette, N., Lee, Y., O'Neill, A.: Order-preserving symmetric encryption. In: Joux, A. (ed.) EUROCRYPT 2009. LNCS, vol. 5479, pp. 224–241. Springer, Heidelberg (2009). https://doi.org/10.1007/978-3-642-01001-9_13

[BCO11] Boldyreva, A., Chenette, N., O'Neill, A.: Order-preserving encryption revisited: improved security analysis and alternative solutions. In: Rogaway, P. (ed.) CRYPTO 2011. LNCS, vol. 6841, pp. 578–595. Springer, Heidelberg (2011). https://doi.org/10.1007/978-3-642-22792-9_33

[BEG+19] Bonawitz, K., et al.: Towards federated learning at scale: system design. Proc. Mach. Learn. Syst. **1**, 374–388 (2019)

[BFOS17] Breiman, L., Friedman, J.H., Olshen, R.A., Stone, C.J.: Classification and Regression Trees. Routledge, London (2017)

[BGV12] Brakerski, Z., Gentry, C., Vaikuntanathan, V.: (Leveled) fully homomorphic encryption without bootstrapping. In ITCS **2012**, 309–325 (2012)

[BGV14] Brakerski, Z., Gentry, C., Vaikuntanathan, V.: (Leveled) fully homomorphic encryption without bootstrapping. ACM Trans. Comput. Theory **6**(3), 13:1–13:36 (2014)

[BMMP18] Bourse, F., Minelli, M., Minihold, M., Paillier, P.: Fast homomorphic evaluation of deep discretized neural networks. In: Shacham, H., Boldyreva, A. (eds.) CRYPTO 2018. LNCS, vol. 10993, pp. 483–512. Springer, Cham (2018). https://doi.org/10.1007/978-3-319-96878-0_17

[Bra12] Brakerski, Z.: Fully homomorphic encryption without modulus switching from classical GapSVP. In: Safavi-Naini, R., Canetti, R. (eds.) CRYPTO 2012. LNCS, vol. 7417, pp. 868–886. Springer, Heidelberg (2012). https://doi.org/10.1007/978-3-642-32009-5_50

[BRAN19] Banerjee, M., Reynolds, E., Andersson, H.B., Nallamothu, B.K.: Tree-based analysis: a practical approach to create clinical decision-making tools. Circ.: Cardiov. Qual. Outcomes **12**(5), e004879 (2019)

[CDPP22] Cong, K., Das, D., Park, J., Pereira, H.V.: SortingHat: efficient private decision tree evaluation via homomorphic encryption and transciphering. In: Proceedings of the 2022 ACM SIGSAC Conference on Computer and Communications Security, CCS 2022, pp. 563–577, New York, NY, USA. Association for Computing Machinery (2022)

[CG16] Chen, T., Guestrin, C.: XGBoost: a scalable tree boosting system. In: Proceedings of the 22nd ACM SIGKDD International Conference on Knowledge Discovery and Data Mining, pp. 785–794 (2016)

[CGGI16] Chillotti, I., Gama, N., Georgieva, M., Izabachène, M.: Faster fully homomorphic encryption: bootstrapping in less than 0.1 seconds. In: Cheon, J.H., Takagi, T. (eds.) ASIACRYPT 2016. LNCS, vol. 10031, pp. 3–33. Springer, Heidelberg (2016). https://doi.org/10.1007/978-3-662-53887-6_1

[CGGI17] Chillotti, I., Gama, N., Georgieva, M., Izabachène, M.: Faster packed homomorphic operations and efficient circuit bootstrapping for TFHE. In: Takagi, T., Peyrin, T. (eds.) ASIACRYPT 2017. LNCS, vol. 10624, pp. 377–408. Springer, Cham (2017). https://doi.org/10.1007/978-3-319-70694-8_14

[CGGI20] Chillotti, I., Gama, N., Georgieva, M., Izabachène, M.: TFHE: fast fully homomorphic encryption over the torus. J. Cryptol. **33**(1), 34–91 (2020)

[CJP21] Chillotti, I., Joye, M., Paillier, P.: Programmable bootstrapping enables efficient homomorphic inference of deep neural networks. In: Dolev, S., Margalit, O., Pinkas, B., Schwarzmann, A. (eds.) CSCML 2021. LNCS, vol. 12716, pp. 1–19. Springer, Cham (2021). https://doi.org/10.1007/978-3-030-78086-9_1

[CKKS17] Cheon, J.H., Kim, A., Kim, M., Song, Y.: Homomorphic encryption for arithmetic of approximate numbers. In: Takagi, T., Peyrin, T. (eds.) ASIACRYPT 2017. LNCS, vol. 10624, pp. 409–437. Springer, Cham (2017). https://doi.org/10.1007/978-3-319-70694-8_15

[DM15] Ducas, L., Micciancio, D.: FHEW: bootstrapping homomorphic encryption in less than a second. In: Oswald, E., Fischlin, M. (eds.) EUROCRYPT 2015. LNCS, vol. 9056, pp. 617–640. Springer, Heidelberg (2015). https://doi.org/10.1007/978-3-662-46800-5_24

[Dwo06]   Dwork, C.: Differential privacy. In: Bugliesi, M., Preneel, B., Sassone, V., Wegener, I. (eds.) ICALP 2006. LNCS, vol. 4052, pp. 1–12. Springer, Heidelberg (2006). https://doi.org/10.1007/11787006_1

[FV12]   Fan, J., Vercauteren, F.: Somewhat practical fully homomorphic encryption. Cryptology ePrint Archive, Report 2012/144 (2012). https://ia.cr/2012/144

[GBY+18]   Gilpin, L.H., Bau, D., Yuan, B.Z., Bajwa, A., Specter, M., Kagal, L.: Explaining explanations: an overview of interpretability of machine learning. In: 2018 IEEE 5th International Conference on Data Science and Advanced Analytics (DSAA), pp. 80–89. IEEE (2018)

[Gen09a]   Gentry, C.: A fully homomorphic encryption scheme. PhD thesis, Stanford University (2009). crypto.stanford.edu/craig

[Gen09b]   Gentry, C.: Fully homomorphic encryption using ideal lattices. In: Proceedings of the 41st Annual ACM Symposium on Theory of Computing, STOC 2009, Bethesda, MD, USA, 31 May–2 June 2009, pp. 169–178 (2009)

[Gol98]   Goldreich, O.: Secure multi-party computation. Manuscript. Preliminary Version **78**(110) (1998)

[GOV22]   Grinsztajn, L., Oyallon, E., Varoquaux, G.: Why do tree-based models still outperform deep learning on typical tabular data? In: Thirty-Sixth Conference on Neural Information Processing Systems Datasets and Benchmarks Track (2022)

[GSW13]   Gentry, C., Sahai, A., Waters, B.: Homomorphic encryption from learning with errors: conceptually-simpler, asymptotically-faster, attribute-based. In: Canetti, R., Garay, J.A. (eds.) CRYPTO 2013. LNCS, vol. 8042, pp. 75–92. Springer, Heidelberg (2013). https://doi.org/10.1007/978-3-642-40041-4_5

[Huy20]   Huynh, D.: Cryptotree: fast and accurate predictions on encrypted structured data. CoRR, abs/2006.08299 (2020)

[JKC+18]   Jacob, B., et al.: Quantization and training of neural networks for efficient integer-arithmetic-only inference. In: Proceedings of the IEEE Conference on Computer Vision and Pattern Recognition, pp. 2704–2713 (2018)

[Joy21]   Joye, M.: Guide to fully homomorphic encryption over the [discretized] torus. Cryptology ePrint Archive, Paper 2021/1402 (2021). https://eprint.iacr.org/2021/1402

[MCMF+2]   Meyre, A., et al.: Concrete-ML: a privacy-preserving machine learning library using fully homomorphic encryption for data scientists (2022). https://github.com/zama-ai/concrete-ml

[MF20]   Meng, X., Feigenbaum, J.: Privacy-preserving xgboost inference. arXiv preprint arXiv:2011.04789 (2020)

[Mic22]   Microsoft: Hummingbird library (2022). https://github.com/microsoft/hummingbird

[Pai99]   Paillier, P.: Public-key cryptosystems based on composite degree residuosity classes. In: Stern, J. (ed.) EUROCRYPT 1999. LNCS, vol. 1592, pp. 223–238. Springer, Berlin (1999). https://doi.org/10.1007/3-540-48910-x_16

[RSA78]   Rivest, R.L., Shamir, A., Adleman, L.M.: A method for obtaining digital signatures and public-key cryptosystems. Commun. ACM **21**(2), 120–126 (1978)

[SZA22]   Shwartz-Ziv, R., Armon, A.: Tabular data: deep learning is not all you need. Inf. Fusion **81**, 84–90 (2022)

[TBK20a] Tueno, A., Boev, Y., Kerschbaum, F.: Non-interactive private decision tree evaluation. In: Singhal, A., Vaidya, J. (eds.) DBSec 2020. LNCS, vol. 12122, pp. 174–194. Springer, Cham (2020). https://doi.org/10.1007/978-3-030-49669-2_10

[Zam22]   Zama: Announcing concrete numpy. Zama Blog (2022). https://www.zama.ai/post/announcing-concrete-numpy

Applying Transfer Testing to Identify Annotation Discrepancies in Facial Emotion Data Sets

Sarah Dreher$^{(\boxtimes)}$, Jens Gebele, and Philipp Brune

Neu-Ulm University of Applied Sciences, Wileystraße 1, 89231 Neu-Ulm, Germany
{Sarah.Dreher,Jens.Gebele,Philipp.Brune}@hnu.com

Abstract. The field of Artificial Intelligence (AI) has a significant impact on the way computers and humans interact. The topic of (facial) emotion recognition has gained a lot of attention in recent years. Majority of research literature focuses on improvement of algorithms and Machine Learning (ML) models for single data sets. Despite the impressive results achieved, the impact of the (training) data quality with its potential biases and annotation discrepancies is often neglected. Therefore, this paper demonstrates an approach to detect and evaluate annotation label discrepancies between three separate (facial) emotion recognition databases by Transfer Testing with three ML architectures. The findings indicate Transfer Testing to be a new promising method to detect inconsistencies in data annotations of emotional states, implying label bias and/or ambiguity. Therefore, Transfer Testing is a method to verify the transferability of trained ML models. Such research is the foundation for developing more accurate AI-based emotion recognition systems, which are also robust in real-life scenarios.

Keywords: Emotion Recognition · Facial Expression Recognition · Emotional Artificial Intelligence · Transfer Testing · Data Quality · Transferability

1 Introduction

Over the past years, there has been significant interest in AI-based emotion recognition both in research and in practical applications. This technology enables machines to identify the emotional state of humans [26,32].

The use of emotion recognition systems has expanded to various fields, including customer service [1], emotional support [3], and human-computer relationships [6,7,18].

Numerous studies have been conducted to develop emotion recognition technology using various data modalities and classification taxonomies [19,31]. Facial expression recognition (FER) is one of the most widely used and promising technologies [14,37], mainly due to the fact that human emotions are strongly conveyed through facial expressions [5,40]. The use of computerized FER has been the subject of extensive research in recent years [26,32].

S. Bouzefrane et al. (Eds.): MSPN 2023, LNCS 14482, pp. 157–174, 2024.
https://doi.org/10.1007/978-3-031-52426-4_11

The primary focus of these studies is to enhance the performance of ML models and their architectures as well as the overall model performance [36]. Although research has mostly centered on individual or a limited number of data sets, not much attention has been given to the underlying data (quality) which affects the transferability. As a result, the significance of inconsistencies in data annotation and/or labeling ambiguity of emotional states remains poorly understood [11] and the models perform badly on additional data sets.

To assess the impact of inconsistencies and/or labeling ambiguity and increase the transferability past research uses Transfer Learning. Transfer Learning uses pre-learned knowledge from a task to improve the performance of a related task [34]. In the context of FER, Transfer Learning is used to improve the performance of a model on a new data set by using a pre-trained model on a different data set [25]. However, Transfer Learning does not provide any information about the quality of the data annotations.

Therefore, in this paper we propose a new method called Transfer Testing to get further insights into quality of the data annotations. This extends and builds on the results some of the authors presented in [13], as we discuss later in Sect. 5. In [13], the same data sets were examined for inconsistencies in data annotation and/or labeling ambiguity. As outlined in Sect. 5, our earlier paper revealed label similarities in RAF-DB and FER2013, whereas AffectNet annotations differed from the other data sets. In the present paper, these earlier results are extended by using more than one ML architecture, as well as by, Transfer Testing to evaluate across databases, while the methodology is not changed.

Transfer Testing is a method to verify the transferability of trained ML models. It is a systematic approach to detect and evaluate annotation label discrepancies between separate (facial) emotion recognition databases. The findings indicate Transfer Testing to be a new promising method to detect inconsistencies in data annotations of emotional states, implying label bias and/or ambiguity. Such research is the foundation for developing more accurate AI-based emotion recognition systems, which are also robust in real-life scenarios.

Our goal is to gain a better understanding of how transferability is affected by different data sets annotations using various model architectures. Therefore, multiply models were trained on one single data set and tested on both other data set. This process is called Transfer Testing. By applying Transfer Testing, we investigate potential discrepancies in data annotations and provide new insights for future research directions in the field of transferability.

The rest of this paper is organized as follows: In Sect. 2, a detailed review of the existing literature on facial emotion recognition is presented, as well as the relevant ML techniques and a description of emotional data sets. The research methodology and data used for the systematic analysis is shown in Sect. 3. In Sect. 4 the accomplished results are presented and discussed in depth in Sect. 5. The conclusions summarize our findings.

2   Related Work

2.1   Facial Expression Recognition

FER combines Psychology [5,9] and Technology (Computer Vision). This inter-disciplinary research field aims to infer human's emotional state to gather highly relevant information contained in facial expressions [12,20].

Most research on facial emotion recognition is based on Paul Ekman's work. He claims, different cultural backgrounds do not affect dependencies between certain facial expressions and human emotional states [9]. Ekman defined six basic emotional states, namely *anger, fear, disgust, happiness, surprise* and *sadness* [5,8]. Focusing on ML, emotion recognition can be differentiated into following four different tasks: Single Label Learning (SLL), SLL Extension (extended by Intensity Estimation), Multi-Label Learning (MLL) and Label Distribution Learning (LDL) [11].

SLL describes a multi-class ML problem. Based on the highest likelihood one emotional class is identified from several possible emotional states in a facial expression. Since, this study focuses on limitations directly linked to SLL [11], the other techniques are not discussed.

Since computers require binary states, research and practice develop ML models, which perform well by assigning one emotional class to a single facial expression. That is still the main focus of research. By taking a closer look on the ML task, there are certain dependencies between the ML approaches, for instance, SLL can be seen as LDL instances [11]. This work deals with a two-sided aspect of data annotations in SLL tasks. Firstly, data annotations (labels) can either be manually or automatically generated which can lead to inconsistencies/biases. Secondly, recent research claims that one facial expression can carry more than one emotional state [11]. From past research is also known that certain emotional states can be recognized better than others [21,35].

These challenges have already been investigated on different facial data sets by some of the authors [13]. By exploring various data sets with one basic CNN model, past research came to the conclusion that not only the size of the data set nor the share of each emotion has influence on the recognition accuracy, the underlying data (label) quality affects this too [13]. In addition, higher image resolution data sets do not necessarily lead to better recognition results [13]. Furthermore, latest research has successfully developed models for FER which discount annotations and still achieve impressive results [25]. These models transform the given emotion into a neutral expression in order to reconstruct the emotion on this basis.

2.2   Machine Learning Techniques

There are different approaches for FER in ML. A general ML process consists of up to three phases. First preprocessing phase, second feature extraction phase, which can be optional, and third emotion recognition or rather classification phase. Different conventional ML and/or modern Deep Learning methods can be applied within each phase. Conventional ML methods consist of Support Vector Machine (SVM), Adaptive Boosting (AdaBoost), Random Forest (RF), Decision Tree [11]. Deep Learning models extract automatically relevant facial features during training [28,41]. In FER Deep Learning models like Convolutional Neural Networks (CNNs) and Recurrent Neural Networks (RNNs) attract attention [11].

A CNN has multiple layers similar to a Deep Neural Network (DNN). A CNN contains convolutional layer(s), pooling layer(s), dense layer(s) and fully connected layer(s). The convolutional layer(s) train the relevant features, starting from low-level features in early layers, up to high-level (abstract) features. The following pooling layer(s), aggregate information and thereby reduce computational complexity [24].

A CNN model automatically extracts features. For this reason, separate feature extraction methods like in traditional ML algorithms are not necessary [11]. Some different popular CNN architectures are listed below in chronological order: LeNet-5 [24], AlexNet [23], GoogleLeNet [39], VGGNet [38], ResNet [16], Xception [4], SENet [17]. The architectures have evolved and got more complex over the time. Further on, convolutional layers have been stacked directly and inception modules, residual learning (with skip connections) and depthwise separable convolution layer have been developed.

2.3 Emotional Facial Databases

Previous research in FER has led to a lot of facial databases. These differ based on data type (static, sequential), data dimension (two-dimensional, three-dimensional), data collection environment (controlled, uncontrolled), and number of facial expressions [11]. Databases set up in a controlled environment are for instance The Extended Cohn-Kanade data set (CK+) [29] and The Japanese Female Facial Expression (JAFFE) database [30]. Since systems based on these data sets reach only lower performance in real-world scenarios, research demanded for databases collected in an uncontrolled setting. Examples are AffectNet [33] and Real-world Affective Faces Database (RAF-DB) [27]. Most of these databases include six basic emotional states [10], usually adding one neutral facial expression. Therefore, emotional labels can be annotated manually by experts [33], by computers or by a combination of these [15].

3 Methodology

3.1 Technical Environment

We implemented all ML models on our institute server. It runs on Ubuntu 20.04 LTS, including the NVIDIA data science stack [2]. The server has two NVIDIA A40 Graphics Processing Units. The code is developed in Python, using Jupyter Notebook as integrated development environment, and made use of these Python frameworks: NumPy, Matplotlib, Pandas, Scikit-Learn, Keras and TensorFlow.

3.2   Data Collection

We consider three different data sets which contain the six basic emotions (*anger, fear, disgust, happiness, surprise* and *sadness*) with an added neutral facial expression [13]. In addition, to receive a sufficient quantity of data, as well as a more realistic and representative data, we excluded databases with a size of less than 10,000 instances and/or the ones collected in a controlled environment. The remaining data sets are FER2013, RAF-DB and AffectNet with eight labels (the so-called Mini Version).

FER2013 contains 35,887 gray images, which are automatically cropped, labeled and then cross-checked by experts. It has seven emotional classes and all images are resized to a format of 48 × 48 pixels [15]. RAF-DB on the other hand has 15,339 aligned colorful RGB-images. All images were manually annotated by about 40 experts and aligned to a size of 100 × 100 pixels [27]. The mini AffectNet consists of 291,650 only manually annotated images in RGB-color with 224 × 224 pixels each. The emotional state contempt was removed in addition to leave us with the same seven emotions as in the other data sets [33].

Table 1. Distribution of Emotional Classes per Data Set

Emotion	FER-2013		RAF-DB		AffectNet	
Pixel Size	48 × 48		100 × 100		224 × 224	
Anger	4,953	(14%)	867	(6%)	25,382	(9%)
Disgust	547	(2%)	877	(6%)	4,303	(1%)
Fear	5,121	(14%)	355	(2%)	6,878	(2%)
Happiness	8,989	(25%)	5,957	(39%)	134,915	(47%)
Sadness	6,077	(17%)	2,460	(16%)	25,959	(9%)
Surprise	4,002	(11%)	1,619	(11%)	14,590	(5%)
Neutral	6,198	(17%)	3,204	(21%)	75,374	(26%)
Total	35,887	(100%)	15,339	(100%)	287,401	(100%)

3.3   Data Pre-processing

The pre-processing stage covers typically different methods. For instance, face detection, facial landmark localization, face normalization and data augmentation [20]. Face localization is the first step. The previously described data sets have already aligned and cropped images. That is why we limit preprocessing to data normalization and augmentation.

To have equal conditions for the comparison, we resize the images of RAF-DB and AffectNet to the pixel size of FER2013. Since we combine normalization and data augmentation method, we divide each pixel by 255, which results in a range from 0 to 1 for each pixel. The total distribution of the emotional classes is presented in Table 1.

The pixel size is similar on the three different data sets. Most emotional states are sufficiently well represented in all data sets, with a few exceptions. Every data set is split into one training and one test set, with ratios of 80 percent to 20 percent. 30 percent of the training set are used as validation set. By stratifying the splits we keep the proportions of each emotional class equal in training, validation and test set. Since AffectNet is provided with a small test set, we first combine training and test set. Afterwards we split it in the same ways as the others. By the end of this publication we address differences in annotation and label ambiguity between the three data sets. Therefore, we use the trained models on each data set and evaluate these on the other two data sets, i.e. AlexNet, which was trained on RAF-DB, is evaluated on AffectNet. Since FER2013 only has decolorized images, we turn all images into black and white.

3.4   Deep Learning Model Architecture

As already mentioned, we implement various CNN architectures. First of all we need to emphasize that our aim is to compare the emotion recognition accuracy for individual emotional states in different data sets, which does not require beating a certain performance threshold. Hence, we have decided to use three architectures which use stacked CNN layers directly. The first one is AlexNet [23]. The second architecture is a standard CNN based on AlexNet [23]. In the following this CNN architecture is called defaultNet. This defaultNet is the same architecture used in [13]. The architecture of defaultNet consists of four blocks, each block contains two convolutional layers followed by one pooling layer. In each convolutional layer, we chose the padding option same and ReLu activation function. The pooling layer uses max pooling, which generally performs better than average pooling. After a stack of these four blocks, the output is flattened and then two dense layers including dropout follow. In the end, we classify between seven possible emotional states. To consider a more complex architecture we decided to use VGGNet [38] as our last architecture.

For training of our models we define 50 epochs and a batch size of 128 for every data set, in order to have the same amount of weight updates. However, the steps per epoch differ due to the different size of the data sets. Furthermore, we use Adam Optimizer starting with a learning rate of 0.0001. This learning rate is dynamic because it is automatically reduced during training, if validation accuracy does not improve for three epochs in a row. At the end, we use on each architecture the model with the highest validation accuracy during training.

3.5   Transfer Testing

All architectures defined in Sect. 3.4 are trained on each data set. After training, the models are initially evaluated on the test set of the data set they were trained on. In addition, we evaluate the trained models on the test sets of the other two data sets. This process is called Transfer Testing. A graphical explanation of the whole process is shown in Fig. 1.

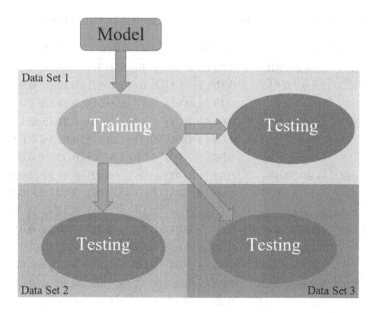

Fig. 1. Evaluation process of one architecture.

Figure 1 show the evaluation of one ML model on the three data sets. This process is done for all three model architectures (AlexNet, defaultNet and VGGNet) among all data sets. For instance, AlexNet is trained on RAF-DB. This trained AlexNet is evaluated on the test set of RAF-DB, FER2013 and AffectNet. This process is repeated for every architecture and each data set. The results are presented in the next Section.

4   Results

In this section, we present emotion recognition accuracy of the seven basic emotional states for every model architecture evaluated on the three data sets. The outcome metrics are limited to precision, recall and F1-score as these are relevant to answering our research question(s). Due to class imbalances, overall accuracy is not very meaningful. Our main focus of the analysis is on the F1-scores, which represents the harmonic mean of precision and recall. The following results evaluate the three trained models on every test set of one of the three data sets, i.e. the AlexNet which was trained on RAF-DB is evaluated on FER2013 and AffectNet. Therefore, the results contain F1-scores of normal testing and Transfer Testing. Table 2 shows the evaluation of the three trained models on the test set of FER2013. Furthermore, the results for RAF-DB are represented in Table 3 and for AffectNet in Table 4.

For each data set, we run the models five times in order to address random model initialization. Additionally, the corresponding standard deviation is shown in brackets for every metric. There is a general tendency for emotional classes

Table 2. Evaluation od Models trained on FER2013 for all three data sets

Count	Emotion	AlexNet	defaultNet	VGGNet
991	Anger-FER	0.34 (± 0.03)	0.49 (± 0.01)	0.46 (± 0.01)
	Anger-RAF	0.16 (± 0.01)	0.16 (± 0.01)	0.12 (± 0.01)
	Anger-Aff	0.19 (± 0.01)	0.17 (± 0.01)	0.12 (± 0.01)
109	Disgust-FER	0.04 (± 0.08)	0.05 (± 0.10)	0.27 (± 0.11)
	Disgust-RAF	0.02 (± 0.01)	0.00 (± 0.01)	0.02 (± 0.01)
	Disgust-Aff	0.02 (± 0.00)	0.01 (± 0.00)	0.02 (± 0.00)
1,024	Fear-FER	0.34 (± 0.02)	0.38 (± 0.02)	0.41 (± 0.02)
	Fear-RAF	0.08 (± 0.04)	0.05 (± 0.02)	0.14 (± 0.03)
	Fear-Aff	0.12 (± 0.04)	0.18 (± 0.01)	0.14 (± 0.03)
1,798	Happiness-FER	0.66 (± 0.01)	0.78 (± 0.01)	0.80 (± 0.01)
	Happiness-RAF	0.43 (± 0.00)	0.50 (± 0.02)	0.52 (± 0.01)
	Happiness-Aff	0.03 (± 0.02)	0.04 (± 0.01)	0.52 (± 0.01)
1,216	Sadness-FER	0.35 (± 0.01)	0.45 (± 0.01)	0.46 (± 0.02)
	Sadness-RAF	0.25 (± 0.02)	0.27 (± 0.02)	0.28 (± 0.01)
	Sadness-Aff	0.01 (± 0.01)	0.02 (± 0.00)	0.28 (± 0.01)
800	Surprise-FER	0.64 (± 0.00)	0.71 (± 0.01)	0.73 (± 0.01)
	Surprise-RAF	0.10 (± 0.02)	0.05 (± 0.01)	0.06 (± 0.03)
	Surprise-Aff	0.00 (± 0.00)	0.00 (± 0.00)	0.06 (± 0.00)
1,240	Neutral-FER	0.44 (± 0.02)	0.53 (± 0.01)	0.52 (± 0.01)
	Neutral-RAF	0.24 (± 0.02)	0.26 (± 0.03)	0.20 (± 0.03)
	Neutral-Aff	0.07 (± 0.02)	0.07 (± 0.01)	0.20 (± 0.01)

with higher occurrence to have lower standard deviations, for instance, *happiness, sadness* and *neutral*. The variation in F1-scores for each trained model on remaining data sets is conspicuous. F1-scores on AffectNet tend to be the lowest, except for the ones trained on AffectNet. For better impression on the impact of the model architectures on the results Table 5 displays the accuracy of each model on every data set. In the table we use the weighted average measured on the quantity of images for each emotion. This means that we first consider the support of each emotion into account and then take the average of the five training cycles.

In the next section, we discuss results, similarities and differences in the recognition accuracy of emotional states and work out possible reasons for this.

5   Discussion

By focusing on the models, we conclude that the impact of the architecture on the result is not the crucial factor. All model architectures tend to the same results. VGGNet, the most complex architecture, tends to have higher accuracy

Table 3. Evaluation od Models trained on RAF-DB for all three data sets

Count	Emotion	AlexNet	defaultNet	VGGNet
173	Anger-FER	0.01 (± 0.01)	0.00 (± 0.00)	0.00 (± 0.00)
	Anger-RAF	0.43 (± 0.03)	0.56 (± 0.02)	0.53 (± 0.03)
	Anger-Aff	0.00 (± 0.00)	0.00 (± 0.00)	0.02 (± 0.04)
175	Disgust-FER	0.07 (± 0.03)	0.05 (± 0.02)	0.05 (± 0.02)
	Disgust-RAF	0.10 (± 0.07)	0.25 (± 0.05)	0.33 (± 0.03)
	Disgust-Aff	0.07 (± 0.03)	0.07 (± 0.01)	0.08 (± 0.03)
71	Fear-FER	0.00 (± 0.01)	0.00 (± 0.00)	0.00 (± 0.02)
	Fear-RAF	0.22 (± 0.03)	0.32 (± 0.08)	0.29 (± 0.05)
	Fear-Aff	0.04 (± 0.01)	0.03 (± 0.01)	0.03 (± 0.00)
1,192	Happiness-FER	0.71 (± 0.01)	0.79 (± 0.01)	0.79 (± 0.01)
	Happiness-RAF	0.83 (± 0.01)	0.87 (± 0.01)	0.88 (± 0.01)
	Happiness-Aff	0.01 (± 0.01)	0.01 (± 0.00)	0.00 (± 0.00)
492	Sadness-FER	0.29 (± 0.01)	0.38 (± 0.01)	0.38 (± 0.03)
	Sadness-RAF	0.50 (± 0.02)	0.54 (± 0.02)	0.57 (± 0.03)
	Sadness-Aff	0.01 (± 0.01)	0.01 (± 0.00)	0.02 (± 0.01)
324	Surprise-FER	0.11 (± 0.02)	0.11 (± 0.02)	0.13 (± 0.02)
	Surprise-RAF	0.63 (± 0.01)	0.67 (± 0.01)	0.67 (± 0.02)
	Surprise-Aff	0.21 (± 0.02)	0.20 (± 0.02)	0.21 (± 0.04)
641	Neutral-FER	0.40 (± 0.06)	0.48 (± 0.03)	0.41 (± 0.02)
	Neutral-RAF	0.61 (± 0.01)	0.68 (± 0.01)	0.67 (± 0.01)
	Neutral-Aff	0.06 (± 0.02)	0.09 (± 0.01)	0.07 (± 0.03)

scores. Obviously the models trained and tested on the same data set provide the best accuracy.

Doing testing and training on the same data set confirms the findings of the previous work [13] for all three architectures. New insights on the overall performance, as well as the emotional states itself, is discussed on the basis of Transfer Testing in the following.

The results of our analysis in Tables 2, 3 and 4 show that the emotional state *happiness* is best recognizable in every data set, independent of the architectures, while testing on the same data set. Using Transfer Testing of FER2013 and RAF-DB trained models on these mutual data sets, still *happiness* is detected best. AffectNet seems to differ from these two data sets, since the recognition ranking vary in order during Transfer Testing on FER2013 or RAF-DB. *Fear* and *disgust* are the most difficult emotional states to recognize in all data sets and for all models except for AffectNet trained ones.

Table 6 illustrates a ranking of recognition accuracy for every emotional state based on F1-score on FER2013. The same information for RAF-DB is shown in Table 8 such as for AffectNet in Table 7. The emotional state *surprise* in the

Table 4. Evaluation od Models trained on AffectNet for all three data sets

Count	Emotion	AlexNet	defaultNet	VGGNet
5,076	Anger-FER	0.14 (± 0.02)	0.12 (± 0.00)	0.10 (± 0.01)
	Anger-RAF	0.13 (± 0.01)	0.15 (± 0.01)	0.11 (± 0.01)
	Anger-Aff	0.41 (± 0.02)	0.54 (± 0.01)	0.53 (± 0.01)
861	Disgust-FER	0.01 (± 0.00)	0.01 (± 0.00)	0.00 (± 0.00)
	Disgust-RAF	0.03 (± 0.00)	0.04 (± 0.00)	0.05 (± 0.01)
	Disgust-Aff	0.00 (± 0.00)	0.00 (± 0.00)	0.07 (± 0.07)
1,376	Fear-FER	0.05 (± 0.00)	0.05 (± 0.00)	0.04 (± 0.00)
	Fear-RAF	0.04 (± 0.00)	0.06 (± 0.01)	0.06 (± 0.01)
	Fear-Aff	0.22 (± 0.02)	0.26 (± 0.03)	0.33 (± 0.03)
26,983	Happiness-FER	0.00 (± 0.01)	0.00 (± 0.00)	0.00 (± 0.00)
	Happiness-RAF	0.04 (± 0.01)	0.00 (± 0.00)	0.04 (± 0.03)
	Happiness-Aff	0.85 (± 0.00)	0.89 (± 0.00)	0.90 (± 0.00)
5,192	Sadness-FER	0.14 (± 0.01)	0.11 (± 0.02)	0.14 (± 0.01)
	Sadness-RAF	0.07 (± 0.04)	0.09 (± 0.02)	0.12 (± 0.01)
	Sadness-Aff	0.32 (± 0.05)	0.49 (± 0.01)	0.49 (± 0.02)
2,918	Surprise-FER	0.04 (± 0.00)	0.04 (± 0.00)	0.04 (± 0.00)
	Surprise-RAF	0.04 (± 0.00)	0.04 (± 0.00)	0.03 (± 0.00)
	Surprise-Aff	0.28 (± 0.03)	0.42 (± 0.01)	0.42 (± 0.02)
15,075	Neutral-FER	0.12 (± 0.03)	0.17 (± 0.01)	0.16 (± 0.03)
	Neutral-RAF	0.23 (± 0.03)	0.18 (± 0.03)	0.18 (± 0.04)
	Neutral-Aff	0.62 (± 0.00)	0.68 (± 0.00)	0.68 (± 0.00)

Table 5. Accuracy as Weighted Average

Test Set	Models trained on	AlexNet	defaultNet	VGGNet
FER2013	FER2013	0.47	0.56	0.58
	RAF-DB	0.24	0.25	0.26
	AffectNet	0.06	0.07	0.07
RAF-DB	FER2013	0.42	0.49	0.47
	RAF-DB	0.63	0.69	0.70
	AffectNet	0.05	0.05	0.05
AffectNet	FER2013	0.06	0.07	0.07
	RAF-DB	0.10	0.07	0.09
	AffectNet	0.65	0.72	0.72

AffectNet data set represents the major exception in the ranking for traditional training and testing. Furthermore, the other emotions hardly vary in order on all three data sets for all architectures. As soon as we evaluate the AffectNet trained models using Transfer Testing we get results which highly vary from the other patterns.

Table 6. Recognition Accuracy Ordinal Ranking for Models trained on FER2013

Trained	Rank	AlexNet	defaultNet	VGGNet
FER	1	Happiness	Happiness	Happiness
	2	Surprise	Surprise	Surprise
	3	Neutral	Neutral	Neutral
	4	Sadness	Anger	Anger
	5	Fear	Sadness	Sadness
	6	Anger	Fear	Fear
	7	Disgust	Disgust	Disgust
RAF	1	Happiness	Happiness	Happiness
	2	Sadness	Sadness	Sadness
	3	Neutral	Neutral	Neutral
	4	Anger	Anger	Fear
	5	Surprise	Surprise	Anger
	6	Fear	Fear	Surprise
	7	Disgust	Disgust	Disgust
Aff	1	Anger	Fear	Fear
	2	Fear	Anger	Anger
	3	Neutral	Neutral	Neutral
	4	Happiness	Happiness	Happiness
	5	Disgust	Sadness	Sadness
	6	Sadness	Disgust	Disgust
	7	Surprise	Surprise	Surprise

Table 7. Recognition Accuracy Ordinal Ranking for Models trained on AffectNet

Trained	Rank	AlexNet	defaultNet	VGGNet
FER	1	Anger	Neutral	Neutral
	2	Sadness	Anger	Sadness
	3	Neutral	Sadness	Anger
	4	Fear	Fear	Fear
	5	Surprise	Surprise	Surprise
	6	Disgust	Disgust	Disgust
	7	Happiness	Happiness	Happiness
RAF	1	Neutral	Neutral	Neutral
	2	Anger	Anger	Sadness
	3	Sadness	Sadness	Anger
	4	Fear	Fear	Fear
	5	Surprise	Disgust	Disgust
	6	Happiness	Surprise	Happiness
	7	Disgust	Happiness	Surprise
Aff	1	Happiness	Happiness	Happiness
	2	Neutral	Neutral	Neutral
	3	Anger	Anger	Anger
	4	Sadness	Sadness	Sadness
	5	Surprise	Surprise	Surprise
	6	Fear	Fear	Fear
	7	Disgust	Disgust	Disgust

The results from trained AffectNet models lead to a totally new order in the recognition ranking. *Fear* is better recognizable whereas *happiness* is not the best emotion to recognize. These outliers in the comparative ranking are the first indications of data inconsistencies.

Table 8. Recognition Accuracy Ordinal Ranking for Models trained on RAF-DB

Trained	Rank	AlexNet	defaultNet	VGGNet
FER	1	Happiness	Happiness	Happiness
	2	Neutral	Neutral	Neutral
	3	Sadness	Sadness	Sadness
	4	Surprise	Surprise	Surprise
	5	Disgust	Disgust	Disgust
	6	Anger	Anger	Anger
	7	Fear	Fear	Fear
RAF	1	Happiness	Happiness	Happiness
	2	Surprise	Neutral	Surprise
	3	Neutral	Surprise	Neutral
	4	Sadness	Anger	Sadness
	5	Anger	Sadness	Anger
	6	Fear	Fear	Disgust
	7	Disgust	Disgust	Fear
Aff	1	Surprise	Surprise	Surprise
	2	Disgust	Neutral	Disgust
	3	Neutral	Disgust	Neutral
	4	Fear	Fear	Fear
	5	Happiness	Happiness	Anger
	6	Sadness	Sadness	Sadness
	7	Anger	Anger	Happiness

Furthermore, it is worth taking a closer look on F1-score intervals at every emotional state. There are differences between the best and worst F1-score for every emotional state in the data sets across all model architectures. The difference in F1-scores are presented in Table 9.

Focusing on *disgust*, the F1-scores differences are the worst for traditional training and testing. Therefore, we can assume that this emotion has the highest label inconsistency. This is also influenced by the low share of this emotion in every data set, see Table 1. *Fear* is underrepresented in AffectNet and RAF-DB as well, and accordingly the F1-score difference is higher. In FER2013 *fear* seems to have some label inconsistency, as the corresponding F1-score differences are always high. The strong F1-score variations in certain emotions is a further sign of potential irregularities in the underlying data sets.

Table 9 leads to the conclusion that trained models on AffectNet tend to worst F1-score ranges among all data sets. This confirms the point that Affect-Net differs from the other data sets with reference to label inconsistency and annotation.

Table 9. F1-score Differences for every Emotional State across all architectures and all data sets

Model trained on	Emotion	Max F1-score differences on		
		FER2013	RAF-DB	AffectNet
FER	Anger	0.15	0.01	0.04
	Disgust	0.23	0.02	0.01
	Fear	0.07	0.00	0.01
	Happiness	0.14	0.08	0.00
	Sadness	0.11	0.09	0.03
	Surprise	0.09	0.02	0.00
	Neutral	0.09	0.08	0.05
RAF	Anger	0.04	0.13	0.04
	Disgust	0.02	0.23	0.02
	Fear	0.09	0.10	0.02
	Happiness	0.09	0.05	0.04
	Sadness	0.03	0.07	0.05
	Surprise	0.05	0.04	0.01
	Neutral	0.06	0.07	0.05
Aff	Anger	0.07	0.02	0.13
	Disgust	0.01	0.01	0.07
	Fear	0.06	0.01	0.11
	Happiness	0.49	0.01	0.05
	Sadness	0.27	0.01	0.17
	Surprise	0.06	0.01	0.14
	Neutral	0.13	0.03	0.06

In accordance to the ranking in Tables 2, 3 and 4, we present a ranking for every emotional state based on F1-scores in every data sets among all models. Table 10 indicates best recognition accuracy, considering the average of F1-scores across all models. All data sets have the best F1-scores across the emotions while training and testing on the same data set, except *disgust* in trained AffectNet. Due to the stratified split into training, validation and test data, class imbalances are present. A reason for *disgust* being more recognizable on RAF-DB for trained AffectNet models is the fact that this class has a very low share in every data set, but is more present in RAF-DB. For trained FER2013 the recognition accuracy in RAF-DB is better than for AffectNet despite the fact RAF-DB has the smallest amount of images. The emotions where RAF-DB ranks have a smaller share. Focusing on RAF-DB trained models, the ranking for *disgust, fear* and *surprise* are the worst on FER2013. Even FER2013 has a higher percentage on the data set for these emotions, AffectNet has a higher recognition accuracy. *Happiness* and *neutral* have higher appearance on AffectNet while the accuracy level is lower. This is an indicator of label inconsistency on this emotions in AffectNet. Overall, this leads to the assumption that RAF-DB has the lowest data inconsistencies, while FER2013 and AffectNet have higher ones.

Table 10. Recognition Accuracy F1-score Ranking

Emotion	FER2013 with trained			RAF-DB with trained			AffectNet with trained		
	FER	RAF	Aff	FER	RAF	Aff	FER	RAF	Aff
Anger	I	II	III	III	I	II	II	III	I
Disgust	I	III	III	III	I	I	II	II	II
Fear	I	III	III	III	I	II	II	II	I
Happiness	I	II	III	II	I	II	III	III	I
Sadness	I	II	II	II	I	III	III	III	I
Surprise	I	III	III	II	I	II	III	II	I
Neutral	I	II	III	II	I	II	III	III	I

The low share of *disgust* might explain the high F1-score differences in Table 9 and the generally low F1-scores in Tables 2, 3 and 4. However, the emotional states *anger* and *fear* also have comparatively small shares, but significantly lower F1-score differences and relatively good F1-scores for all models. Emotional states with lower proportions can also achieve quite satisfactory recognition accuracy, for instance, *surprise* on FER2013 and RAF-DB. Beyond, *happiness* with its high appearance in all data sets has small accuracy levels on FER2013 for trained AffectNet models (see Table 9).

The emotional classes are largely equally distributed across all data sets. In all three data sets, *happiness* is the emotional state with the highest share followed by *neutral* and *sadness*. For this reason, we believe that a comparison without further adjustment of the class weights in the training set is valid. However, we are also aware that our analysis has limitations and suggest future research considering class imbalances. This could help to understand the potential impact of class imbalances on our findings. Generally speaking, our analysis provides convincing evidence that recognition accuracy of individual emotional states differs. On the one hand, between individual emotional states, which is known from previous studies as well [14]. On the other hand, recognition accuracy of individual emotions vary (strongly) between different data sets while the image features (e.g. size, color) and training parameters (e.g. epochs) are kept constant. The used model architectures slightly vary in the accuracy, therefore the results lead to the same conclusions. AffectNet data set indicates higher (F1-score) differences. The least data inconsistencies can be assumed on RAF-DB. Our findings imply data inconsistencies and/or label ambiguity. Possible reasons for these variations in emotional data can be multifactorial. Three potential factors follow.

First, the number of total support and the proportion of emotional classes tend to have an influence on the recognition accuracy of emotional states. This does not apply to all emotional states. The AffectNet data set with most support, reaches the lowest recognition accuracy for three emotions.

Second, reducing the image size and color range of RAF-DB and AffectNet to fit the size of FER2013 could potentially lead to losses of information content. However, interestingly initial experiments without pixel reduction showed the opposite. The AffectNet data set with the highest image resolution and detail information, had generally the lowest recognition accuracy scores.

Third, our findings show that certain emotions, i.e., disgust and *fear*, have lower recognition accuracy. This is in line with previous publications [21,22]. It is worth mentioning that emotions can have different intensities. Plus, differences between certain emotions are not very obvious. Some emotions are very similar and their expressions can be closely related to other emotions. Recently, research has also questioned whether it is valid to assume that facial expressions only contain single emotional states [11]. As consequence, data annotations can be biased and/or incorrect. This can be possible for images carrying higher information content, which leads to higher ambiguity, variability and variance. Therefore, manual image annotation is more difficult and subject to a higher error rate.

The previous analysis clearly shows that Transfer Testing reveals differences between the databases. Through these findings, trained models can be tested for their transferability to other databases. However, further research on Transfer Testing is necessary to determine a measure of transferability and to apply this to real-world scenarios. Overall, the transfer test is a valid method for detecting inconsistencies and/or label ambiguity.

6 Conclusion

In conclusion, this paper presents a comparative analysis to detect label inconsistencies in three commonly used facial expression datasets by Transfer Testing with three different ML model architectures. For this, the data sets have been processed using the same resolution to classify the contained facial images with respect to the expressed emotions. To eliminate possible influences of model architectures, we considered three different types of architectures. Our experiments indicate that the complexity of the ML architectures does not have a significant impact on the overall performance. The transferability among the data sets, on the other hand, deserved a closer look. By Transfer Testing, the presented results demonstrate that recognition accuracy is influenced by the size of the data set and the share for each emotion in it. Furthermore, transferability seems to be (strongly) influenced by the underlying data (label) quality. Transfer testing shows the existence of label biases and/or ambiguity. Furthermore, Transfer Testing shows that the transferability is decisively influenced by this.

All in all, this leads to several future research directions. First, more empirical analysis is required, comparing more data sets. Class imbalances should also be taken into account. Second, investigations are necessary to understand why certain emotions have low recognition accuracy and possible solutions for this challenge. Third, based on our results, it is necessary to investigate a potential relationship between annotation inconsistencies and transferability of ML architectures. Fourth, research is required to minimize and/or distinguish data annotation inconsistencies and label ambiguity as well as the implications which entail with each of them.

AI-based emotion recognition is in general a promising technique for applications. Nonetheless, our results show that AI needs to be applied with great care. On the one hand we should always critically reflect its outcomes, and on the other hand its data input (quality).

References

1. Affectiva - Humanizing Technology (2021). https://www.affectiva.com/
2. NVIDIA Data Science Stack. NVIDIA Corporation (2021)
3. Replika (2021). https://replika.com
4. Chollet, F.: Xception: deep learning with depthwise separable convolutions. In: Proceedings of the IEEE Conference on Computer Vision and Pattern Recognition, pp. 1251–1258 (2017)
5. Darwin, C.: The Expression of the Emotions in Man and Animals. John Murray, London (1872)
6. Davenport, T., Guha, A., Grewal, D., Bressgott, T.: How artificial intelligence will change the future of marketing. J. Acad. Mark. Sci. **48**(1), 24–42 (2020)
7. Davoli, L., et al.: On driver behavior recognition for increased safety: a roadmap. Safety **6**(4) (2020). https://doi.org/10.3390/safety6040055
8. Ekman, P.: Basic emotions. In: Handbook of Cognition and Emotion, pp. 301–320. Wiley, New York (1999)
9. Ekman, P., Friesen, W.V.: Constants across cultures in the face and emotion. J. Pers. Soc. Psychol. **17**(2), 124 (1971)
10. Ekman, P., Friesen, W.V.: Unmasking the Face: A Guide to Recognizing Emotions from Facial Clues, vol. 10. ISHK (2003)
11. Ekundayo, O.S., Viriri, S.: Facial expression recognition: a review of trends and techniques. IEEE Access **9**, 136944–136973 (2021). https://doi.org/10.1109/ACCESS.2021.3113464
12. Ekweariri, A.N., Yurtkan, K.: Facial expression recognition using enhanced local binary patterns. In: 2017 9th International Conference on Computational Intelligence and Communication Networks (CICN), pp. 43–47. IEEE (2017)
13. Gebele, J., Brune, P., Fau ßer, S.: Face value: on the impact of annotation (in-)consistencies and label ambiguity in facial data on emotion recognition. In: IEEE 26th International Conference on Pattern Recognition (2022)
14. Generosi, A., Ceccacci, S., Mengoni, M.: A deep learning-based system to track and analyze customer behavior in retail store. In: 2018 IEEE 8th International Conference on Consumer Electronics-Berlin (ICCE-Berlin), pp. 1–6. IEEE (2018)
15. Goodfellow, I.J., et al.: Challenges in Representation Learning: A report on three machine learning contests. arXiv:1307.0414 (2013)

16. He, K., Zhang, X., Ren, S., Sun, J.: Deep residual learning for image recognition. In: 2016 IEEE Conference on Computer Vision and Pattern Recognition (CVPR), pp. 770–778 (2016). https://doi.org/10.1109/CVPR.2016.90
17. Hu, J., Shen, L., Sun, G.: Squeeze-and-excitation networks. In: 2018 IEEE/CVF Conference on Computer Vision and Pattern Recognition, pp. 7132–7141 (2018). https://doi.org/10.1109/CVPR.2018.00745
18. Huang, M.H., Rust, R.T.: Artificial intelligence in service. J. Serv. Res. **21**(2), 155–172 (2018)
19. Huang, M.H., Rust, R.T.: A strategic framework for artificial intelligence in marketing. J. Acad. Mark. Sci. **49**(1), 30–50 (2021). https://doi.org/10.1007/s11747-020-00749-9
20. Jaison, A., Deepa, C.: A review on facial emotion recognition and classification analysis with deep learning. Biosci. Biotechnol. Res. Commun. **14**(5), 154–161 (2021). https://doi.org/10.21786/bbrc/14.5/29
21. Khaireddin, Y., Chen, Z.: Facial Emotion Recognition: State of the Art Performance on FER2013. arXiv:2105.03588 (2021)
22. Knyazev, B., Shvetsov, R., Efremova, N., Kuharenko, A.: Convolutional neural networks pretrained on large face recognition datasets for emotion classification from video. arXiv:1711.04598 (2017)
23. Krizhevsky, A., Sutskever, I., Hinton, G.E.: Imagenet classification with deep convolutional neural networks. Adv. Neural. Inf. Process. Syst. **25**, 1097–1105 (2012)
24. Lecun, Y., Bottou, L., Bengio, Y., Haffner, P.: Gradient-based learning applied to document recognition. Proc. IEEE **86**(11), 2278–2324 (1998). https://doi.org/10.1109/5.726791
25. Li, J., Nie, J., Guo, D., Hong, R., Wang, M.: Emotion Separation and Recognition from a Facial Expression by Generating the Poker Face with Vision Transformers. http://arxiv.org/abs/2207.11081
26. Li, S., Deng, W.: Deep facial expression recognition: a survey. IEEE Trans. Affect. Comput. **13**(3), 1195–1215 (2020)
27. Li, S., Deng, W., Du, J.: Reliable crowdsourcing and deep locality-preserving learning for expression recognition in the wild. In: 2017 IEEE Conference on Computer Vision and Pattern Recognition (CVPR), Honolulu, HI, pp. 2584–2593. IEEE (2017). https://doi.org/10.1109/CVPR.2017.277
28. Liu, X., Kumar, B.V.K.V., You, J., Jia, P.: Adaptive deep metric learning for identity-aware facial expression recognition. In: 2017 IEEE Conference on Computer Vision and Pattern Recognition Workshops (CVPRW), pp. 522–531 (2017). https://doi.org/10.1109/CVPRW.2017.79
29. Lucey, P., Cohn, J.F., Kanade, T., Saragih, J., Ambadar, Z., Matthews, I.: The extended Cohn-Kanade dataset (CK+): a complete dataset for action unit and emotion-specified expression. In: 2010 IEEE Computer Society Conference on Computer Vision and Pattern Recognition - Workshops, pp. 94–101 (2010). https://doi.org/10.1109/CVPRW.2010.5543262
30. Lyons, M., Akamatsu, S., Kamachi, M., Gyoba, J.: Coding facial expressions with Gabor wavelets. In: Proceedings Third IEEE International Conference on Automatic Face and Gesture Recognition, pp. 200–205 (1998). https://doi.org/10.1109/AFGR.1998.670949
31. Marín-Morales, J., et al.: Affective computing in virtual reality: emotion recognition from brain and heartbeat dynamics using wearable sensors. Sci. Rep. **8**(1), 1–15 (2018)
32. Mellouk, W., Handouzi, W.: Facial emotion recognition using deep learning: Review and insights. Procedia Comput. Sci. **175**, 689–694 (2020)

33. Mollahosseini, A., Hasani, B., Mahoor, M.H.: Affectnet: a database for facial expression, valence, and arousal computing in the wild. IEEE Trans. Affect. Comput. **10**(1), 18–31 (2017)
34. Pan, S.J., Yang, Q.: A survey on transfer learning. IEEE Trans. Knowl. Data Eng. **22**(10), 1345–1359 (2010). https://doi.org/10.1109/TKDE.2009.191
35. Quinn, M.A., Sivesind, G., Reis, G.: Real-time emotion recognition from facial expressions. Standford University (2017)
36. Rouast, P.V., Adam, M., Chiong, R.: Deep learning for human affect recognition: insights and new developments. IEEE Trans. Affect. Comput. **12**(2), 524–543 (2019)
37. Shao, J., Qian, Y.: Three convolutional neural network models for facial expression recognition in the wild. Neurocomputing **355**, 82–92 (2019)
38. Simonyan, K., Zisserman, A.: Very Deep Convolutional Networks for Large-Scale Image Recognition. arXiv:1409.1556 (2015)
39. Szegedy, C., et al.: Going deeper with convolutions. In: Proceedings of the IEEE Conference on Computer Vision and Pattern Recognition, pp. 1–9 (2015)
40. Tian, Y.I., Kanade, T., Cohn, J.F.: Recognizing action units for facial expression analysis. IEEE Trans. Pattern Anal. Mach. Intell. **23**(2), 97–115 (2001)
41. Yang, H., Ciftci, U., Yin, L.: Facial expression recognition by de-expression residue learning. In: 2018 IEEE/CVF Conference on Computer Vision and Pattern Recognition, pp. 2168–2177 (2018). https://doi.org/10.1109/CVPR.2018.00231

Multiple Person Tracking Based on Gait Identification Using Kinect and OpenPose

Ryotaro Toma, Terumi Yaguchi, and Hiroaki Kikuchi[✉]

School of Interdisciplinary Mathematical Sciences, Meiji University,
4-21-1 Nakano, Tokyo 164-8525, Japan
kikn@meiji.ac.jp

Abstract. A gait provides the characteristics of a person's walking style and hence is classified as personal identifiable information. There have been several studies for personal identification using gait, including works using hardware such as depth sensors and studies using silhouette image sequences of gait. However, these methods were designed specialized for tracking a single walking person and the accuracy reduction when multiple people are simultaneously reflected in several angles of view is not clear yet. In addition, dependencies on hardware-based methods is not clarified yet. In this study, we focus on Kinect and OpenPose, the representative gait identification techniques with a function to detect multiple people simultaneously in real time. We investigate how many people can be identified for these devices and with the accuracy for tracking.

1 Introduction

Multiple human tracking refers to the task of simultaneously detecting and tracking multiple individuals in a given scene or video. The objective is to accurately locate and follow each person's movement throughout the sequence of frames or time. The goal of multiple human tracking is to provide a comprehensive understanding of the activities and interactions of multiple people in various applications, such as surveillance [1], crowd analysis [2], behavior understanding, human-computer interaction, and augmented reality.

The process of multiple human tracking typically involves several steps. First, individual humans need to be detected or localized in each frame, often using computer vision techniques such as object detection [3,4], face detection [5–7,13,34], attribute estimation [24–26] or pose estimation [8,28,35]. Next, these detection or pose estimates are linked across frames to establish trajectories, ensuring consistent and accurate tracking over time. Various methods and algorithms are employed for data association and tracking. Muaaz et al. [31] proposed a person identification method using a smartphone-based accelerator. They used the acceleration information of an Android device in a person's front pocket as data. Preis et al. proposed a gait recognition method using Kinect [9]. They used a decision tree and a Naive Bayes classifier to recognize the gait. Han et al. [10] proposed the gait energy image (GEI). The advantages of GEI are the reduction of processing time, reduction of storage requirements, and robustness of obstacles. Backchy et al. [11] proposed a gait authentication method using Kohonen's

S. Bouzefrane et al. (Eds.): MSPN 2023, LNCS 14482, pp. 175–187, 2024.
https://doi.org/10.1007/978-3-031-52426-4_12

self-organizing mapping (K-SOM). In this work, the authors used K-SOM to classify GEI and reported a 57% recognition rate. Shiraga et al. proposed the GEINet [12] using a convolutional neural network to classify GEI images. The best EER obtained was 0.01.

In this study, we consider two approaches: the computer vision approach using OpenPose [20] and the depth sensor approach such as Kinect [14]. Computer vision approaches can be applied to a variety of applications and provide rich information including joint positions without any additional sensors or equipment, relying solely on visual data captured by cameras. However, computer vision methods primarily rely on 2D image data, which may lack depth information required for precise depth-related analysis. In contrast, depth sensors, like Kinect, provide depth data, enabling more accurate and detailed 3D tracking of human movements and positions. But, depth sensors often have limited tracking ranges, which may restrict their applicability to certain scenarios. The pros and cons are can vary depending on specific applications and implementations for tracking. Hence, it is not trivial to determine which is superior than others.

To evaluate the effectiveness of these two approaches, we employ the Dynamic Time Warping (DTW) [15,22,23] algorithm for individual identification. The DTW algorithm leverages the 3-dimensional coordinates obtained from either approach to recognize individuals. By calculating the DTW distance of time series data representing a complete walking cycle, it enables multiple human tracking, accommodating crowded scenes, and addressing environmental variations. Our objective is to utilize DTW for reliable and precise human tracking, facilitating a comprehensive understanding of behaviors and enabling in-depth analysis of human movements in urban environments.

In this study, we develop a testbed for human tracking, implementing two representative approaches: OpenPose and Kinect. We conduct small-scale experiments to assess the robustness and accuracy of estimation provided by these approaches in the context of multiple human tracking.

2   Preliminary

2.1   OpenPose

OpenPose [20] is an open-source computer vision library that enables real-time multi-person tracking from video and image data. OpenPose is capable of estimating the 25 positions of body joints, such as the shoulders, elbows, wrists, hips, knees, and ankles, for multiple individuals in a frame.

OpenPose utilizes convolutional neural networks (CNNs) to analyze visual data and extract keypoint information. The library employs a two-step process: first, it generates a set of body part candidates through a body part detector, and then it associates these candidates to corresponding body parts and individuals through a series of refinement stages.

Figure 1 shows the example of keypoint detection in OpenPose. It offers several advantages for person tracking: First, tracking multiple individuals simultaneously in real-time. It is a significant advantage for application that captures the movement of guest in shopping malls. Second, it detect human from images without any special equipment such as 3D depth sensors.

 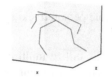 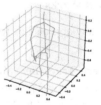

Fig. 1. Sample OpenPose execution

Fig. 2. Sample 3d-pose-baseline execution

Fig. 3. Sample 3D skeleton data via Kinect

Despite its advantages, it has some limitations: (i) Limited to 2D Keypoint Estimation: OpenPose focuses on 2D keypoint estimation, meaning it provides positional information for body joints in the image plane. It lacks depth information and hence suffers low estimation accuracy. Its performance can be affected by image quality and variations in camera viewpoints. (ii) Resource Intensive: Real-time multi-person tracking with OpenPose can be computationally demanding. It requires substantial computational resources, including a powerful GPU, to achieve real-time performance.

To estimate 3D points from 2D keypoint estimated from OpenPose, Julieta et al. [29] proposed an effective model and developed open-source software, 3D-Pose-Baseline. It is based on an assumption that a 3D pose can be represented as a linear combination of a set of 3D basis points. Figure 2 shows the sample of estimated 3D points of human. It demonstrates that some joints are accurately estimated.

2.2 Kinect

Kinect [14] is a motion-sensing input device developed by Microsoft for use with gaming. It was initially released as an accessory for the Xbox 360 gaming console in 2010. The Kinect sensor combines a depth camera, RGB camera, and multi-array microphone to provide a range of interactive and immersive experiences.

Kinect utilizes a structured light or time-of-flight technology to capture depth information of the surrounding environment. It measures the distance between the sensor and objects, enabling 3D depth perception. Kinect has built-in algorithms and software libraries for robust human body tracking and gesture recognition. It can detect and track the movements of multiple individuals within its field of view, allowing for natural and intuitive interaction in gaming, fitness, and person tracking. Figure 3 shows the sample of 3D skeleton data captured via Kinect. We utilize Microsoft library Kinect for Windows v2 for retrieving the 3D points for this study.

Tracking more than six individuals becomes challenging due to the complexity of processing the depth data, distinguishing individual bodies, and maintaining accurate tracking in real-time. The hardware and computational resources of the Kinect sensor are optimized to handle a limited number of tracked bodies. Although the tracking limitation of six individuals is specific to the Kinect sensor, it apply to other depth-sensing devices or motion-tracking systems.

2.3   Related Works

There are many approaches for multiple person tracking using various devices.

Multi-camera Tracking. Many works utilize multiple cameras to improve tracking accuracy. Each camera provides a different viewpoint, and sophisticated algorithms are used to use data from these cameras to track individuals as they move across different views. This is especially common in surveillance systems. Amosa et al. [16] categorized existing works based on six crucial facets and summarized 30 state-of-the-art MCT algorithms on common datasets.

Depth Sensors. Depth sensors have been widely used for multiple person tracking. They provide accurate depth information, which helps in distinguishing between individuals and handling occlusions more effectively. Preis et al. proposed a gait recognition method using Kinect [9]. They used a decision tree and a Naive Bayes classifier to recognize the gait. In their work, a success rate of 91.0% was achieved for nine subjects. Studies using depth sensors include [17, 18, 21, 27].

Device-Based Tracking. Each smartphone continuously records accelerometer and gyroscope data, allowing us to capture motion patterns and changes in orientation. Muaaz et al. [31] introduced a multiple person tracking approach utilizing smartphone accelerometer data. Their method focuses on identifying individuals based on the accelerometer readings of an Android device placed in the front pocket of a person. During the registration phase, walking cycles are defined as templates, and multiple templates are enrolled. In the subsequent authentication phase, the system assesses the distances from all registered templates and considers the user as the correct individual if more than half of the templates fall within the predefined threshold.

3   Person Tracking Based on Gait

Person tracking becomes feasible by utilizing gait data, which comprises a time-sequence of 3D points representing the primary joints of the human body. In this section, we describe the approach introduced by [18], which incorporates metrics quantifying the Dynamic Time Warping (DTW) [15]. This approach aims to recognize individuals by utilizing 3-dimensional coordinates obtained from motion capture sensors. It involves calculating the DTW distance of the time series data representing one complete cycle of walking. The method encompasses four key steps: cycle extraction, calculation of relative coordinates, computation of DTW distance, and person recognition.

3.1   Cycle Extraction

Let $a_\ell(t) = (x, y, z)$ be a time series of 3-dimensional absolute coordinates of joint ℓ in time t. The collection of these time series data, representing absolute coordinates at different points in time, is referred to as *skeleton data*.

From the skeleton data, we extract a single cycle of walking. In our specific context, each video stream observation typically contains approximately two complete walking cycles.

First, let $\Delta(t)$ be the distance between both feet in time t, defined using $a_{LF}(t)$ and $a_{RF}(t)$ as

$$\Delta(t) = \pm \|a_{RF}(t) - a_{LF}(t)\|. \tag{1}$$

If the right foot is in front, The sign of $\Delta(t)$ determines whether the right foot is positioned in front (positive) or not (negative).

Next, we apply Fourier transformation to the time series $\Delta(1), \ldots, \Delta(n)$ and employ a low pass filter to reduce noise and identify a single cycle. The resulting low-frequency components at a rate of $1/30$ are processed further. For cycle extraction, we define a *cycle* of walking as the period between peaks. It is important to note that the low-pass filter is solely used for cycle extraction purposes, while the DTW algorithm operates on the non-filtered data. In the cycle extraction phase, time t is a unit corresponding to the frame rate of the motion capture sensor. The frame rate is 30 fps. Suppose that we have one cycle as a series of features from the first peak ($t = 37$) to the second peak ($t = 70$). The data is normalized from t_1 to t_{35}.

3.2 DTW Distance

We compute the relative coordinates of joints while walking, with the choice of the coordinate origin being stable joints located at the center of the body (SpineMid). Given an absolute coordinate of center joints c at time t $a_c(t)$, the relative coordinate r is defined as $r_\ell(t) = a_\ell(t) - a_c(t)$.

We use a multi-dimensional Dynamic Time Warping [30], which is a technique used to measure the similarity between two temporal sequences. It is commonly employed in various fields, including time series analysis, speech recognition, gesture recognition, and pattern recognition. The goal of DTW is to find an optimal alignment or warping path between two sequences by stretching or compressing the time axes. This alignment aims to minimize the differences between corresponding elements of the sequences, allowing for comparison and similarity estimation even when the sequences have variations in length or speed.

Dynamic programming is used to find the optimal warping path through the cost matrix, providing distance between elements of two sequences. The algorithm iteratively computes the cumulative cost along different paths and identifies the path with the minimum total cost as follows.

Consider two sets of time series data denoted as $P = (p_1, p_2, \ldots, p_{n_P})$ and $Q = (q_1, q_2, \ldots, q_{n_Q})$. The distance between them, represented by $d(P, Q)$, is defined as $d(P, Q) = f(n_P, n_Q)$. The cost function $f(i, j)$ is calculated recursively as

$$f(i, j) = \|p_i - q_j\| + \min(f(i, j-1), f(i-1, j), f(i-1, j-1),) \tag{2}$$

with initial conditions; $f(0, 0) = 0$, and $f(i, 0) = f(0, j) = \infty$. When several features are aggregated, the distance is calculated as follows. Given two data sets (R_ℓ, R_m) and (R'_ℓ, R'_m), and data of joints ℓ and m, the integrated DTW distance $D((R_\ell, R_m), (R'_\ell, R'_m))$ is defined as an Euclidean distance of all DTW distances.

3.3 Human Identification

Consider the set U representing all users. Let $R^{(u)}$ denote the time series data of k pieces of normalized relative coordinates for user u. Given a set of s data pieces $(R^u 1, \ldots, R^u s)$, we define one of them as the template data $R^{(u)}$. Two users, u and v, are considered identical if the integrated DTW distance $D(R^{(u)}, R^{(v)})$ between their respective sets of time series data, $R^{(u)}$ and $R^{(v)}$, is less than a threshold value θ. The threshold θ^ℓ is determined using the Equal Error Rate (EER), which is an error rate at which the False Acceptance Rate (FAR) equals the False Rejection Rate (FRR).

4 Evaluation

4.1 Objectives

Our experiment aims to achieve the following objectives:

1. Evaluate the baseline accuracy of gait tracking using DTW distance for multiple humans.
2. Compare two tracking approaches: the computer vision approach utilizing Open-Pose and the deep sensor approach using Kinect.

We have developed a testbed system to capture the 3D time-series data of walking humans. For the essential features, we the Processing V3 with the KinectPV2 library, which provides access to Kinect for Windows V2 [14].

4.2 Data

The experimental conditions are presented in Table 1, outlining the specifications. The data collected includes two types of scenarios: walking by a single individual and walking by multiple individuals. The observations took place in a gymnastic hall, where subjects walked without encountering any obstacles. During the experiment, the subjects were instructed to walk while being recorded from three different camera viewpoints: front camera, as well as cameras positioned obliquely at plus and minus 30°.

We conducted a multiple person tracking evaluation by observing a varying number of walking subjects, denoted by m, ranging from 1 to 6. For each number of subjects, we explored different variations, including scenarios where all subjects walked in the same direction and cases where some subjects walked in a direction opposite to others. For each variation, we repeated the tracking process three times to ensure reliable results.

4.3 Methodology

We conducted an evaluation of two tracking approaches: one using computer vision with OpenPose and the other using a depth sensor with Kinect.

In the initial stage, we examined the quality of 3D skeleton data obtained from both methods. We observed that the accuracy of 3D estimation using OpenPose might be affected by the camera viewpoints due to the absence of depth information. On the other

Table 1. Experimental condition

item	value
date	July 16, 2022
venue	gymnastic hall, Meiji University
age	20's
population	7 (4 male, 3 female)

hand, the depth sensor method with Kinect had limitations in tracking the number of humans due to the complexity involved in processing depth data. Consequently, the 3D points estimated from these devices may contain erroneous data. To evaluate this, we analyzed the occurrence of detection failures by manually classifying three randomly sampled frames from three camera viewpoints into three categories: (a) *normal*, (b) *partially malfunctioning*, and (c) *completely malfunctioning* frames. Figure 4 provides examples of these frames, including normal data with accurately estimated 3D points (Fig. 4a), partially malfunctioning frames with failed detection of a specific joint (e.g., left knee) (Fig. 4b), and completely malfunctioning frames (Fig. 4c) where most of the points are incorrect.

For the analysis involving a single walking subject, we investigated a total of n subjects captured from three viewpoints across three randomly chosen frames, resulting in a total of 63 frames ($7 \times 3 \times 3$). In the case of multiple subjects, we examined n subjects based on two randomly selected frames.

In the next stage, we applied the DTW human identification algorithm using 3D time-series data as described in Sect. 3. By varying the number of subjects m from 1 to 6, we tested the accuracy of identification using the 3D point data obtained from Kinect and OpenPose. The accuracy of identification was measured as the fraction of correctly identified subjects. Additionally, we evaluated the *top-k accuracy*, which is a common performance metric used in classification tasks. The top-k accuracy measures the proportion of correct identifications where the correct person label is among the top-k predicted labels. In other words, if the true class label is among the k highest-ranked persons based on the DTW distance to the given data, the tracking is considered correct. We calculated the top-k accuracy for values of k ranging from 1 to 5.

4.4 Results

Quality of Detection. Table 2 shows the successful tracking rate using Kinect. It is evident that the rate of successful tracking decreases significantly when the camera viewpoint is not frontal. When the camera is positioned obliquely, 33% of the frames exhibit partial malfunctions, while 19% of the frames are not utilized at all.

Table 3 shows the successful tracking rate in relation to the number of walking individuals simultaneously. The rate of success decreases as the number of walking persons m increases. Specifically, at $m = 4$, the success rate is 0.36, which is half of the rate observed at $m = 3$ (0.64). It should be noted that the maximum number of individuals that Kinect can track is specified as 6. The findings reveal that the quality of 3D

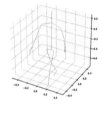

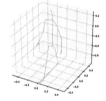

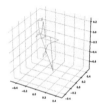

(a) Normal   (b) partially malfunctioning   (c) completely malfunction-
                        frames   ing frames

Fig. 4. Detection failures

Table 2. successful tracking rate with regard to orientation (Kinect)

| orientation | success | malfunctioning | |
		partially	totally
front	1.0 (21/21)	0.0 (0/21)	0.0 (0/21)
side	0.48 (20/42)	0.33 (14/42)	0.19 (8/42)
total	0.65 (41/63)	0.22 (14/63)	0.13 (8/63)

point detection diminishes even before reaching the specified tracking limitation of 6 individuals.

As a result, the accuracy of 3D point estimations is negatively affected when the camera viewpoint is not frontal or when there are multiple individuals walking in different directions. The accuracy of person tracking, therefore, depends on these factors, including the orientation of walking and the number of individuals being tracked.

Multiple Person Tracking. Figure 5a shows the tracking accuracy based on DTW, for different top-k values ranging from 1 to 5. Confidence intervals are included for both tracking approaches, Kinect and OpenPose. It can be observed that as the top-k value

Table 3. successful tracking rate with regard to population

| population m | success | failure | |
		partially	totally
1	0.65 (41/63)	0.22 (14/63)	0.13 (8/63)
2	0.67 (8/12)	0.17 (2/12)	0.17 (2/12)
3	0.64 (9/14)	0.29 (4/14)	0.071 (1/14)
4	0.36 (5/14)	0.43 (6/14)	0.21 (3/14)
5	0.29 (4/14)	0.50 (7/14)	0.21 (3/14)
6	0.43 (6/14)	0.29 (4/14)	0.29 (4/14)

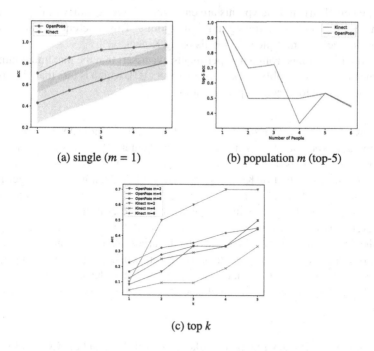

(a) single ($m = 1$)   (b) population m (top-5)

(c) top k

Fig. 5. Person tracking accuracy

increases, the accuracy for both approaches improve. Overall, the accuracy of Kinect is superior to that of OpenPose, with a difference ranging from 0.3 to 0.2.

Figure 5b illustrates the distribution of top-5 accuracy while varying the number of individuals m from 1 to 6. Similar to the results obtained for 3D point quality, the accuracy of person tracking substantially decreases with an increasing number of individuals. When comparing the accuracies of OpenPose and Kinect, the reduction in accuracy with Kinect is more strongly influenced by the number of individuals. The accuracy of Kinect appears to be more unstable with respect to m. Therefore, we concluded that OpenPose demonstrates greater robustness in handling different numbers of individuals, although the overall accuracy is relatively lower.

Figure 5c shows the accuracy plot for the number of individuals, specifically for $m = 2$, $m = 4$, and $m = 6$. The differences in accuracy are evident when multiple people are simultaneously tracked using Kinect. In particular, the accuracy for $m = 4$ is consistently the lowest across all top-k values. This finding provides evidence of the robustness of OpenPose in comparison to Kinect.

4.5 Discussion

Kinect's Sensing Error. Through our observations, we noticed a significant decline in tracking accuracy when using Kinect as the number of individuals increased. In Kinect, the estimation of joint locations relies on depth information captured by the sensor.

However, when obstructed viewpoints are encountered, the accuracy of depth measurement can be compromised, resulting in missing joints. This inherent limitation leads to difficulties in tracking multiple individuals using Kinect.

Based on the findings from our experiments, we assert that the maximum number of individuals that can be reliably tracked using Kinect is 3, which is less than the specified limitation according to Kinect's specifications.

Robustness of Multiple Person Tracking. Our findings indicate that the computer vision approach, specifically OpenPose, exhibits greater robustness when considering the number of individuals being tracked. The experiment demonstrates that the accuracy of OpenPose surpasses that of Kinect, particularly when dealing with a larger number of individuals. This observation aligns with the fact that the computer vision approach possesses a higher tracking capacity, as specified by its capabilities.

However, it is important to acknowledge the limitations of our experiment. These include the limited number of subjects involved, variations in environmental conditions such as brightness, and the impact of obstacles on sensing accuracy. Additionally, it should be noted that the performance of a specific device, Kinect, cannot be generalized to other depth sensors, as different sensors may have varying characteristics and performance.

Privacy Concerns. Privacy regulations like the GDPR [32] and the CCPA [33] strictly forbid the collection of personal information without explicit individual consent. Gait information is categorized as a form of personal data. Consequently, employing multiple person tracking methods based on gait information raises concerns regarding privacy regulation compliance. To harness the insights derived from tracking individuals, it becomes imperative to adopt privacy-enhancing technologies, including techniques such as data anonymization and obfuscation.

An illustrative approach, "VideoDP" proposed by Wang et al. [19], offers a potential method for identifying individuals within video data by incorporating noise into statistical data, ensuring the application of differential privacy principles. However, there is a pressing need for specialized privacy-enhanced technologies tailored to the unique characteristics of gait information.

5   Conclusions

In this study, we have examined the performance of multiple human tracking using two approaches: OpenPose and Kinect. By employing the DTW distance metric, we have demonstrated the feasibility of tracking multiple humans based on time-series 3D point data. Our experimental results indicate that the depth sensor, Kinect, is capable of accurately tracking multiple individuals. However, its accuracy diminishes when there are more than three individuals walking simultaneously or when their walking orientations differ. Consequently, we conclude that person tracking is influenced by factors such as the orientation of walking and the number of individuals being tracked.

As a future area of investigation, we plan to explore algorithms for large-scale human tracking. Additionally, we are interested in addressing privacy concerns arising from this type of tracking.

Acknowledgment. Part of this work was supported by JSPS KAKENHI Grant Number 23K11110 and JST, CREST Grant Number JPMJCR21M1, Japan.

References

1. Kim, D., Park, S.: A study on face masking scheme in video surveillance system. In: Tenth International Conference on Ubiquitous and Future Networks (ICUFN 2018), pp. 871–873 (2018)
2. Crețu, A.M., Monti, F., Marrone, S., et al.: Interaction data are identifiable even across long periods of time. Nat. Commun. **13**, 313 (2022). https://doi.org/10.1038/s41467-021-27714-6
3. Viola, P., Jones, M.: Rapid object detection using a boosted cascade of simple features. In: Proceedings Computer Vision and Pattern Recognition (CVPR 2001), pp. I-511–I-518 (2001)
4. Shakhnarovich, G., Viola, P., Moghaddam, B.: A unified learning framework for real time face detection and classification. In: Proceedings of the Automatic Face and Gesture Recognition (FG 2002) (2002)
5. Viola, P., Jones, M.: Robust real-time face detection. Int. J. Comput. Vis. (IJCV) **57**(2), 134–157 (2004)
6. Simonyan, K., Zissserman, A.: Very deep convolutional networks for large-scale image recognition. In: ICLR 2014, pp. 1409–1556 (2014)
7. Wang, J., Li, Z.: Research on face recognition based on CNN. In: IOP Conference Series: Earth and Environmental Science, vol. 170, no. 3 (2018)
8. Kazemi, V., Sullivan, J.: One millisecond face alignment with an ensemble of regression trees. In: The IEEE Conference on Computer Vision and Pattern Recognition (CVPR), pp. 1867–1874 (2014)
9. Preis, J., Kessel, M., Werner, M., Linnhoff-Popien, C.: Gait recognition with Kinect. In: Proceedings of the First Workshop on Kinect in Pervasive Computing (2012)
10. Han, J., Bhanu, B.: Individual recognition using gait energy image. IEEE Trans. Pattern Anal. Mach. Intell. **28**(2), 316–322 (2006)
11. Bakchy, S.C., Islam, M.R., Sayeed, A.: Human identification on the basis of gait analysis using Kohonen self-organizing mapping technique. In: 2nd International Conference on Electrical, Computer and Telecommunication Engineering (ICECTE), pp. 1–4 (2016)
12. Shiraga, K., Makihara, Y., Muramatsu, D., Echigo, T., Yagi, Y.: GEINet: view-invariant gait recognition using a convolutional neural network. In: 2016 International Conference on Biometrics (ICB), pp. 1–8 (2016)
13. Amos, B., Ludwiczuk, B., Satyanarayanan, M.: OpenFace: a general- purpose face recognition library with mobile applications. Technical report, CMU School of Computer Science, CMU-CS-16-118 (2016)
14. MicroSoft. Kinect v2 library for Processing (2016). https://github.com/ThomasLengeling/KinectPV2
15. Berndt, D.J., Clifford, J.: Using dynamic time warping to find patterns in time series. In: The Third International Conference on Knowledge Discovery and Data Mining, pp. 359–370 (1994)

16. Amosa, T.I., et al.: Multi-camera multi-object tracking: a review of current trends and future advances. Neurocomputing **552** (2023)

17. Mori, T., Kikuchi, H.: Person tracking based on gait features from depth sensors. In: The 21st International Conference on Network-Based Information Systems (NBiS-2018), vol. 22, pp. 743–751 (2018)

18. Mori, T., Kikuchi, H.: Robust person identification based on DTW distance of multiple-joint gait pattern. In: Mori, P., Furnell, S., Camp, O. (eds.) Proceedings of the 5th International Conference on Information Systems Security and Privacy, ICISSP 2019, pp. 221–229 (2019)

19. Wang, H., Xie, S., Hong, Y.: VideoDP: a flexible platform for video analytics with differential privacy. Proc. Priv. Enhancing Technol. **2020**(4), 277–296 (2020)

20. Cao, Z., Hidalgo, G., Simon, T., Wei, S.-E., Sheikh, Y.: OpenPose: realtime multi-person 2D pose estimation using part affinity fields. IEEE Trans. Pattern Anal. Mach. Intell. **43**(1), 172–186 (2021)

21. Espitia-Contreras, A., Sanchez-Caiman, P., Uribe-Quevedo, A.: Development of a Kinect-based anthropometric measurement application. In: 2014 IEEE Virtual Reality (VR), pp. 71–72 (2014). https://doi.org/10.1109/VR.2014.6802056

22. Booij, M.M., et al.: Dynamic time warp analysis of individual symptom trajectories in depressed patients treated with electroconvulsive therapy. J. Affect. Disord. **293**, 435–443 (2021). https://doi.org/10.1016/j.jad.2021.06.068

23. Tang, J., Cheng, H., Zhao, Y., Guo, H.: Structured dynamic time warping for continuous hand trajectory gesture recognition. Pattern Recogn. **80**, 21–31 (2018). https://doi.org/10.1016/j.patcog.2018.02.011

24. Martınez-Felez, R., Alberto-Mollineda, R., Salvador-Sanchez, J.: Gender classification from pose-based GEIs. In: Proceedings of the Computer Vision and Graphics (ICCVG), pp. 501–508 (2012)

25. Barra, P., Bisogni, C., Nappi, M., Freire-Obregón, D., Castrillón-Santana, M.: Gender classification on 2D human skeleton. In: 2019 3rd International Conference on Bio-engineering for Smart Technologies (BioSMART), pp. 1–4 (2019). https://doi.org/10.1109/BIOSMART.2019.8734198

26. Bewes, J., Low, A., Morphett, A., Pate, F.D., Henneberg, M.: Artificial intelligence for sex determination of skeletal remains: application of a deep learning artificial neural network to human skulls. J. Forensic Leg. Med. **62**, 40–43 (2019)

27. Hukkelås, H., Mester, R., Lindseth, F.: DeepPrivacy: a generative adversarial network for face anonymization. In: Bebis, G., et al. (eds.) ISVC 2019. LNCS, vol. 11844, pp. 565–578. Springer, Cham (2019). https://doi.org/10.1007/978-3-030-33720-9_44

28. Liu, J., Shahroudy, A., Perez, M., Wang, G., Duan, L.-Y., Kot, A.C.: NTU RGB+D 120: a large-scale benchmark for 3D human activity understanding. IEEE Trans. Pattern Anal. Mach. Intell. (TPAMI) **42**, 2684–2701 (2019)

29. Martinez, J., Hossain, R., Romero, J., Little, J.J.: A simple yet effective baseline for 3D human pose estimation. In: ICCV, pp. 2640–2649 (2017)

30. Ten Holt, G.A., Reinders, M.J.T., Hendriks, E.A.: Multi-dimensional dynamic time warping for gesture recognition. In: Thirteenth Annual Conference of the Advanced School for Computing and Imaging (2007)

31. Muaaz, M., Mayrhofer, R.: Smartphone-based gait recognition: from authentication to imitation. IEEE Trans. Mob. Comput. **16**(11), 3209–3221 (2017)

32. European Parliament, Council of the European Union. General Data Protection Regulation (2016). https://eur-lex.europa.eu/eli/reg/2016/679/oj)

33. California Consumer Privacy Act of 2018. Civil Code, Division 3, Part 4, Title 1.81.5 (2020). https://leginfo.legislature.ca.gov/faces/codes_displayText.xhtml?lawCode=CIV&division=3.&title=1.81.5.&part=4.&chapter=&article=

34. Mishra, R.: Persuasive boundary point based face detection using normalized edge detection in regular expression face morphing. In: 2023 International Conference on Distributed Computing and Electrical Circuits and Electronics (ICDCECE), Ballar, India, pp. 1–4 (2023)
35. Wong, S.W., Chiu, Y.C., Tsai, C.Y.: A real-time affordance-based object pose estimation approach for robotic grasp pose estimation. In: 2023 International Conference on System Science and Engineering (ICSSE), Ho Chi Minh, Vietnam, pp. 614–619 (2023)

Evaluating Image Similarity Using Contextual Information of Images with Pre-trained Models

Juyeon Kim[1], Sungwon Park[2,3], Byunghoon Park[3], and B. Sooyeon Shin[4(✉)]

[1] Sorbonne University, Paris, France
juyeon.kim@etu.sorbonne-universite.fr
[2] Korea University, Sejong, South Korea
apcm05@korea.ac.kr
[3] T3Q Co., Ltd., Seoul, South Korea
warmpark@t3q.com
[4] Center for Creative Convergence Education, Hanyang University,
Seoul, South Korea
shinsy@hanyang.ac.kr

Abstract. This study proposes an integrated approach to image similarity measurement by extending traditional methods that concentrate on local features to incorporate global information. Global information, including background, colors, spatial representation, and object relations, can leverage the ability to distinguish similarity based on the overall context of an image using natural process techniques. We employ Video-LLaMA model to extract textual descriptions of images through question prompts, and apply cosine similarity metrics, BERTScore, to quantify image similarities. We conduct experiments on images of the same and different topics using various pre-trained language model configurations. To validate the coherence of the generated text descriptions with the actual theme of the image, we generate images using DALL-E 2 and evaluate them using human judgement. Key findings demonstrate the effectiveness of pre-trained language models in distinguishing between images depicting similar and different topics with a clear gap in similarity.

Keywords: Vision language · Image similarity · Natural language processing · Computer Vision · Vision Transformer · Large language model

1 Introduction

Vision language models integrate both vision and language modalities in a single model, enabling the processing of images and natural language texts. They find application in diverse tasks, including visual question answering and image captioning [2].

S. Bouzefrane et al. (Eds.): MSPN 2023, LNCS 14482, pp. 188–204, 2024.
https://doi.org/10.1007/978-3-031-52426-4_13

The field of image understanding and representation has witnessed significant advancements, with notable approaches including Convolutional Neural Networks (CNNs) and Vision Transformers (ViT). CNNs are known for their deep architecture, capable of detecting diverse image features through filter operations. ViT, alternatively, partitions images into patches and processes them as sequences, employing multi-layer transformers for efficient feature extraction. In the domain of large language models, Video-LLaMA merges language and vision understanding through its Vision-Language Branch, featuring a pre-trained image encoder and contextualising temporal information. BERT stands out for its contextual interpretation of text, leveraging transformers with self-attention to capture rich contextual information within the text.

Our research primarily aims to use the vision transformer's image understanding capabilities and combine them with text generated by language models to compute image similarities. This paper is organised as follows. We review some important studies on image understanding methods related to our methodology in Sect. 2. Section 3 presents our methods based on Video-LLaMA and BERTScore (Sect. 3.1) and our approach to generate image descriptions with contextual global information (Sect. 3.2) and measure image similarity scores (Sect. 3.3). Section 4 presents the experimental setup of the image dataset (Sect. 4.1) and its procedures (Sect. 4.2). The results of our experiment are presented in Sect. 5: images of the same topic in Sect. 5.1 and different topics in Sect. 5.2. A comparison of the pre-trained language models is discussed in Sect. 5.3. Finally, we conclude our study and provide prospects for future advancements in image similarity in Sect. 6.

2 Related Works

CNN. Convolutional neural networks (CNN) [3] consist of multiple layers, each dedicated to detecting distinct image features. Various filters with different resolutions are applied to the training images, and the output from each convolutional layer serves as the input for the subsequent layer. Filters are used to detect special patterns, such as brightness and boundaries, in an image by detecting changes in the intensity values of the image. They allow the network to learn the hierarchical representations of the input image. By stacking multiple convolutional layers with different filters, CNNs can learn increasingly complex features of the input image, leading to a higher accuracy in image recognition tasks.

ViT. In Vision Transformer (ViT) [4], input images are partitioned into fixed-size patches, with each patch undergoing tokenization. These tokenized patches are constructed as sequences and subjected to linear embedding before their incorporation into the transformer model. This contrasts with CNNs, which directly use raw pixel values. Within the ViT architecture, the transformer model comprises multiple encoder layers. Each encoder unit comprises multi-head self-attention and Multi-Layer Perceptron (MLP) blocks. Layer normalisation was uniformly applied to all the blocks, with residual connections introduced following each block. This design empowers ViT to discern the intricate hierarchical features within the input images. Upon traversing the transformer encoders, the initial vector of the encoder's terminal output plays a crucial role in classification. This vector is directed through an MLP Head that features a single hidden layer for classification tasks. During fine-tuning, it traverses a single linear layer, instead of the aforementioned MLP head. ViT's strategy of image partitioning into patches and subsequent treatment as sequential data has been shown as a computationally efficient and accurate approach compared to CNNs.

Video-LLaMA. In prior research efforts, Large Language Models (LLMs) have been trained with varying parameters, ranging from 7 billion to 65 billion. The Vision-Language Branch within the architecture of Video-LLaMA [6] is designed to allow LLMs to understand visual content. This branch consists of a frozen pre-trained image encoder, which is fixed and extracts features from video frames (see Fig. 1). In addition, a position embedding layer was employed to inject temporal information into the video frames. The video Q-former shares architectural similarities with the query transformer (Q-former) used in BLIP-2 [7]. This process results in a video embedding vector that encapsulates the representations of the input video. To ensure compatibility with the language model, a linear layer is introduced, which transforms the video embedding vector into a video query vector of the same dimensions as the LLM's text embedding. During the Forward Pass, a video soft prompt establishes a connection between the input text embedding and frozen LLM, guiding it to generate contextually relevant text based on the video content. In the implementation of the Vision-Language Branch, the visual components of the pre-trained BLIP-2 model serve as a frozen visual encoder. This includes ViT-G/14 from EVAPLIP and pre-trained Q-formers. Notably, the remaining components, such as the position embedding layers, video Q-formers, and linear layers, are initialized randomly and subsequently optimised to seamlessly integrate with the frozen LLM.

BERT Contextual Interpretation. BERT, or Bidirectional Encoder Representations from Transformers [8], relies on contextual embeddings to process input. Initially, input tokens are transformed into embedding vectors, where the dimensionality of these vectors, known as d_{model}, serves as an input for BERT. These embedding vectors are computed for each word in the input sequence following internal operations. The resulting output embeddings in BERT encapsulate contextual information that extends across the entire sentence, referencing all words within the context. This process, in which each word interacts with every other word, is achieved through a self-attention mechanism. In essence, BERT's use of contextual embeddings and the self-attention mechanism across its transformer encoder layers enables it to capture and represent the contextual nuances of input text comprehensively, yielding output embeddings that reflect the context of the entire textual input.

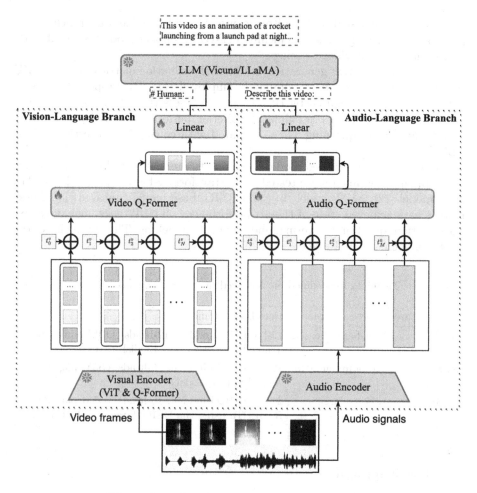

Fig. 1. Overall architecture of Video-LLaMA [6]

3 Methods

In this section, we detail our methodology, starting with an overview of our approach for generating textual image descriptions and computing image similarity scores.

3.1 Video-LLaMA and BERTScore Methodology

The Video-LLaMA [6] framework consists of two integral components: the Vision-Language and Audio-Language branches. For the scope of this paper, we focus solely on the elements within the Vision-Language (VL) branch. Our specific interest lies in comparing images and text. Video-LLaMA, as a multimodal framework, is designed to enhance language models with the ability to understand both visual and auditory content in videos. The VL branch uses a pre-trained image encoder, specifically ViT-G/14 [5], to encode visual information from the input video or image.

In the context of text generation, traditional evaluation metrics such as BLEU [10] and ROUGE have been commonly employed [11]. We propose the use of automated metrics inspired by BERTScore to assess the quality of text generation. Notably, BERTScore exhibited superior performance in machine translation and image captioning when compared with conventional metrics such as BLEU [1].

We employ a pre-trained model to encode the reference and candidate input texts. In our experiments, we tested three transformer-based models, RoBERTa large model [13], XLM model [14], and BERT base model (uncased) [8]. These models have achieved state-of-the-art performance on NLP tasks, including text classification, question answering, and language modelling. The specificity of the models is included in Table 1.

Table 1. Pre-trained models used in our experiments [14, 16]

Architecture	Shortcut name	Details of the model
BERT	bert-base-uncased	12-layer, 768-hidden, 12-heads, 110M parameters Trained on lower-cased English text
XLM	xlm-mlm-en-2048	12-layer, 2048-hidden, 16-heads, 665M parameters XLM English model
RoBERTa	roberta-large	24-layer, 1024-hidden, 16-heads, 355M parameters RoBERTa using the BERT-large architecture

3.2 Our Approach

The proposed system follows the architecture of Video-LLaMA as illustrated in Fig. 2. The procedure begins with the input of a reference image, which is transformed into vectors using the Video-LLaMA image encoder, resulting in representations of specific dimensions. In the initial stage, the user poses a single question prompt for all input images. Subsequently, the model generates a descriptive text output containing contextual information regarding the image. We repeat the same process for the candidate image using the contextual information generated from both the reference and the candidate images to calculate cosine similarity.

BERTScore, introduced by Zhang et al. (2020) [1], was initially designed to evaluate machine translation outputs and image captioning. The core concept in BERTScore involves encoding the candidate and reference separately using a BERT-based model, and assigning a score based on the similarity between individual encoded tokens. Each word in the reference sentence is compared for cosine similarity with all the words in the candidate sentence, constituting the 'reference and candidate token-pair' evaluation mechanism. BERTScore leverages BERT to generate contextualised word representations. Our approach generally aligns with that of BERTScore.

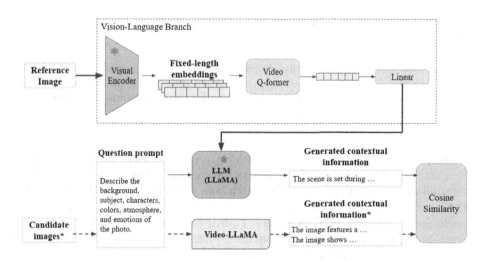

Fig. 2. Illustration of our approach.

3.3   Similarity Measure and Score

Given a reference sentence $x = \{x_1, \ldots, x_n\}$ and a candidate sentence $\hat{x} = \{\hat{x_1}, \ldots, \hat{x_m}\}$, we employ contextual embeddings to represent the tokens. We use different models and tokenizers according to each model. Matching is computed through cosine similarity as illustrated in Fig. 3.

The cosine similarity calculation between the encoded reference and encoded candidate tokens, as described by Zhang et al. (2020) [1], is expressed as: $sim(x_i, \hat{x}_i) = \frac{\mathbf{x}_i^\top \cdot \hat{\mathbf{x}}_j}{||\mathbf{x}_i|| \cdot ||\hat{\mathbf{x}}_j||}$. Although this involves a comparison of individual tokens x_i and $\hat{x}_i$, their vector representations $\mathbf{x_i}$ and $\hat{\mathbf{x}}_j$ encapsulate contextual information.

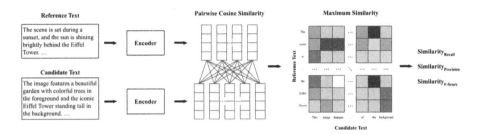

Fig. 3. Illustration of the similarity scores computation: when provided with the reference text x and candidate $\hat{x}$, we calculate BERT embeddings and pairwise cosine similarity. We proceed with greedy matching, choosing the maximum value from both rows and columns of the similarity matrix. [1].

To calculate the similarity score recall S_R, we match each token in the reference text x to its corresponding token in the candidate text $\hat{x}$ and to calculate the similarity score precision S_P, we match each token in the candidate text $\hat{x}$ to its corresponding token in the reference text x. We use a greedy matching approach, pairing each token with its most similar counterpart in another sentence. The F-score is then computed by combining precision and recall. We apply these techniques using the following equations:

$$S_R = \frac{1}{|x|} \sum_{x_i \in x} \max_{\hat{x}_j \in \hat{x}} \mathbf{x}_i^\top \hat{\mathbf{x}}_j, S_P = \frac{1}{|\hat{x}|} \sum_{\hat{x}_j \in \hat{x}} \max_{x_i \in x} \mathbf{x}_i^\top \hat{\mathbf{x}}_j, S_F = 2\frac{S_P \cdot S_R}{S_P + S_R} \quad (1)$$

We observe that the computed scores are confined to a narrow range. To enhance the score readability, following Zhang et al. (2020) [1], we proceed with min-max normalisation. We use the experimental lower threshold b and upper threshold h to linearly rescale S_R. For example, the normalised value $\hat{S_R}$ of S_R is:

$$\hat{S_R} = \frac{S_R - b}{h - b} \quad (2)$$

Following this process, the scores typically fell within the range of 0 to 1. We apply the identical procedure to both S_P and S_F.

4   Experiments

For our experiment, we used Video-LLaMA Demo [6] to process the collected image dataset. By posing questions using the Video-LLaMA Demo prompt, we obtained text-based answers. We then employed BERTScore to assess the textual outputs in terms of their relevance to original image themes. In addition, we explored the possibility of transforming text-based descriptions back into images resembling the originals using the DALL-E 2 model. This enabled a comparative analysis of the original and generated images based on subjective assessment.

4.1   Data Collection and Preparation

Before data collection, we chose five image topics to compute the image similarity scores. We then sourced image data related to these five topics from Kaggle [15] and curated a dataset consisting of 25 images, which are provided in Table 2.

Table 2. Topics of image dataset.

Theme	Topic
1. Sculpture	Eiffel Tower
2. Animal	Butterfly
3. Human Activity	Eating Ice Cream
4. Landscape	Rainbow
5. History	Pyramid

4.2   Procedures

Question Prompt for Video-LLaMA. Upon feeding the images into the Video-LLaMA model, we presented a single question: "Describe the background, subject, characters, colors, atmosphere, and emotions of the photo.". This question was posed collectively for all images, aiming to capture the overall context of each image, including the typical elements found in such visuals. The formulation of this prompt aims to encapsulate contextual details from the visual attributes of the object or event, covering elements like color, and the overall description of the scene [12].

DALL-E 2 Text-to-Image Transformation. To validate the text generated by Video-LLaMA, we employed DALL-E 2, a text-to-image conversion model. Considering text length constraints (540 characters and 76 words), we used a segment of the original text output from Video-LLaMA to generate corresponding images.

Comparison of DALL-E 2 Generated Images with Originals. We compared the images generated by DALL-E 2 with the original images by using direct human judgement to evaluate the fidelity and accuracy of the generated images. The process is illustrated in Fig. 4.

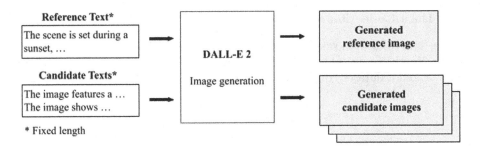

Fig. 4. Illustration of validation process using DALL-E 2

Cosine Similarity Analysis. The text outputs are compared to the corresponding image themes using cosine similarity, allowing us to quantify the alignment between the generated descriptions and the expected themes. This study investigates contextual embedding models that create embeddings at various layers within an encoder network. Prior research by Liu et al. (2019) [9] has highlighted the efficacy of intermediate layers for semantic tasks. We adopted the recommended representation layer for the similarity score, a selection made using the validation set outlined in prior studies by Zhang et al. (2020) [1], namely, the WMT16 dataset.

5   Results

The results of our experiments are described in detail in the following sections. Initially, we compared images within the same topic, followed by a comparison of images across different topics.

5.1   Images of the Same Topic

We show three sample images centered around the Eiffel Tower, as presented in Fig. 5.

Generated Image Descriptions

Question: Describe the background, subject, characters, colors, atmosphere, and emotions of the photo.

Reference Image 0 (Fig. 5a): The background of the image is the Eiffel Tower at night. The tower is lit up in the colors of the French flag, red, white, and blue. The fountains in front of the tower are also lit up in the same colors. The atmosphere of the image is romantic and beautiful. The emotions of the image are awe and wonder at the sight of the Eiffel Tower lit up in the colors of the French flag.

(a) Reference image 0   (b) Candidate image 1   (c) Candidate image 2

Fig. 5. Reference and candidate images of Eiffel Tower (Color figure online)

Candidate Image 1 (Fig. 5b): The scene is set during a sunset, and the sun is shining brightly behind the Eiffel Tower. The tower appears to be the main focus of the photo, towering over the landscape in front of it. There is a car parked in the foreground, with two cars visible to the left of the Eiffel Tower, and two cars visible to the right of it. Additionally, there are two bird silhouettes present in the scene, one on the right and one on the left of the tower. The overall atmosphere is serene and peaceful, with the golden sunset illuminating the Eiffel Tower and the surrounding area. There is no indication of any people or other objects in the scene, but one might imagine the tower attracting crowds of tourists and locals to admire its beauty.

Candidate Image 2 (Fig. 5c): The image features a beautiful garden with colorful trees in the foreground and the iconic Eiffel Tower standing tall in the background. The Eiffel Tower is an iron tower located in Paris, France, and it is an iconic landmark known throughout the world. It is a symbol of romance and Parisian culture, attracting millions of visitors annually. The garden is well-maintained with green grass, providing an ideal setting for a leisurely stroll. A path leads the viewer through the garden, making it easier to enjoy the scenery and take in the beauty of the Eiffel Tower. The trees are decorated with leaves of varying hues, adding to the vibrant and colorful atmosphere. The scene is peaceful, allowing visitors to relax and enjoy the surrounding beauty.

DALL-E 2 Input Text and Generated Images
We verified the context2image using images from the same topic.

Generated Image of Reference 0 (Fig. 6a): The background of the image is the Eiffel Tower at night. The tower is lit up in the colors of the French flag, red, white, and blue. The fountains in front of the tower are also lit up in the same colors. The atmosphere of the image is romantic and beautiful. The emotions of the image are awe and wonder at the sight of the Eiffel Tower lit up in the colors of the French flag.

Generated Image of Candidate 1 (Fig. 6b): The scene is set during a sunset, and the sun is shining brightly behind the Eiffel Tower. The tower appears to be the main focus of the photo, towering over the landscape in front of it. There is a car parked in the foreground, with two cars visible to the left of the Eiffel Tower, and two cars visible to the right of it. Additionally, there are two bird silhouettes present in the scene, one on the right and one on the left of the tower.

Generated Image of Candidate 2 (Fig. 6c): The image features a beautiful garden with colorful trees in the foreground and the iconic Eiffel Tower standing tall in the background. The Eiffel Tower is an iron tower located in Paris, France, and it is an iconic landmark known throughout the world. It is a symbol of romance and Parisian culture, attracting millions of visitors annually. The garden is well-maintained with green grass, providing an ideal setting for a leisurely stroll. A path leads the viewer through.

(a) New Eiffel Tower 1-1   (b) New Eiffel Tower 1-2   (c) New Eiffel Tower 1-3

Fig. 6. Generated image outputs from DALL-E 2 (Color figure online)

5.2   Images of Different Topics

In this context, we illustrate our comparative analysis by juxtaposing images Fig. 7) from four different topics with the reference image of the Eiffel Tower.

Generated Image Descriptions

Question: Describe the background, subject, characters, colors, atmosphere, and emotions of the photo.

Butterfly (Fig. 7a): The background of the image is a pink flower garden with white and purple pink flowers. The subject of the image is a black butterfly sitting on a pink flower with its wings open, showcasing its vibrant colors. The colors used in the image are primarily pink and purple, with the butterfly's wings and the flowers being the most prominent. The atmosphere of the image is peaceful and serene, with the butterfly appearing to be in a state of contemplation as it rests on the flower. The emotions conveyed in the image are serenity and tranquility.

Eating Ice Cream (Fig. 7b): The scene features a young girl wearing a white dress, standing in a park, eating a green and white ice cream cone. The ice

(a) Butterfly   (b) Eating ice cream

(c) Rainbow   (d) Pyramid of Djoser

Fig. 7. Images of different topics: Butterfly, Eating ice-cream, Rainbow, Pyramid (Color figure online)

cream cone stands out from her dress due to its bright color, and the contrast is visually appealing. Her expression shows she is delighted, possibly tasting a flavor she enjoys. In the background, there is a building or structure, possibly an amusement park, providing an entertaining setting for the girl to enjoy her ice cream.

Rainbow (Fig. 7c): The scene features an incredible double rainbow over a beach, accompanied by some trees and sand. The rainbow seems to have started just a few seconds ago, with a beautiful arc of colors spanning the horizon. It appears that the sunset has started, creating a warm and serene atmosphere in the scene. The rainbow is visibly captivating the beachgoers' attention, bringing a sense of wonder and delight to the picture. The colors of the rainbow, combined with the sunset, make the scene very pleasant, making it a momentous and memorable sight for those present.

Pyramid (Fig. 7d): The image shows the ruins of a large stone structure, which appears to be a pyramid. The structure is made of large, rough stone blocks and is surrounded by sand dunes in the desert. The pyramid has several chambers and entrances, and it appears to be in a state of disrepair. There are no people or animals in the image. The atmosphere is arid and desolate, with the only vegetation in the image being the small shrubs and cacti that can be seen growing around the base of the pyramid. The emotions conveyed in the image are of awe and reverence for the ancient structure.

DALL-E 2 Input Text and Generated Images
We verified the context2image using images from the different topics.

(a) Generated Butterfly   (b) Generated Eating ice cream

(c) Generated Rainbow   (d) Generated Pyramid of Djoser

Fig. 8. Generated image outputs from DALL-E 2 (Images of different topics): Butterfly, Eating ice-cream, Rainbow, Pyramid (Color figure online)

Generated Image of Butterfly (Fig. 8a): The background of the image is a pink flower garden with white and purple pink flowers. The subject of the image is a black butterfly sitting on a pink flower with its wings open, showcasing its vibrant colors. The colors used in the image are primarily pink and purple, with the butterfly's wings and the flowers being the most prominent. The atmosphere of the image is peaceful and serene, with the butterfly appearing to be in a state of contemplation as it rests on the flower.

Generated Image of Eating Ice Cream (Fig. 8b): The scene features a young girl wearing a white dress, standing in a park, eating a green and white ice cream cone. The ice cream cone stands out from her dress due to its bright color, and the contrast is visually appealing. Her expression shows she is delighted, possibly tasting a flavor she enjoys. In the background, there is a building or structure, possibly an amusement park, providing an entertaining setting for the girl to enjoy her ice cream.

Generated Image of Rainbow (Fig. 8c): The scene features an incredible double rainbow over a beach, accompanied by some trees and sand. The rainbow seems to have started just a few seconds ago, with a beautiful arc of colors spanning the horizon. It appears that the sunset has started, creating a warm and

serene atmosphere in the scene. The rainbow is visibly captivating the beachgoers' attention, bringing a sense of wonder and delight to the picture. The colors
of the rainbow, combined with the sunset.

Generated Image of Pyramid (Fig. 8d): The image shows the ruins of a
large stone structure, which appears to be a pyramid. The structure is made of
large, rough stone blocks and is surrounded by sand dunes in the desert. The
pyramid has several chambers and entrances, and it appears to be in a state of
disrepair. There are no people or animals in the image. The atmosphere is arid
and desolate, with the only vegetation in the image being the small shrubs and
cacti that can be seen growing around the base of the pyram.

5.3 Comparison of Language Models

Our experiment involves two sets of images for the comparison of language models: Eiffel Tower images, representing similarity, and images depicting the act
of eating ice cream, representing dissimilarity to the Eiffel Tower. To assess the
image similarity, we leveraged specific pre-trained models, which are detailed in
Table 1.

For English text generation evaluation, the recommended choice is the
24-layer RoBERTa-large model for computing BERTSCORE [1]. BERT-base-
uncased is the base model of the BERT language model, and is learned with
little data [8]. Xlm-mlm-en-2048 performs well in cross-lingual classification, and
supervised and unsupervised machine translation. [14] We computed similarity
scores of the images of the same topic and different topic scores in three BERT
language models.

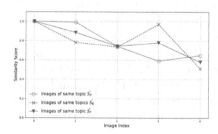
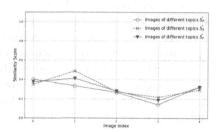

(a) Images of the same topic: five images of Eiffel Tower compared to the
reference image of Eifel Tower with image index 0

(b) Images of different topics: five candidate images of Eating ice cream compared to the reference image of Eiffel
Tower

Fig. 9. Rescaled similarity scores with RoBERTa-large. Each image index corresponds
to an individual image within the dataset.

For RoBERTa-large (Fig. 9), images of the same topic showed a score of 0.5 or
higher, and 0.4 or lower for images of different topics. Using BERT-base-uncased,

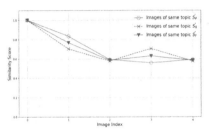

(a) Images of same topic with BERT-base-uncased

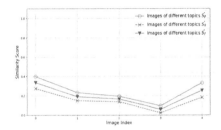

(b) Images of different topics with BERT-base-uncased

Fig. 10. Rescaled similarity scores with BERT-base-uncased

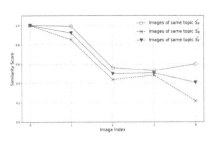

(a) Images of same topic with xlm-mlm-en-2048

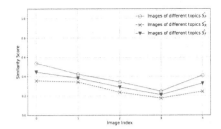

(b) Images of different topics with xlm-mlm-en-2048

Fig. 11. Rescaled similarity scores with xlm-mlm-en-2048

we found that the similarity scores were above 0.6 for images considered as the same topic, and below 0.4 for images from various topics after rescaling, as shown in Fig. 10. For xlm-mlm-en-2048 shown in Fig. 11, scores for images of the same topic range from 0.2 to 1.0, whereas images of different topics receive scores of 0.6 or lower. Unlike other models, the score data for both the same topic and different topic images make it challenging to discern the relationship between the images. The language model that exhibits the most distinguishable image similarity scores among the experimental models is bert-base-uncased.

5.4   Comparison of Topics

With bert-base-uncased, we compared the F1 Similarity Score $\hat{S}_F$ for images of the same topic and different topics, as illustrated in Fig. 12. The comparison involved 25 images across five topics from our dataset, with each image index corresponding to a unique image of its topic. The Eiffel Tower, represented as a hollow circle ○, serves as the reference at an image index of 0. Similarity scores between the reference image and other Eiffel Tower images are plotted along the solid line. We repeated the comparison using the same Eiffel Tower reference image with images of different topics as candidate images, for example, the Butterfly topic represented as 'x' along the dashed lines, the Eating ice cream topic in ●, Rainbow in ▽, Pyramid in △.

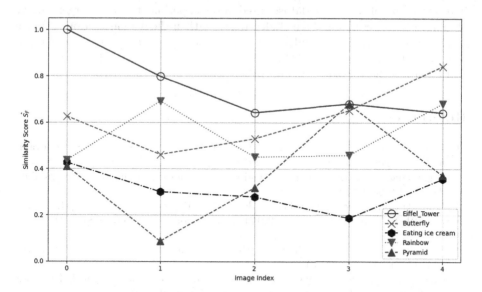

Fig. 12. Comparison of different topics (bert-base-uncased) with Fig. 5a as the reference image represented at image index 0 in ○.

We observed a cosine similarity score of 0.6 or higher for images categorised as the same topic, whereas scores below 0.6 indicated different topics. However, outliers exist where images of different topics score higher than 0.6. At image index 3, where a consistent similarity score is observed, we noticed shared information among images of the Eiffel Tower and the Pyramid. This shared information includes details about the blue sky, architectural structures, and a variety of colors depicted in all three images of the Eiffel Tower, the Butterfly, and the Pyramid. Further experiments using larger image datasets and varied rescaling techniques with different models are essential to comprehensively examine and address these cases.

6   Conclusion

We introduced an integrated approach that efficiently calculates image similarities by harnessing the capabilities of vision transformers and language models. Using BERTScore and Video-LLaMA, we extracted textual descriptions through question prompts, experimented with diverse pre-trained language model configurations, and quantified similarities with cosine similarity metrics. Our results highlight the effectiveness of specific pre-trained language models in distinguishing between images of the same and different topics, revealing a clear gap in similarity scores. We verified the coherence of the generated text by generating images using DALL-E 2 from the original image descriptions and subsequently comparing the generated images with the originals. However, this study is limited by the size of the image dataset used in the experiments, and a larger variety of image categories should be included to strengthen the demonstration of image similarity score. To further enhance our approach, we will explore various question prompts and diverse BERTScore models, optimise layers within each model, and integrate the similarity computations within Video-LLaMA.

References

1. Zhang, T., Kishore, V., Wu, F., Weinberger, K.Q., Artzi, Y.: BERTScore: evaluating text generation with BERT (2019)
2. Huggingface blog. https://huggingface.co/blog/vision_language_pretraining. Accessed 8 Sept 2023
3. Kim, P.: Convolutional neural network. In: Kim, P. (ed.) MATLAB Deep Learning, pp. 121–147. Apress, Berkeley (2017). https://doi.org/10.1007/978-1-4842-2845-6_6
4. Dosovitskiy, A., et al.: An image is worth 16×16 words: transformers for image recognition at scale (2020)
5. Zhai, X., et al.: Scaling vision transformers. In: Proceedings of the IEEE/CVF Conference on Computer Vision and Pattern Recognition (2022)
6. Zhang, H., Li, X., Bing, L.: Video-llama: an instruction-tuned audio-visual language model for video understanding (2023)
7. Li, J., et al.: Blip-2: bootstrapping language-image pre-training with frozen image encoders and large language models (2023). https://doi.org/10.48550/arXiv.2301.12597
8. Devlin, J., et al. BERT: pre-training of deep bidirectional transformers for language understanding (2018)
9. Liu, N.F., et al.: Linguistic knowledge and transferability of contextual representations (2019). https://doi.org/10.18653/v1/N19-1112
10. Papineni, K., Roukos, S., Ward, T., Zhu, W.-J.: Bleu: a method for automatic evaluation of machine translation. In: Proceedings of the 40th Annual Meeting of the Association for Computational Linguistics, Philadelphia, Pennsylvania, USA, pp. 311–318. Association for Computational Linguistics (2002). https://doi.org/10.3115/1073083.1073135
11. Eddine, M.K., et al.: FrugalScore: learning cheaper, lighter, and faster evaluation metrics for automatic text generation. In: Proceedings of the 60th Annual Meeting of the Association for Computational Linguistics (Volume 1: Long Papers) (2022)
12. Wang, X., Zhu, Z.: Context understanding in computer vision: a survey. Comput. Vis. Image Understanding **229** (2023)
13. Liu, Y., et al.: RoBERTa: a robustly optimized BERT pretraining approach (2019)
14. Lample, G., Conneau, A.: Cross-lingual language model pretraining (2019)
15. Griffin, G., Holub, A.D., Perona, P.: Caltech 256 Image Dataset
16. Huggingface docs, pre-trained models. https://huggingface.co/transformers/v3.4.0/pretrained_models.html

AI vs. Dinosaurs – Automated Re-implementation of Legacy Mainframe Applications in Java by Combining Program Synthesis and GPT

Simon Fischer-Heselhaus[1] and Philipp Brune[1,2(✉)] [iD]

[1] SQ Solutions GmbH, Platz der Einheit 2, 60327 Frankfurt am Main, Germany
Simon.Fischer@sq-solutions.de
[2] Neu-Ulm University of Applied Sciences, Wileystraße 1, 89231 Neu-Ulm, Germany
Philipp.Brune@hnu.de
https://sq-solutions.de, https://hnu.de

Abstract. Large-scale mainframe applications written in outdated languages such as COBOL still form the core of the enterprise IT in many organizations, even though their flexibility and maintainability declines continuously. Their manual re-implementation in modern languages like Java is usually economically not feasible. Automated code conversion of legacy programs usually produces poor quality code in the target language, even with recent AI tools such as ChatGPT. In addition, code conversion recovers dead or unnecessary code artifacts in the new language. Therefore, in this paper we explore a novel approach, which does not convert the legacy code, but instead uses the existing input/output data to generate program tokens through program synthesis. These tokens are subsequently translated into input tokens and submitted to ChatGPT to produce the target code. The approach is illustrated and evaluated by means of a semi-realistic example program. The obtained results look promising, but need to be further investigated.

Keywords: Program Synthesis · Legacy Modernization · AI · COBOL · GPT · Large Language Models

1 Introduction

For many years, possible ways how to deal with the growing amount of program code considered "legacy" is one of the grand challenges of software engineering [21]. State-of-the-art architectures and technologies are often a prerequisite for moving applications to the cloud, create new digital services and business models, and integrate with new technologies like e.g. blockchain or AI [3, 28].

However, modernization of legacy applications remains a big challenge for various reasons. One is the lack of developers who are familiar with its code and have the skills to maintain and update it. This is getting worse when developers

© The Author(s), under exclusive license to Springer Nature Switzerland AG 2024
S. Bouzefrane et al. (Eds.): MSPN 2023, LNCS 14482, pp. 205–221, 2024.
https://doi.org/10.1007/978-3-031-52426-4_14

retire or move to other fields, thus losing their specific knowledge [32]. Another challenge is the lack or inadequacy of documentation [?]. In some extreme cases, even the source code may be missing, meaning that the program cannot be changed at all.

Additionally, legacy code can lead to vendor lock-in. This means that companies are constrained by specific programming languages, platforms, or technologies that were selected in the past. This can make it difficult to switch to more modern technologies or vendors and create additional costs and risks.

Legacy code represents a significant burden for many organizations, and the pressure to transform or migrate such systems continuously grows. One reason is the sheer volume of existing code. It is estimated that there are between 180 and 200 billion lines of such code worldwide [8]. This figure becomes even worse considering that the global code base is growing by billions of lines annually [7].

Automating transformation and reimplementation projects in software development are a major challenge, and many of these projects encounter significant difficulties [28, 33]. One important reason is that many programs depend on proprietary middleware considered outdated today., like e.g., old database systems or transaction monitors.

The use of exotic or less common programming languages can also be an obstacle, as expertise in such languages is scarce, and transformation tools may be lacking. In addition, the quality of legacy code is often already poor, and automated transformation could actually degrade code quality further. In addition, there are concepts related to programming languages that cannot be easily transferred to other programming languages. A typical example is imperative code that cannot be directly transferred to object-oriented programming languages, leading to ineffective code after an automated transformation [29].

However, given the growing amount of legacy code, automated code transformation nevertheless remains an increasingly important topic in research and practice [29]. Manual code transformation is usually both time-consuming and costly [13]. Moreover, it requires specialized knowledge and, for large code bases, can lead to errors that are difficult to detect and fix [3].

Therefore, it is essential to develop more effective tools for automated code transformation to efficiently and cost-effectively transition legacy code into modern systems [13].

Recent advances in large language models (LLM) due to the introduction of generative pretrained transformer (GPT) architectures using attention mechanisms [10, 35], popularized by services like ChatGPT[1], have revolutionized the art of programming and transformed software development in many ways. Despite these advances, there are some restrictions limiting their usefulness for legacy code transformation:

- LLM can translate code, but often do so without a deep understanding of the underlying concept or original purpose [18].
- There is a risk that LLM translate code that may be redundant or no longer have a use in modern systems.

---

[1] https://openai.com.

- Even if LLM are able to translate legacy code, different programming paradigms (e.g., imperative vs. object-oriented) may cause the performance of the transformed code to suffer.
- For a successful code transformation, LLM often require the full source code or specific details from the documentation describing what functions the code should perform.

Instead of LLM, in order to reproduce the relationships between inputs and outputs, deep learning models could be used, but the resulting program surrogate, in the form of a trained neural network, could neither guarantee that inputs always generate the expected outputs, nor is it verifiable or testable [9,27,31].

Therefore, in this paper a hybrid approach is proposed, which combines program synthesis, which can establish relationships between inputs and outputs but does not suffer from the black box problem, and use a LLM to generate the surrounding code.

The rest of this paper is organized as follows: In Sect. 2 the related work is analyzed in more detail. Section 3 describes the proposed solutions, which is experimentally evaluated by applying it to a semi-realistic COBOL program as described in Sect. 4. The results of the evaluation are presented in Sect. 5. We conclude with a summary of our findings.

2   Related Work

Legacy application modernization has been a topic for many years in research and practice [3,15,21,28].

Various approaches to automatic code transformation have been considered in the literature over the years. However, mainly symbolic, rule-based [15] or simple statistical methods have been investigated, mostly also only for restricted problem classes such as clone detection [19,34].

Only few recent works discuss approaches for using ML or AI methods in the context of code analysis or transformation, e.g., again for code clone detection [36–38]. However, approaches that use e.g. new approaches like GPT are missing so far. On the other hand, initiatives such as AI for Code are currently in the process of establishing a basis for such approaches by creating corresponding databases of program code (Codenet) [22].

As only little previous work exists on the use of AI for legacy application modernization, in this paper a novel hybrid approach is proposed, combining the earlier works on program synthesis with the recent LLM breakthrough by ChatGPT.

The theory of program synthesis dates back to the 1950s [11]. It was extensively defined and elaborated in the 1970s. The main problem of program synthesis, to automatically construct programs to match a given specification, has long been a research topic in computer science [4,20,30].

Thanks to increased computing power, the implementation of these ideas is more feasible today. A wide variety of approaches exist in the area of program synthesis, but a unified definition is lacking so far [16,23,40].

The predominant approaches as described by Si et al. [27] can be classified into three types: The **neural approach**, in which pseudocode is generated from input-output examples, the **symbolic approach**, which synthesizes based on specifications, and the **inductive approach**, in which a neural network acts as a surrogate for a program.

In particular, the symbolic approach can be a promising way forward in certain circumstances, but only if the specifications are sufficiently concrete and precise.

In the case of legacy code, as already mentioned, this is often not the case. The inductive approach, on the other hand, confronts researchers and developers with the well-known black box problem and is therefore often not applicable in sectors with extremely strict regulations, such as banking and insurance.

In this work, we focus on the Programming by Example (PBE) approach [39]. Well-known implementations include *RobustFill* (for string analysis), *AlphaRegex* (for regular expression generation), and *DeepCoder* (for integer and integer list analysis).

A particular advantage of program synthesis is evident in the legacy context: Many large corporations, banks, and insurance companies that use legacy code have an extensive database of input-output examples. These IO-based approaches theoretically do not require code. Moreover, they are language-independent and can therefore be applied to different programming languages. Despite the black-box nature of the underlying AI model, the results are editable and validatable [17].

However, there are challenges. These include problems due to "noise" in data [27], difficulties in handling loops [12], limited model availability, and limited mapping capability through Domain Specific Languages (DSL) [23].

Criticism also includes the overuse of synthetic data and the resulting insufficient semantic mastery, as well as limited generalization and accuracy rates [24]. In addition, the models are currently limited to integers, which leads to problems in representing floating point numbers and other data types.

In conclusion, the flexibility of DSL is both an advantage and a challenge. While it can be extended to include arbitrary constructs, an overly elaborate DSL increases model complexity.

All these points illustrate, that program synthesis alone is not sufficient to build a solution for legacy code transformation, which would be useful in practice. However, combining it with the power of LLM, e.g. in the form of ChatGPT, could bring a new quality to it.

Therefore, in this paper the question is addressed, how a combination of an existing approach for program synthesis with ChatGPT for the actual code generation could be applied to transform legacy code to modern languages like e.g. Java, and what could be expected with respect to the quality of the resulting code.

3   Design of the Solution

The functional core of the program candidate to be replaced, and thus the starting point for the LLM query shall be the relationship between input and output established by the program synthesis.

This core shall then be enriched step by step by further information, as illustrated in Fig. 1.

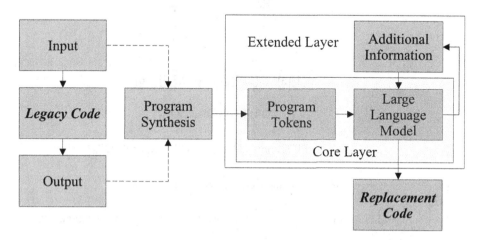

Fig. 1. Hybrid and multi-layered approach, with information generated by program synthesis at the core, enhanced with further information (e.g. embedding in desired framework).

The implementation of program synthesis in a real-world context follows a multistep process. This process can be divided into the following steps, as shown in Fig. 2.

1. **Extraction of inputs and outputs:** First, the necessary inputs and outputs are extracted from the available data.
2. **Generation of data combinations:** A Data Variator is used to generate all possible combinations of inputs and outputs. This allows to identify potential sub-combinations in the data.
3. **Application of program synthesis:** The next step is to perform the actual program synthesis.
4. **Translation to LLM query:** The result of the program synthesis is translated into an LLM query and submitted to the LLM system
5. **Code generation:** Based on the query, the LLM system generates the associated code.
6. **Optimization of query:**
   (a) **Refining:** Optimize the query by adding additional information from source code, comments, documentation and other sources.

(b) **Extension:** For more comprehensive code generation, information about frameworks, interfaces and other relevant aspects are integrated into the query.

This approach ensures a structured and comprehensive approach to program synthesis, generating high-quality and relevant code.

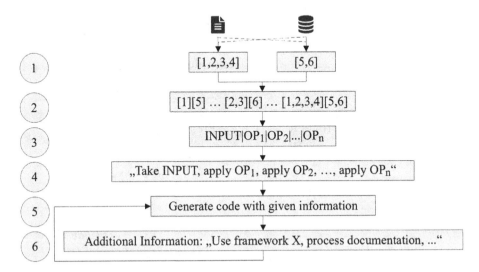

Fig. 2. Procedure to generate code using LLM and program synthesis, restricted to (lists of) integer values from different data sources

Program Synthesis: Per-Example Program Synthesis

PEPS (Per-Example program synthesis) aims to create a pseudo-program p_g that satisfies a set X consisting of N IO examples, each represented as an input-output pair. This program, consisting of T lines, is identified within a specified time limit. The behavior and structure of this program are influenced by a domain-specific language (DSL) originally introduced for DeepCoder [2].

The DSL presented by Balog et al. includes first-order functions such as SORT and REVERSE and higher-order functions such as MAP and FILTER. These functions can handle lambda functions as inputs. The DSL supports both integers and lists of integers as inputs and outputs.

Unlike PCCoder, which is based on a *Global Program Search (GPS)* approach and processes all IO examples simultaneously, N-PEPS implements an approach that handles each example individually. In this approach, PCCoder builds programs incrementally based on a concept of a program state. The state of this program is a $N \times (\nu + 1)$ dimensional memory created by executing t program steps over N inputs. The model consists of two neural components: H_θ and W_ϕ.

While H_θ generates the embedding of the current state, W_ϕ predicts three key variables for the next program line.

The model is trained with multiple instances of the specification X and the actual program p_g. For inference, complete anytime bar search (CAB) is used, stopping either when a solution is reached or when the maximum time is reached.

The main idea behind N-PEPS is to decompose the given N IO examples into N individual subproblems and then reassemble them later. Within N-PEPS, the module responsible for detecting PE solutions is called the PE search module.

The Cross Aggregator (CA) approach aims to detect the next line in the global solution p_g based on the execution data of individual programs. This is done using a cross-attention mechanism where the key and value matrices are generated from the PE program state embeddings and their subsequent lines.

To achieve the synthesis of a global solution p_g, the Cross Aggregator (CA) employs a neural network-based architecture with a multi-head attention mechanism. Instead of relying on elementary aggregation methods, the CA harnesses program execution state information, comparing the global solution's current state to those of preliminary solutions (PE solutions). By using a cross-attention mechanism, it determines the relevance of PE solution states, positing that a closely aligned PE state can provide significant cues for the next line of the global solution. This strategy ensures optimal combinations of PE solutions, proving especially crucial in scenarios where the comprehensive solution requires non-trivial combinations or introduces statements not found in the PE solutions.

The N-PEPS model mirrors one layer of the transformer encoder block. However, due to computation time constraints, the framework consists of only one layer. The key-to-value mapping in the N-PEPS model plays a critical role in the process.

Overall, N-PEPS enables efficient synthesis of programs based on IO examples. By combining domain-specific languages, neural models, and specialized search techniques, N-PEPS offers some improvements in program synthesis compared to previous models.

In the context of the development of program synthesis models, the evolution of the models can be seen as a progressive process that started with DeepCoder, evolved through PCCoder, and finally culminated in the development of N-PEPS. In this process, N-PEPS builds directly on the DSL originally developed for DeepCoder.

This ensures continuity in the application and development of the models, while allowing to build on the knowledge and functionality of the previous models. In terms of performance, significant improvements were observed; the results of N-PEPS outperformed those of PCCoder, which ultimately led to N-PEPS being selected as the preferred model. This indicates that the ongoing development and refinement of models in the field of program synthesis is leading to increasingly efficient and powerful solutions.

Large Language Models: General Pretrained Transformer

For the natural language processing application domain, the LLM in the form of ChatGPT (version 4) was chosen. The reasons for this choice are:

- Availability: ChatGPT is currently widely available.
- API access: ChatGPT's interface provides user-friendly and easy access, which facilitates integration and application in various contexts.
- ChatGPT is able to generate working code, often of good quality [1,5].
- ChatGPT has limited learning capabilities (few-shot/zero-shot learning) [5, 6,14]

Prompt

Is there a relationship between the following inputs and outputs of a program?
Input=7,2,0, Output=18

ChatGPT Response

Given the provided input and output:
Input: 7, 2, 0 Output: 18
Let's explore possible relationships:
Looking at the numbers, a straightforward operation like addition results in:
7+2+0=9
However, that's not 18. So, addition doesn't seem to be the operation in question.
Another approach could be multiplication:
7×2×0=0
That's not the desired output either.
One might also consider other operations such as concatenation, but 7,2,0 would concatenate to 720720, which isn't 18.
With the information provided, there isn't a clear and direct arithmetic relationship that gives an output of 18 from the given input. It's possible that the program uses a more complex or non-trivial operation, or there might be an error in the provided data.
If you have more input-output pairs or additional context, it would be easier to deduce a potential relationship.

Fig. 3. An example of ChatGPTs limited reasoning abilities.

ChatGPT has significant capabilities in terms of generating coherent code. Nevertheless, it has inherent limitations in terms of deep understanding of context, especially when it comes to complex links between inputs and outputs. Although it is capable of responding to the information provided to it and generating responses based on its extensive training, it lacks the human ability to intuit and consider context beyond the immediate data, as seen in Fig. 3.

A simple solution, which is not directly obvious to ChatGPT, is to add all the numbers and then multiply by two. ChatGPT itself points out that there is *(a)* a lack of additional information and *(b)* a lack of input-output pairs. Even with an additional input-output pair, ChatGPT does not manage to establish a simple connection between input and output. The multiplier that might be "hidden" in a program is invisible to ChatGPT's analysis capabilities.

4   Experimental Evaluation

COBOL modules, which perform Db2 and dataset accesses, form the basis of this study. Publicly available repositories often only provide technology demonstrations or are too complex for demonstration purposes.

Therefore, self-created modules are used as a basis. A JCL batch job is composed of two COBOL modules: *TXPROC* and *SCORES*. *TXPROC* reads one transaction record each from a dataset. This record consists of a "type", a "minimum rating", a "maximum rating" and a "value". Depending on the "type", different processes are triggered, as illustrated in Fig. 4. The input lists of the IO pairs for the program synthesis are generated from the respective transaction record and the unchanged rows from the table CUSTACOT.

The table CUSTACOT represents a backup of CUSTACC before changes were made by TXPROC. The output lists of the IO pairs consist of the rows from CUSTACC changed by TXPROC, i.e. the delta between CUSTACC and CUSTACOT.

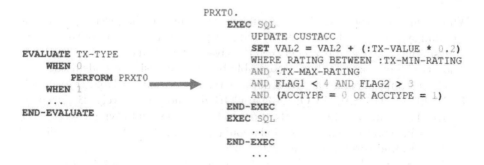

Fig. 4. Code excerpt of COBOL module *TXPROC*

SCORES calculates a SCORE for each customer and records it in the corresponding dataset. This is calculated from (RATING + FLAG1 + FLAG2) * 2. Customers with a negative rating receive an additional entry in a BADRATING dataset. Following the SCORE processing, another dataset with HIGHSCORES is created. For this purpose, all entries with a score > 20 are transferred from the SCORE dataset to the HIGHSCORE dataset, as shown in Fig. 5.

```
FETCH-RECORD.
    ...
    IF SQLCODE = 100                                    READ-AND-FILTER.
        SET END-OF-DATA TO TRUE                             READ SCORE-FILE INTO WS-SC-REC
    ELSE                                                    ....
        IF RATING < 0                                       IF WS-SCORE > 20
            MOVE CUSTID TO WS-BADRAT          ━━━━▶             MOVE WS-SC-REC TO HIGHSCORER-RECORD
            WRITE WS-BADRAT                                     WRITE HIGHSCORER-RECORD
        END-IF                                              END-IF
        COMPUTE WS-SCORE = (RATING + FLAG1 + FLAG2) * 2  END-READ.
        ...
        WRITE SCORE-RECORD
    END-IF.
```

Fig. 5. Code excerpt of COBOL module *SCORES*

The pre-trained model "E2" from the N-PEPS authors' Git repository [25] is used for synthesis. Default parameters, see [26], are used and synthesis is applied directly to the inputs and outputs of the COBOL modules. The Data Variator is used to prepare the input-output pairs. The main goal is to identify partial relations between the different IO pairs. One challenge here is the combinatorial explosion, which allows up to $n!$ for $n = |InputVariables| + |OutputVariables|$ combination possibilities. This makes it difficult to check all combinations, especially for large programs.

The output of the program synthesis is transformed into tokens using a Python script, which can then be processed by ChatGPT.

Applying program synthesis methods to the given COBOL modules revealed some interesting observations.

Module 1: TXPROC

While examining the *TXPROC* module, we encountered the several difficulties. Program synthesis could not identify a direct path from inputs to outputs. This suggests that the relationship between the given inputs and outputs in *TXPROC* is non-trivial or not directly representable by the synthesis methods used.

The module partially accesses data of type 'Decimal' in Db2, respectively 'PIC S9(5)V9(4) USAGE COMP-3' in COBOL, and respectively 'BigDecimal' in Java. The mapping of these data types to the 'Integer' data type was required, resulting in compression losses. This could have an impact on the ability of synthesis to find correct and accurate paths.

Furthermore, the application of the Data Variator was only possible to a limited extent in this case. The main problem was the sheer number of possible combinations that could be generated by the Data Variator. This makes it impractical to analyze all possible combinations in an efficient amount of time.

Module 2: *SCORES*

As described the module is able to write entries in three datasets. This is achieved by the processing steps already described. In the following, the steps are divided into three logical units: SCORE, to calculate the score, HIGHSCORE, if the score is greater than 20 and BADRATING, if the rating is negative.

To calculate the SCORE, input data from the database were first connected to the corresponding output data from the dataset. For simplicity, it was assumed that the customer ID in the database has an equivalent in the dataset.

The resulting IO pairs were processed with the Data Variator and inputs for program synthesis were generated from them. An input for the program synthesis could look as follows:

```
1   {"examples":[
2           {"output":[38,99],"inputs":[[99,1,5,7,7,
                -245,-230]]},
3           {"output":[24,17],"inputs":[[17,3,0,5,7,
                -251,-253]]},
4           {"output":[22,7],"inputs":[[7,0,3,7,1,
                -177,-200]]}
5       ]
6   }
```

The program synthesis applied to the IO pairs shown here could not produce a result. Since we assume that one value of the output is the customer ID in each case, the focus is on the other value of the output list.

So the crucial "examples" are the following:

```
1   {"examples":[
2           {"output":38,"inputs":[[5,7,7]]},
3           {"output":24,"inputs":[[0,5,7]]},
4           {"output":22,"inputs":[[3,7,1]]}
5       ]
6   }
```

In the first test run, the following token, using the said DSL, was generated:

```
LIST|MAXIMUM,0|TAKE,1,0|ZIPWITH,+,2,2|SUM,3
```

For the first IO pair, this would mean the following: Take the maximum of the list $a = [5, 7, 7]$. Create a new *list b* containing all elements of the input list after the maximum (here: 7). Take the *list b* and the *list b*, add all elements in order, create *list c* from it. Sum all elements of *list c*. For the specified IO pairs, this procedure makes sense, but the first two steps do not seem necessary, since the lists are shorter than the "maximum". Apart from this, this could cause errors under corresponding conditions.

After adding another IO pair, namely {"output":6, "inputs":[[1, 1,1]]}, the program synthesis was able to generate a shortened, permissible token:

```
LIST|ZIPWITH,+,0,0|SUM,1
```

Using Python script, a prompt for ChatGPT is automatically generated from the pseudocode. When ChatGPT is asked to apply the steps to a given input, it is able to generate a corresponding output, as illustrated in Fig. 6 and Fig. 7.

Prompt

Apply the following logic if $Input_0 = [7, 2, 0]$ and give a solution which is equal to the last $input_x$:

1. $Input_1$ = Take $Input_0$ and $Input_0$, add both elements of the lists according to their order.

2. $Input_2$ = Sum up all elements of $Input_1$.

Fig. 6. Example for ChatGPT query with token generated by program synthesis translated into natural language

---

ChatGPT Response

```
public int compute(int[] input_0) {
    int[] input_1 = new int[input_0.length];
    for (int i = 0; i < input_0.length; i++) {
        input_1[i] = input_0[i] + input_0[i];
    }
    int input_2 = 0;
    for (int value : input_1) {
        input_2 += value;
    }
    return input_2;
}
```

Fig. 7. Response to ChatGPT query with token generated by program synthesis translated into natural language

When asked to translate the functions into Java code as compact as possible, ChatGPT responds as follows:

In the last step we feed ChatGPT with additional information: We assume that we know that the data is taken from a database with a table named "CUS-TACC" and the columns "RATING", "FLAG1" and "FLAG2" are evaluated. With this information ChatGPT is able to deliver a SQL query that is close to the original query, as shown in Fig. 8:

ChatGPT Response

Given the requirements, it seems you want to double the values of each column in the tuple and then sum them up. Here's how this can be represented using a Db2 SQL query:

```
SELECT
        SUM(2 * RATING + 2 * FLAG1 + 2 * FLAG2) AS INPUT_2
FROM
        CUSTACC;
```

Explanation:

- We multiply each column in the tuple (RATING, FLAG1, FLAG2) by 2 to simulate adding the column to itself.
- We then sum up all these doubled values to produce Input_2.

This will give you the sum of the doubled values of all rows in the CUSTACC table. **Note:** This query assumes that RATING, FLAG1, and FLAG2 are numeric fields in your database. If they are not, this query might not run as intended.

Fig. 8. Response from ChatGPT when asked for a SQL query after enriching the original ChatGPT query with details such as the table layout.

It was not possible to generate results for the HIGHSCORE routine by means of program synthesis. Although HIGHSCORE works similarly to SCORE, not all customer IDs appear in the HIGHSCORE dataset. Accordingly, the IO pairs sometimes look different:

```
1    {"examples":[
2            {"output":38,"inputs":[[5,7,7]]},
3            {"output":[],"inputs":[[5,1,0]]},
4            {...}
5         ]
6    }
```

If only the entries present in the HIGHSCORE dataset are matched with the database, a subset of the functionally equivalent IO pairs of the SCORE routine is created; accordingly, the control structure of HIGHSCORE would be lost.

There is no negative rating (BADRATING) in the table used, so no entry is created in the corresponding dataset. In a realistic scenario, there would be two explanations for this: Either it is dead code that is no longer applied or the occurrence of a negative rating it is a rare, if not critical, event.

5   Results

Applying program synthesis to legacy code provides an impressive way to automatically generate tokens, which can be used as a starting point for code generation via LLM.

The tokens generated by program synthesis offer the advantage of transparency. This differs from "black box" approaches and allows direct comparison with the original legacy code. A notable advantage of program synthesis is the automatic elimination of dead code. However, there is a risk that certain edge cases could be overlooked if insufficient I/O examples are provided.

In theory, program synthesis can be applied at any level - be it IO within a JCL job, within a COBOL module, a process or a subroutine. The only requirement is the ability to create a relation between inputs and outputs.

The case study highlighted the advantages and some pitfalls of the multi-layered AI approach. In particular, program synthesis can react very strongly to small changes in input-output pairs. It should be noted that the case study chosen is deliberately simple. Shrivastava et al. give other, much more complex examples [26].

Among the challenges is the need to map various data types to the 'integer' type, which in some cases can prevent the use of program synthesis.

Although there are theorems for mapping data types into congruent (number) spaces by approximation, there is no way to map floating point numbers effectively, i.e. without loss of information, which means that correlations between inputs and outputs are easily lost [?].

Furthermore, data preparation requires a lot of time and effort. Nevertheless, a detailed knowledge of inputs and outputs enables the creation of input-output pairs suitable for program synthesis. A completely open application to inputs and outputs is possible, but the processing time increases considerably if every conceivable combination is evaluated by means of program synthesis.

In addition, it has been observed that program synthesis generates overly complex tokens in some situations, which could make the process inefficient. It could be shown that linking program synthesis and LLM provides an approach to migrate legacy code to other programming languages even with little information.

In addition, the use of an LLM ensures that there is flexibility with regard to the target environment, represented here in the form of Java code and SQL query. However, it also became apparent that the code quality increases if the LLM is provided with appropriate additional information.

6   Conclusion

In conclusion, in this paper a new hybrid approach for AI-based transformation of legacy code to modern programming languages was presented. By combining program synthesis with GPT, it avoids translating the original legacy code, but recovers its actual functionality and generates a new program for it. The approach was evaluated in an explorative way in first experimental setup using a semi-realistic COBOL program as example.

The results are promising, but further research and development are needed to improve and expand it regarding the following aspects: First, stochastic methods, in particular cluster analysis, should be integrated into the overall workflow. By pre-analyzing the relationships between inputs and outputs, it would enable to perform inferences about control structures in legacy code. It could also help reduce the sheer volume of possible combinations for the Data Variator. If certain inputs have particularly strong relationships to specific outputs, these correlations could be brought to the forefront, leading to more efficient and targeted analyses.

Second, the constraints of the input and output values to an integer number range needs to be removed. The key questions are: What limits are reasonable? What range of values actually occurs in real inputs and outputs? And can there be alternative models or more efficient mappings that exceed or replace the integer number range?

Finally, the approach needs to be integrated in a software tool to provide a higher degree of automation and to make the program synthesis process more efficient and user-friendly. This will help to achieve faster and more accurate results, especially in complex legacy code environments.

References

1. Aljanabi, M., Ghazi, M., Ali, A.H., Abed, S.A., ChatGpt: ChatGpt: open possibilities. Iraqi J. Comput. Sci. Math. **4**(1), 62–64 (2023). https://doi.org/10.52866/20ijcsm.2023.01.01.0018. https://journal.esj.edu.iq/index.php/IJCM/article/view/539
2. Balog, M., Gaunt, A.L., Brockschmidt, M., Nowozin, S., Tarlow, D.: DeepCoder: Learning to Write Programs (2017). eprint: 1611.01989
3. Bandara, C., Perera, I.: Transforming monolithic systems to microservices - an analysis toolkit for legacy code evaluation. In: 2020 20th International Conference on Advances in ICT for Emerging Regions (ICTer), pp. 95–100 (2020). https://doi.org/10.1109/ICTer51097.2020.9325443
4. Biermann, A.W.: The inference of regular LISP programs from examples. IEEE Trans. Syst. Man Cybern. **8**(8), 585–600 (1978). https://doi.org/10.1109/TSMC.1978.4310035
5. Borji, A.: A Categorical Archive of ChatGPT Failures (2023). eprint: 2302.03494
6. Brown, T.B., et al.: Language Models are Few-Shot Learners (2020). eprint: 2005.14165
7. Ciborowska, A., Chakarov, A., Pandita, R.: Contemporary COBOL: developers' perspectives on defects and defect location. In: 2021 IEEE International Conference on Software Maintenance and Evolution (ICSME), pp. 227–238 (2021). https://doi.org/10.1109/ICSME52107.2021.00027
8. Di Nucci, D., et al.: A Language-Parametric Modular Framework for Mining Idiomatic Code Patterns (2019)
9. Dwivedi, R., et al.: Explainable AI (XAI): core ideas, techniques, and solutions. ACM Comput. Surv. **55**(9) (2023). https://doi.org/10.1145/3561048

10. Floridi, L., Chiriatti, M.: GPT-3: its nature, scope, limits, and consequences. Mind. Mach. **30**, 681–694 (2020)
11. Friedman, J.: Alonzo Church. Application of recursive arithmetic to the problem of circuit synthesisSummaries of talks presented at the Summer Institute for Symbolic Logic Cornell University, 1957, 2nd edn., Communications Research Division, Institute for Defense Analyses, Princeton, NJ, 1960, pp. 3–50. 3a–45a. J. Symb. Logic **28**(4), 289–290 (1963)
12. Gupta, K., Christensen, P.E., Chen, X., Song, D.: Synthesize, Execute and Debug: Learning to Repair for Neural Program Synthesis (2020). eprint: 2007.08095
13. Kiran Mallidi, R., Sharma, M., Singh, J.: Legacy digital transformation: TCO and ROI analysis. Int. J. Electr. Comput. Eng. Syst. **12**(3), 163–170 (2021)
14. Kojima, T., Gu, S.S., Reid, M., Matsuo, Y., Iwasawa, Y.: Large Language Models are Zero-Shot Reasoners (2023). eprint: 2205.11916
15. Kontogiannis, K.A., DeMori, R., Merlo, E., Galler, M., Bernstein, M.: Pattern matching for clone and concept detection. Autom. Softw. Eng. **3**(1), 77–108 (1996)
16. Laich, L., Bielik, P., Vechev, M.: Guiding program synthesis by learning to generate examples. In: International Conference on Learning Representations (2020). https://openreview.net/forum?id=BJl07ySKvS
17. Liventsev, V., Grishina, A., Härmä, A., Moonen, L.: Fully autonomous programming with large language models. In: Proceedings of the Genetic and Evolutionary Computation Conference. ACM (2023). https://doi.org/10.1145/3583131.3590481
18. Mahowald, K., Ivanova, A.A., Blank, I.A., Kanwisher, N., Tenenbaum, J.B., Fedorenko, E.: Dissociating language and thought in large language models: a cognitive perspective (2023). eprint: 2301.06627
19. Manilov, S.Z.: Analysis and transformation of legacy code (2018)
20. Manna, Z., Waldinger, R.J.: Toward automatic program synthesis. Commun. ACM **14**(3), 151–165 (1971)
21. Montakab, C.: Legacy transformation white paper. Technical report, softwaremining (2009). https://softwaremining.com/download/pdf/SM_Legacy_Transformation_whitepaper.pdf
22. Puri, R., et al.: Project codenet: a large-scale AI for code dataset for learning a diversity of coding tasks. arXiv preprint arXiv:2105.12655 1035 (2021)
23. Shi, K., Hong, J., Zaheer, M., Yin, P., Sutton, C.: Compositional Generalization and Decomposition in Neural Program Synthesis (2022). eprint: 2204.03758
24. Shin, R., et al.: Synthetic Datasets for Neural Program Synthesis. CoRR abs/1912.12345 (2019). http://arxiv.org/abs/1912.12345
25. Shrivastava, D., Larochelle, H., Tarlow, D.: N-PEPS. https://github.com/shrivastavadisha/N-PEPS
26. Shrivastava, D., Larochelle, H., Tarlow, D.: Learning to combine per-example solutions for neural program synthesis. In: Beygelzimer, A., Dauphin, Y., Liang, P., Vaughan, J.W. (eds.) Advances in Neural Information Processing Systems (2021). https://openreview.net/forum?id=4PK-St2iVZn
27. Si, X., Yang, Y., Dai, H., Naik, M., Song, L.: Learning a meta-solver for syntax-guided program synthesis. In: International Conference on Learning Representations (2019). https://openreview.net/forum?id=Syl8Sn0cK7
28. Sneed, H., Verhoef, C.: Re-implementing a legacy system. J. Syst. Softw. **155**, 162–184 (2019). https://doi.org/10.1016/j.jss.2019.05.012. https://www.sciencedirect.com/science/article/pii/S0164121219301050
29. Strobl, S., Zoffi, C., Haselmann, C., Bernhart, M., Grechenig, T.: Automated code transformations: dealing with the aftermath. In: 2020 IEEE 27th International

Conference on Software Analysis, Evolution and Reengineering (SANER), pp. 627–631 (2020). https://doi.org/10.1109/SANER48275.2020.9054813. ISSN 1534-5351

30. Summers, P.D.: A methodology for LISP program construction from examples. J. ACM **24**(1), 161–175 (1977). https://doi.org/10.1145/321992.322002

31. Sun, J., et al.: Investigating explainability of generative AI for code through scenario-based design. In: 27th International Conference on Intelligent User Interfaces, Helsinki, Finland, IUI 2022, pp. 212–228. Association for Computing Machinery, New York (2022). https://doi.org/10.1145/3490099.3511119

32. Teplitzky, P.: Closing the COBOL Programming Skills Gap (2019). https://techchannel.com/Enterprise/10/2019/closing-cobol-programming-skills-gap

33. Terekhov, A., Verhoef, C.: The realities of language conversions. IEEE Softw. **17**(6), 111–124 (2000). https://doi.org/10.1109/52.895180

34. Trudel, M.: Automatic translation and object-oriented reengineering of legacy code (2013)

35. Vaswani, A., et al.: Attention is all you need. In: Advances in Neural Information Processing Systems, vol. 30 (2017)

36. Wavresky, F., Lee, S.W.: A methodology towards the adaptization of legacy systems using agent-oriented software engineering. In: Proceedings of the 31st Annual ACM Symposium on Applied Computing, pp. 1407–1414 (2016)

37. Weisz, J.D., et al.: Perfection not required? Human-AI partnerships in code translation. In: 26th International Conference on Intelligent User Interfaces, pp. 402–412 (2021)

38. White, M., Tufano, M., Vendome, C., Poshyvanyk, D.: Deep learning code fragments for code clone detection. In: 2016 31st IEEE/ACM International Conference on Automated Software Engineering (ASE), pp. 87–98. IEEE (2016)

39. Ye, X., Chen, Q., Dillig, I., Durrett, G.: Optimal Neural Program Synthesis from Multimodal Specifications (2021). eprint: 2010.01678

40. Zhang, Y., Wang, D., Dong, W.: MerIt: improving neural program synthesis by merging collective intelligence. Autom. Softw. Eng. **29**(2), 45 (2022). https://doi.org/10.1007/s10515-022-00343-z

Fully Distributed Deep Neural Network: F2D2N

Ernesto Leite[1]([⊠]), Fabrice Mourlin[2], and Pierre Paradinas[1]

[1] Conservatoire National des Arts et Métiers, 292 rue Saint Martin,
75141 Paris, France
{ernesto.leite,pierre.paradinas}@lecnam.net
[2] UPEC, 61 Av. du Général de Gaulle, 94000 Créteil, France
fabrice.mourlin@u-pec.fr

Abstract. Recent advances in Artificial Intelligence (AI) have accelerated the adoption of AI at a pace never seen before. Large Language Models (LLM) trained on tens of billions of parameters show the crucial importance of parallelizing models. Different techniques exist for distributing Deep Neural Networks but they are challenging to implement. The cost of training GPU-based architectures is also becoming prohibitive. In this document we present a distributed approach that is easier to implement where data and model are distributed in processing units hosted on a cluster of machines based on CPUs or GPUs. Communication is done by message passing. The model is distributed over the cluster and stored locally or on a datalake. We prototyped this approach using open sources libraries and we present the benefits this implementation can bring.

Keywords: F2D2N · model parallelism · data parallelism · Deep Neural Network

1 Introduction

Data has become one of the most valuable asset a company can have and it's actually producing a lot of expectation. It brings several challenges like how data should be extracted, stored, cleaned and transformed. When the amount of data is huge or grows exponentially, it brings new challenges like how to scale or how to train AI models in a reasonable amount of time and money. Data volumes are growing every day. Deep learning models are struggling to ingest the increased amount of data without reaching the hardware limits of the training machines. GPUs are intensely used for matrix computation but the increased size of the models makes the training phase no more possible with standard techniques because the size of the models cannot fit anymore in GPUs memory even the largest. Data, model, pipeline and tensor parallelism are widely used to answer these challenges. Tensor parallelism is actually one of the best approaches but it is challenging to implement and requires a lot of engineering effort.

S. Bouzefrane et al. (Eds.): MSPN 2023, LNCS 14482, pp. 222–236, 2024.
https://doi.org/10.1007/978-3-031-52426-4_15

We prototyped the F2D2N where fragments of weights, bias, activation and gradients are fully distributed and stored in remote machines. This allow the model to be distributed over the network. These machines do not require GPUs hardware even GPUs can of course speed up the training process. Feedforward and back-propagation phases are done using an event messaging mechanism. This implementation is also ready for future improvements like Reinforcement Learning, Forward-Forward approach [4] and Generative AI.

Reducing the size of the models negatively impact the precision of the models, that's why continuing exploring how to efficiently distribute the model is an urgent need in the AI field.

But actually implementing model parallelism techniques are not straightforward and require a lot of engineering effort. In this paper we give a brief review of different techniques used to overcome DNN training challenges over the years. We present shortly what data, model, pipeline and tensor parallelism are and we will introduce an innovative way to organize and compute DNN in a distributed cluster.

2   Related Work

Scaling a DNN is hard and a lot of techniques have been implemented over the years to address this challenge. We give a short presentation of those who are actually widely used in the AI field.

2.1   Data Parallelism

The goal of data parallelism [1,2,6,9] is to distribute the training data across multiple processors or machines. The model is replicated on each processor, and each replica processes a different subset of the training data. Each device processes locally different mini-batches and then synchronized its local gradients with the other devices before updating the model parameters. This is probably the easiest way to train a DNN but this brings some important limitations while scaling up the network.

For example, Data parallelism requires each device to hold a copy of the entire model parameters, which can be a memory-intensive task for large models which is also redundant and not efficient in terms of storage. While training DNN on large datasets, it often leads to an out of memory (OOM) exception when the training model exceeds the memory limits of the device. Mini-batches need to remain as small as possible but this ends up in convergence issues.

2.2   Model Parallelism

Model parallelism [2,8] tries to resolve some of the challenges data parallelism brings when the size of the model does not fit anymore on the device. One simple technique is to split the layers of the model among available GPUs. Each GPU will compute the feed-forward *(Fx)* pass of the hidden layer at a time. Then after the back-propagation pass *(Bx)*, it will update the gradients at a time too.

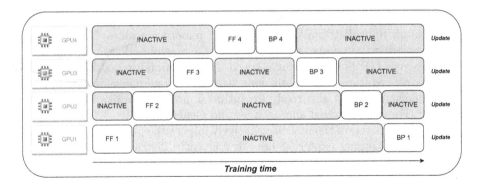

Fig. 1. Feed-Forward (FF) and Back-propagation (BP) tasks usage over 4 GPUs.

The Fig. 1 represents a model with 4 layers placed on 4 different GPUs (vertical axis). The horizontal axis represents training this model through time, demonstrating that only 1 GPU is utilized at a time.

As the graph shows, the main problem of this naive implementation is that it is not efficient and costly for large training as only one GPU is used at a time. It does not resolve the problem it tries to solve if one part of the model overfits again the physical memory of the device.

2.3   Pipeline Parallelism

To overcome model parallelism limits, Google was the first introducing the concept of pipeline parallelism [2,5,10]. GPipe is actually implemented in Pytorch. The goal is to split the mini-batch into multiple micro-batches and pipelines the execution of these micro-batches across multiple GPUs. This approach leads to a better utilization of the hardware resources because it allows the DNN to train the model in parallel. This is outlined in the Fig. 2.

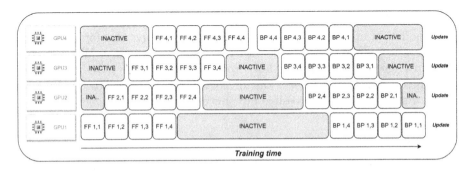

Fig. 2. Optimized pipeline parallelism over 4 GPUs.

The Fig. 2 represents a model with 4 layers placed on 4 different GPUs (vertical axis). The horizontal axis represents training this model through time demonstrating that the GPUs are utilized much more efficiently. Pipeline parallelism divides the input mini-batch into smaller micro-batches, enabling different accelerators to work on different micro-batches simultaneously. Gradients are applied synchronously at the end. However, there still exists a bubble (as demonstrated in the figure) where certain GPUs are not utilized [5].

Gpipe requires additional logic to handle the efficient pipelining of these communication and computation operations, and suffers from pipeline bubbles that reduce efficiency, or changes to the optimizer itself which impact accuracy.

2.4 Tensor Parallelism (TP)

Tensor parallelism [11,12] (and its variants) is a method to speed up the training of deep neural networks by parallelizing the computation of tensors. A tensor is a multi-dimensional array of numerical values that is used to represent data in deep learning. TP helps to scale up the training of deep neural networks to larger datasets and more complex models. TP is widely used while training huge amount of data and it's already implemented by major cloud providers like Amazon Web Services (AWS) (Fig. 3).

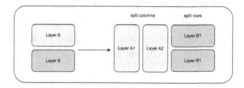

Fig. 3. Tensor parallelism applied to 2 layers A et B

TP involves dividing particular model parameters, gradients, and optimizer states among different devices.

Nethertheless, TP requires more complex software and hardware infrastructure to distribute the computation across multiple devices or GPUs. This can increase the complexity of the training process and require more expertise to set up and maintain. Not all deep learning frameworks and libraries support tensor parallelism (like transformers), so it may not be compatible with all the tools and libraries a Deep Learning project requires.

3 Proposed Architecture

3.1 Concepts

As we saw in the introduction, data is already huge in terms of volumes and it will continue to grow. An important aspect is to be able to **parallelize** the DNN as much as possible and to make it *more easy* to distribute and train.

Tensor Parallelism is actually one of the most widely solutions used to scale up and distribute the computation of a DNN, but it suffers from being complex to implement. Parallelizing data or model with these different techniques is often challenging because of the complexity of the configuration, the costly architecture and the engineering efforts it implies.

Based on that need, we intend to simplify the process of parallelization as much as possible for three reasons:

- First of all: to be able to train complex and big DNN (or Convolutional Neural Networks) with CPUs and/or GPUs machines.
- Secondly: to split the DNN in small units of computing (UC).
- Thirdly: to use open source libraries that can work in different environments like Windows, Linux or Mac OS.

A basic DNN is composed by 3 types of layers: an input layer, one or more hidden layers and an output layer which outputs the final predictions.

Each hidden layer will compute on the feed-forward pass an activation function σ (relu, leakyRelu, sigmoid, tanH, etc.) having w (weights), x (inputs) and b (bias):

$$a = \sigma(w_1 x_1 + ... + w_n x_n + b) \tag{1}$$

The weighted function is a sum of a matrix product. So we can distribute this function across a cluster of machines as the sum is commutative. The position of each UC determines the position of the matrix array the UC will compute. For the back-propagation, the derivative can be applied to the portion of weights or bias hosted by each UC as it produces the same results if it was applied to the whole set.

L is the layer, y the true label, z (weighted sum + bias) and σ' is the derivative of the activation function:

$$\delta^L = (a^L - y) \odot \sigma'(z^L) \tag{2}$$

The error can be propagated from the output layer to the first input layer using the transpose of the upper layer $l+1$ of w.

$$\delta^l = ((w^{l+1})^T \delta^{l+1}) \odot \sigma'(z^l) \tag{3}$$

By combining (3) with (2) we can compute the error δ^l for any layer in the network.

$$\frac{\partial C}{\partial w_{jk}^l} = a_k^{l-1} \delta_j^l \tag{4}$$

In the context of an UC, we need to compute the portion of the matrix using the chain rule.

$$\delta^{l,uc} = ((w^{l,uc+1})^T \delta^{l,uc+1}) \odot \sigma'(z^{l,uc}) \tag{5}$$

n.b.: More detailed information of the formulas can be found here [9].

3.2 Parallelized Approach

We introduce in this paper a Fully Distributed Deep Neural Network (*F2D2N*). The goal is to have units of computing (UC) that can handle a small piece of the DNN. This architecture is close to micro-services. Each UC is responsible of initializing the portion of weights or bias using the best algorithm like random, Xavier, HE, etc. It stores its data (weights, bias, activation, gradients, etc.) locally or in a data lake. The grouping of all these pieces constitute the model itself.

This approach allows the model to grow without reaching the hardware limits of any device because the architecture can be scaled in *advance* to cover the final training size of the model. This because we can calculate the number of parameters the model will hold at its final stages and calibrate the needed network to compute it.

For distributing the matrix computation (Eq. 1), we divided the hidden layer into two different layers:

Weighted Layer (WL): this layer holds the portion of weights. The size and the dimension of the matrix is calculated considering how the next layer is divided and the size of the activation matrix it receives. It is exclusively connected to its corresponding Activation layer (same index) and fully connected to the next Activation layer. WL basically distributes the computation of the splitted weighted matrix over a cluster of UCs. Each UC is dedicated to a specific portion of the matrix. In Eq. 6, s is the startIndex and e is the lastIndex of the portion of the matrix. This operation is repeated for each UC in the Layer.

$$wm_{uc} = (w_s * x_s + ... + w_e * x_e) \tag{6}$$

Activation Layer (AL): this layer holds the portion of bias and activation. The size and the dimension of the matrix is calculated considering how the next weighted layer is divided and the size of the activation matrix it receives from the previous layer. It is fully connected to the previous weighted layer and exclusively connected to the weighted layer of it same index position.

Equation 7: AL sums all the weighted matrix wm from layer $l - 1$. uc_1 is the first UC and uc_n is the last UC in the layer $l - 1$. Then it add a bias b and compute the activation function σ.

$$a = \sigma((wm_{uc_1} + ... + wm_{uc_n}) + b) \tag{7}$$

Each UC processes its small piece of work (weighted computation or activation computation) then triggers an event to the next UC until reaching the output layer. Figure 4 shows a simplified schema of the F2D2N based on a DNN with 1 hidden layer. It contains: one Input layer (green), 2 weighted layers (purple):

one for the input layer, one for the activation layer, 1 activation layer (orange) and one output layer (blue)

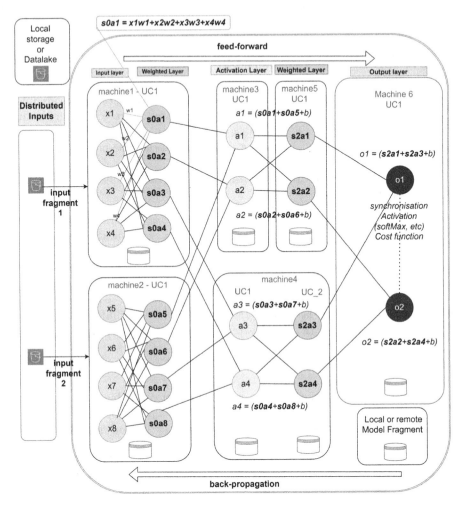

Fig. 4. Simple F2D2N with 1 hidden layer using a cluster of 6 machines (Color figure online)

As other approaches, F2D2N has some *synchronous* states. For example, an AL UC has to wait until receiving the *complete* set of the weighted matrix from the previous layer before computing the activation function in the forward pass. This is only for a training sample but does not block the UC to continue to process another sample.

Figure 5 shows activation neuron *a1* has to wait to receive weighted matrix *s0a1* from actor *machine1-UC1* and weighted matrix *soa5* from *machine2-UC1* to compute the activation function.

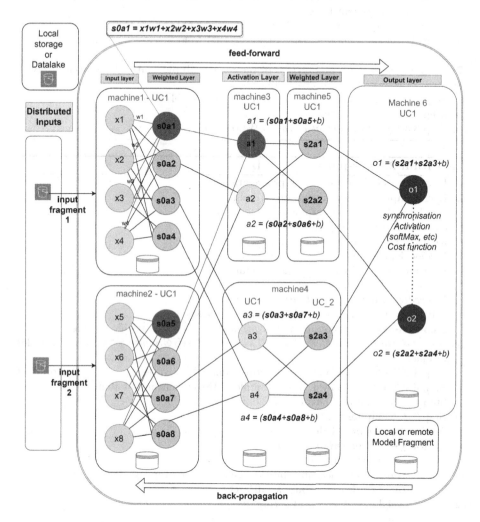

Fig. 5. Activation layer in *machine3-UC1* waiting for Weighted matrix from 2 UCs *machine1-UC1*, *machine2-UC1*

For the back-propagation pass, the AL and WL UC have to detect when it receives the last sample of a mini-batch to apply the gradients to the portions of weights or bias it holds. Each UC has an internal buffer that tracks how many back-propagation events it received and when the counter is equal to the size of the mini-batch it will apply the gradients to the local weight or bias it contains.

Algorithm 1. Feed-forward AL

1: Each sample has its unique correlationId
2: Initialize b matrix
3: Initialize UC hashMap variables: activation, weighted, shardsReceived
4: Layer l is the current layer
5: $ucIndex$ is the current vertical position of the UC in the L l
6: Step 1 : sum $weightedInput$ matrix received from layer -1 and update $weighted$ matrix
7: Step 2 : check if all the portions of the weightedInput matrix have been received
8: Step 3 : When shardsReceived are complete do :
9: Step 3.1 : $z[correlationId] = weighted(\text{correlationId}) + b$
10: Step 3.2 : $a[correlationId] = \sigma(z)$
11: Step 3.3 : Send $a[correlationId]$ to WL(l+1, $ucIndex$)

Algorithm 2. Back-propagation WL

Updating weights during back-propagation
2: Each sample has its unique correlationId
$regularisation$: hyperparameter
4: $learningRate$: hyperparameter
$nInput$: size of the training sample
6: Init local variables
$neuronCount = NeuronsInLayer.\text{count}$
8: $ucCount = UCInLayer.\text{count}$
$layerStep = neuronCount/ucCount$
10: Initialize UC hashMap variables: $weights$, $nablasw$
Step 1. Receive gradients from activation layer +1 for a specific sample.
12: Step 2. Compute $newDelta[layerSize] = $ weights($UCSender$) * delta)   ▷ dot product
Step 3. Compute $nablaw[delta.length] = $ delta * activation   ▷ dot product
14: Step 4. Case UC received all the sample of the current mini-batch
Step 4.1. Sum all the matrices of the mini-batch
16: Step 4.2. Compute gradients
for $i \leftarrow 0\, ucCount - 1$ **do**
18:    **for** $j \leftarrow 0\ layerStep - 1$ **do**
$tmp \leftarrow$ weights$[i][j]$;
20:      $tmp1 \leftarrow (1 - $ learningRate $\cdot$ (regularisation/nInput)) $\cdot tmp$);
$tmp2 \leftarrow$ (learningRate/MiniBatch) $\cdot$ nabla$_w[i][j]$;
22:      weights$[i][j] \leftarrow (tmp1 - tmp2)$;
   end for
24: **end for**
Step 4.3. clean buffer

Figure 6 shows the events flow during the training process of an epoch. Some context parameters are sent during the feed-forward or back-propagation event (min, max, avg, etc.).

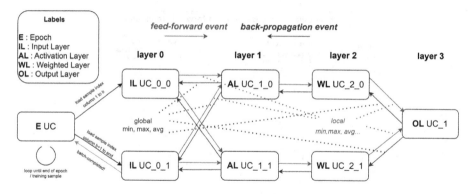

Fig. 6. Feed-forward and back-propagation event flow

4   Communication Scheme

4.1   Graph Messaging Overview

A F2D2N is a graph that computes the feed-forward pass and back-propagation pass by a message passing system. The neural network is divided *horizontally* (the layers) and *vertically* (the UCs). If we want to scale up the cluster we need to add vertically more UCs. Theoretically each UC can reach another UC in the cluster. It is easy to scale up verticaly the cluster by adding new UCs to a specific layer.

Epoch UC is the *root* of the graph. It is connected to at least one input UC which will load and compute the initial input weighted matrix. Input UC will be fully connected to at least one activation UC. This UC will sum all the weighted matrix it received from the previous layer, will add the bias and will send the activation results to its dedicated weighed UC. Weighted UC will be fully connected to all the activation UC of the next level until reaching the output UC. This architecture can also support vertical communication when UC in the same layer needs to synchronized their data like batch normalization. This will allow the architecture to support also Recurrent Neural Networks, Variational Autoencoders (VAE), Generative Adversarial Networks (GAN), etc.

4.2   Benefits

This architecture brings some interesting benefits (Fig. 7):

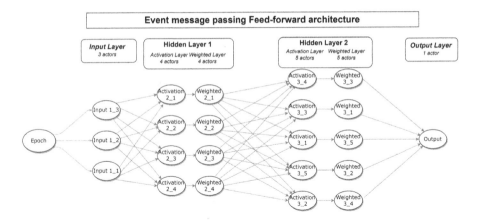

Fig. 7. F2D2N as a graph from the epoch UC to Output UC

- Model size: it is distributed on a data lake and can grow linearly with the size of cluster. It is not limited to the physical size of a machine as the load is distributed across UCs.
- Check-pointing: each UC can save its memory state on a storage like a data lake and the node manager can recreate the dead UC from it.
- Contextual variables: min, max, avg, and many more information can be transmitted in the message event. This allows the UC that receives these information to determine the global min, max, avg of the full matrix because it has the full vision of it. This removes the need for a costly parameter server [7] for example as regularization or normalization techniques can be applied during the back-propagation stage.
- The F2D2N can remain live allowing new training phases to be processed like reinforcement learning or to respond live to a request.
- The F2D2N can be reconstructed in advance based on a specific configuration.
- Modularity: each piece of the F2D2N is a local or remote UC. This allow the F2D2N to be completely divided into small units of computating and to decide where they would be placed over the network. This allows also the architect to determine which intensive compute units of the network should go to specific machines (GPUs, CPUs).
- Asynchronous: all the training samples of a batch are triggered asynchronously allowing part of the feed-forward pass to parallelize the computation of the training samples.
- Continuous Integration /Continuous deployment (CI/CD) ready: F2D2N is close to a micro-service architecture. This allow the entire architecture to be stored in a git repository, hosted in a development project under an IDE like Intellij, tested, validated and delivered using a CI/CD pipeline

5   Performance Evaluation

We prototyped this approach using Akka server implementation [14] which can scale to 400 nodes without the need to put a lot of engineering effort. Akka cluster can go beyong that size (over 1000 nodes) but this will need the help of technical specialists. We believe that for most usecases Akka implementation will handle any F2D2N implementation. But this choice allowed us to not focus on the cluster implementation itself. Note that Lightbend recently changed Akka product licensing (https://www.lightbend.com/akka/pricing). The feedforward and backpropagation pass are based on the Akka event messaging system. An actor (UC) runs in a machine and it holds its *own* memory. A machine contains one or several actors.

We prototyped a sample of a F2D2N using the MNIST dataset [3]. The solution is designed in scala and needs Simple Build Tool (SBT) to compile and run the solution. The external libraries (Maven) are defined in the build.sbt file. Additional libraries are needed as NVIDIA drivers (CUDA) if we want to activate the GPU support. This dataset has: 784 input neurons, 60 000 training samples, 10 000 test samples.

We defined 2 actors for the input layer, 2 actors for the first hidden layer, 2 actors for the 2nd input layer and 1 actor for the output layer using a cluster of 3 machines.

We ran the lab in 3 modes.

Table 1 shows the training duration of the MNIST database. Actually, the cluster mode takes longer compared to the local mode because of the messages being passed through the network and the size of the data not really significant. The cluster mode will perform better on bigger training volumes where the model would need to be splitted among the cluster.

We trained the prototype in 3 DELL R730 E5-2690 v4 @ 2.60GHz with 96GB Ram & 1Tb SSD. The instances need to run a Java runtime (11 or higher) and Scala Build Tool (SBT) in order to compile the git sources. A build.sbt file contains the references to the maven packages.

Table 1. Training duration

Mode	Duration (min)
Local: Pytorch/Jupyter	13.3
Local: F2D2N	24.2
Cluster (3 machines): F2D2N	29.2

Table 2 shows the parameters used to train the MNIST samples. We used the Categorical Cross Entropy as we are dealing with a multi-class classification problem. The prototype will handle more cost functions in the future.

Table 2. Hyperparameters

Parameters	Value
Epochs	50
Learning rate	0.195
Activation	Relu, Relu, Softmax
Cost function	CategoricalCrossEntropy
Minibatch	50
Regularisation	0.5
Input Neurons	784
Hidden Layer 1 Neurons	128
Hidden Layer 2 Neurons	64
Output Neurons	10

Table 3 shows F2D2N using 9 UCs on the local mode and the cluster mode to train the MNIST database.

Table 3. Cluster configuration

Layer	UC
Input	4 UCs
Hidden 1	2 UCs
Hidden 2	2 UCs
Output	1 UCs
Total	9 UCs (local or remote)

Table 4 shows the list of the main libraries used in the prototype. They are listed in the build.sbt and available in maven repository.

Figure 8 shows the training results for a F2D2N in a local mode. Blue columns represent the execution time of an epoch (average of 36 s per epoch) and the curve represents the cost function (categorical cross entropy) which decrease over the time. The accuracy for that training is 96.10% for a total execution time of 29 min.

Table 4. Main scala libraries

Library	Version
sbt	1.9.2
scala	2.13.12
akka	2.8.5
Amazon Coretto	20
IDE	Intellij 2023
ML	ai.dlj

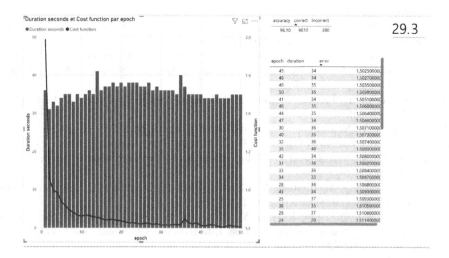

Fig. 8. Training of a F2D2N during 50 epochs (Color figure online)

6 Conclusion

In this paper, we reviewed different techniques that implement data and model parallelism. Tensor parallelism is actually widely used to tackle the challenges of model parallelism but it suffers from being very complex to implement or to extend it with new features.

We demonstrate that it is possible to parallelize a DNN into small units of computing (UCs) and to distribute the training process in an event messaging system. This modularity makes it more easy to implement new features like encoders, RNN and reinforcement learning. It also makes possible to integrate the solution in a DevOps workflow (CI/CD, tests, git, etc.).

Our tests showed that expanding horizontally the DNN can have better performance compared to vertical scaling even it can bring other challenges like exploding gradients.

As future work, we aim to train F2D2N with larger datasets and make some improvements like reducing the number of messages for better efficiency.

References

1. Ben-Nun, T., Hoefler, T.: Demystifying Parallel and Distributed Deep Learning: An In-Depth Concurrency Analysis (2018)
2. Chen, C.-C., Yang, C.-L., Cheng, H.-Y.: Efficient and Robust Parallel DNN Training through Model Parallelism on Multi-GPU Platform (2019)
3. Deng, L.: The MNIST database of handwritten digit images for machine learning research [best of the web]. IEEE Signal Process. Mag. **29**(6), 141–142 (2012)
4. Hinton, G.: The Forward-Forward Algorithm: Some Preliminary Investigations (2022)
5. Huang, Y., et al.: GPipe: Efficient Training of Giant Neural Networks using Pipeline Parallelism (2019)
6. Jiang, Y., Fu, F., Miao, X., Nie, X., Cui, B.: OSDP: Optimal Sharded Data Parallel for Distributed Deep Learning (2023)
7. Li, M.: Scaling distributed machine learning with the parameter server. In: Proceedings of the 2014 International Conference on Big Data Science and Computing, Beijing China, p. 1. ACM (2014)
8. Li, S., et al.: PyTorch Distributed: Experiences on Accelerating Data Parallel Training (2020)
9. Nielsen, M.A.: Neural Networks and Deep Learning (2015)
10. Shoeybi, M., Patwary, M., Puri, R., LeGresley, P., Casper, J., Catanzaro, B.: Megatron-LM: Training Multi-Billion Parameter Language Models Using Model Parallelism (2020)
11. Singh, S., Sating, Z., Bhatele, A.: Communication-minimizing Asynchronous Tensor Parallelism (2023). arXiv:2305.13525 [cs]
12. Wang, B., Xu, Q., Bian, Z., You, Y.: Tesseract: parallelize the tensor parallelism efficiently. In: Proceedings of the 51st International Conference on Parallel Processing, pp. 1–11 (2022)

Author Index

Printed in the United States
by Baker & Taylor Publisher Services